For

The great grandchildren of Tom Rutledge

Antonia, James, Edward, Harry and Jack Parker

Alex, Zara and Marcus Lowe

Finn and Sam Campbell

And

Florence Rutledge

Born 100 Years after her great grandfather

set off for the Great War

Tom's letters written
during the war —

I would not like to have
them burnt - years hence
they will be of great interest -

Note by Jean left in box of letters.

Jane Ruth (Jean) Rutledge, Tom's mother; the recipient of most of the letters.

Socks *from* Bungendore

The letters of Tom Rutledge
from the First World War

Edited by Martha Rutledge
and William Rutledge

First published in 2015 by Willrut Pty Ltd trading as Wusofar Books, with Barrallier Books Pty Ltd, trading as Echo Books.

Registered Office: 35-37 Gordon Avenue, West Geelong, Victoria 3220, Australia.

www.echobooks.com.au

Edited by Martha Rutledge and William Rutledge

National Library of Australia Cataloguing-in-Publication entry

Creator: Rutledge, Tom, author.

Title: Socks from Bungendore : the letters of Tom Rutledge from the first World War / editor: Martha Rutledge ; contributor: William Rutledge.

ISBN: 9780994232328 (hardback)

Subjects: Rutledge, Tom--Correspondence. World War, 1914-1918--Personal narratives, Australian. World War, 1914-1918--Participation, Australian. World War, 1914-1918--New South Wales--Bungendore. Bungendore (N.S.W.)--History, Military--20th century.

Other Creators/Contributors: Rutledge, Martha, editor.

Rutledge, William.

Dewey Number: 940.48194

Book and cover design by Peter Gamble, Ink Pot Graphic Design, Canberra.
Set in Garamond Premier Pro Display, 13/17 and Optima, regular.

www.echobooks.com.au

Contents

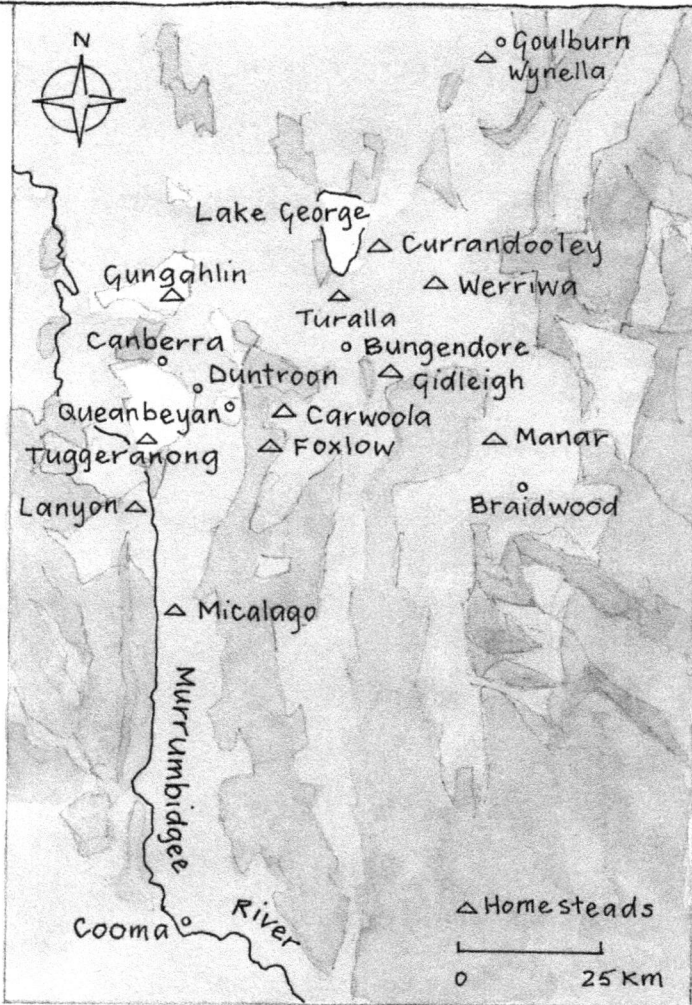

The SOUTHERN TABLELANDS and AUSTRALIAN CAPITAL TERRITORY

N

o Goulburn
△ Wynella

Lake George

△ Currandooley

Gungahlin
△

△ Werriwa
△
Turalla

Canberra
o
o Bungendore

△ Duntroon
o
△ Gidleigh

Queanbeyan o
△ Carwoola

Tuggeranong
△
△ Foxlow

△ Manar

Lanyon △

o
Braidwood

△ Micalago

Murrumbidgee

River

△ Homesteads

Cooma o

0   25 Km

Map by Catherine Gordon.

Preface

When, with mixed feelings, my family decided to sell Gidleigh which had been in Rutledge ownership for one hundred and fifty years, we had to deal with a large accumulation of possessions. There were attics and lofts where objects had been stowed away and forgotten.

One day, tucked away in a corner of one of the lofts, I came across a chest which was full of letters. I took one out of its envelope and found that it had been written in pencil by my father, from his dugout on Gallipoli, to his brother discussing, of all things, wool prices. It turned out that this chest contained all the surviving letters that my father had written home while he had been away at the First World War.

At the time, being pre-occupied with moving and settling into a new environment, I handed the letters over to my sister, Martha. She had spent most of her working life on the editorial staff of the *Australian Dictionary of Biography*. With her husband, Charles Campbell, they read the letters and realised their value.

The letters describe aspects of the day to day life of the soldiers, both at the front and away from it. They also give an insight into how the family and community were coping on the home front.

Martha then started to prepare the letters for possible publication. In her research for the footnotes she managed to identify nearly all the names mentioned. Sadly, neither Martha nor Charles has survived to see the published work: Charles died in 2011 and Martha in 2014. It has been a labour of love, as well as a challenge, to bring their work to fruition.

The letters were often hurriedly written, from uncomfortable places. The original text has been closely followed except for correction of minor errors to improve readability. Where an irregular spelling has been retained, it has been indicated by the expression 'sic'. To avoid too much repetition of footnotes, a listing of names that recur often has been included as an appendix. Where it is not clear to whom a christian name refers, the surname has been added in square brackets.

The general policy with names is to use final rank and decorations, not those that would have applied at the time.

There are numerous people to thank who have made this publication possible.

Martha's son, Daniel typed the letters from the original, and they were meticulously checked back to the originals by Martha and Charles. My wife, Julia, and my sister, Caroline Parker, were diligent proof readers, and made many valuable suggestions. Their support and encouragement kept me going when I felt overwhelmed by the project.

The publication has been in the capable hands of Ian Gordon, and, being able to draw on his advice and experience, has been invaluable. I am also indebted to Peter Gamble for design and type setting, and to Cathy Gordon for drawing the maps.

My late sister Martha did most of the research for the footnotes. She died before she could complete the Introduction. This, the Preface, Biographical Notes and some of the footnotes are my work, but the overall credit for producing this book belongs to Martha.

William Rutledge
Bungendore
MMXV

Tom's father, William (Forster) with baby Tom in front of Gidleigh 1890.

Introduction

Tom Rutledge came from an Anglo-Irish family, which arrived in Australia in the first half of the nineteenth century and established themselves on the land. The family's origins were around the Scottish border, but they had been in Ireland living in County Cavan. The first member of the family to come to Australia was William Rutledge. He left his home in the village of Ballymagirl which is near the present day border with Northern Ireland, and arrived in Sydney in the eighteen-twenties. He gradually made his way south, acquiring land on the way, and finally settled at Port Fairy which was then called Belfast.

Three of his brothers followed him to Australia. One of them, Thomas, settled at Carwoola, near Bungendore, which had been acquired by William from Edward John Eyre[1]. In 1855, he purchased Gidleigh from Phillip Parker

---

1   Griffiths, G. Nesta, *Some Southern Homes of New South Wales*, Sydney, The Shepherd Press, 1952.

King[2] . Thomas married his cousin, Martha Forster and they produced a large family. He eventually made Gidleigh over to his eldest son, William Forster, who was always known as Forster.

Forster married Jane Ruth Morphy in 1887. Jane, or Jean as she was known, was the daughter of Richard John Morphy, who had served in the Madras Native Infantry, and Emma Styles of Reevesdale, near Bungonia. Forster and Jean had four children: Tom, the author of the letters, Harry Forster (Pat) who was killed at Passchendaele in 1917, Lloyd who died as the result of a riding accident aged seven, and (Alice) Elma.

Before the First World War, Tom served in the Citizen Military Forces as a Lieutenant in the 11th Light Horse. When war was declared, Tom was posted to the 7th Light Horse and was quickly promoted to Major. The regiment departed just before Christmas 1914. After spending time in Egypt, training and waiting for deployment, they were sent to Gallipoli—without horses.

After several months, Tom was invalided off with a severe bronchial infection which developed into pneumonia. At that time, there were no antibiotics to treat such infections, and he was out of action for about nine months, firstly in Malta and then Florence.

On his recovery, he returned to Egypt. There were no letters surviving from this period. Apparently he was unattached doing various training and administrative jobs before being sent to

---

2   Rear Adm Phillip Parker King, FRS, son of Philip Gidley King, 3rd Governor of NSW; he was a noted hydrographer who charted much of the Australian coast and the Magellan Straits; he was the first Australian born Admiral. [see B D Abbott, *Phillip Parker King 1791-1856: A most Admirable Australian*]

England and, after another period in limbo, was appointed to command a Pioneer Training Battalion which moved around various camps on the Salisbury Plains.

Late in 1917, he was posted to France with the 2nd Pioneer Battalion. In 1918 he was transferred to the 4th Pioneers as their commanding officer and promoted Lieutenant Colonel. The battalion served in and around Villers-Bretonneux before moving up the Somme valley towards St Quentin. They helped prepare for the attack on Hamel but did not take part in the battle itself.[3]

He left France before the armistice. Mr Hughes, the Prime Minister, had insisted that all the troops who had been away from home since 1914 should be given home leave. This was resisted by General Monash who argued that the end of the war was close, and he needed every available man to speed up the victory. However the Prime Minister prevailed.[4]

Tom was one of those granted home leave. He was placed in command of the troops on SS Port Lyttleton. By the time the ship arrived off Albany at the end of 1918, the war was over. Due to the outbreak of the Spanish flu epidemic, instructions were given that no one could disembark. Tom sent off a series of telegrams to the authorities stating that it was impossible to enforce that order and many of the men found their way to land.

Tom had been running Gidleigh since his father's death in 1912. When he joined the army, his brother Pat, who had been

---

3   *Australian Imperial Force unit war diaries, 1914-18 War*, AWM4 14/16/29 PART 1 – July 1918.

4   Carlyon, Les, *The Great War*, Sydney, Macmillan, 2006.

jackerooing in Queensland, managed the property until he enlisted in 1916.

The business enjoyed good seasons and wool prices during the war. Tom is continually surprised by the prices received for the wool. As a war time measure, the British Government acquired the entire Australian wool clip. Above average rainfall was recorded in 1915, 16 and 17 with 1916 being a particularly wet year, one of the twenty wettest recorded at Gidleigh between 1886 and 2005. As a result, Tom came home to find Gidleigh in great order and the financial position very sound.

Chapter One
To Egypt

Tom, Elma and Pat Rutledge

7th Light Horse
Holsworthy
nr Liverpool
16-11-14

My dear Mother

I have not had a word from you yet & suppose your letters have gone astray. I am wondering if you have got my letter. Yesterday after Church Parade I went with Major Onslow[1] to Camden Park & stayed the night. Cherie Gordon[2] was staying there & she told me that she had been at Gidleigh. I had a very pleasant time & only arrived back in Camp for lunch. I will be able to get some leave later on but there is not any hurry as it seems certain we will not leave till January. It has been frightfully hot here & we have a small thunderstorm here every evening but I don't think the weather [will] clear till we get a good one. I will be given command of a squadron which is better than I ever dreamt but it has not been officially announced yet & the Colonel[3] does not want it to get about till he makes his official announcement. I was examined by the Doctor on Saturday and passed him all right.

Your loving son,
Tom.

I left a small mirror on the table in my room will you please send it to me.

---

1   Brig. Gen. George Macleay Onslow, CMG, DSO, (1875-1931) of Camden Park, CO 7th LH Aug 1915 to Sept 1918

2   Cherie Gordon, b.1890; d. of William Forbes & Beatrice Deuchar Gordon of Manar, Braidwood.

3   Col. John McLean Arnott, CO 7th LH Oct1914 to Aug 1915, RTA 28-5-19. [see J D Richardson, *The History of the 7th Light Horse Regiment, A.I.F.*]

7th Light Horse
Holsworthy
nr Liverpool
19-11-14

My dear Mother

Everything is going on well here & I expect to get word that I have been officially appointed in a day or two. The Colonel has picked all the officers except two and has sent the names to Melbourne for confirmation. I think they will be a pretty good lot.

Will you please send my green uniform (coat & trousers) down tomorrow addressed to the Union Club. I have to go to Randwick for about 10 days to learn musketry & after Monday my address will be School of Musketry, Randwick. Will you also please have my military saddle sent to Walther & Stevenson[4] & they had better put in the bridle as well. I want a few little things done to it & will call in & see them about it. With love

Your loving son,
Tom.

You may not get this letter till Saturday in which case please send the uniform direct to Randwick.

---

4   Walther and Stevenson Ltd, manufacturers of saddlery, George and Hunter Streets, Sydney

Off Coast
Tues 12 noon
[22-12-1914]

My dear Mother

I scribbled a hurried note to you to send back by the pilot but I don't know whether you will get it or not. This is our third day out and everything is going on well. We have had good weather so far and everything seems to point to it continuing. Things are settling down to a general routine now and life is not very eventful. However after we finish fixing up the horses there is not much time left to think about amusements & so far everyone has been so sleepy at night that they go to bed almost directly after dinner which takes place at 6-30. Our day is filled in somewhat after this manner:

6-45 [sic] get up & do 10 minutes physical exercise then turn a hose on and give one another a bath on the top deck. After that, dress & have coffee. At 6-30 groom, feed and water horses which fills in time till 7-30 when men have breakfast. We breakfast at 8-30 & fill in the time before shaving &c. At 9-30 turn in to stables again & clean them out thoroughly then hose down the decks & groom. By this time it is time to feed & water again after which at 12 o'clock comes the men's dinner. We have lunch at one & in the afternoon repeat the same performance as the morning interspersed with a little instruction if there is time. Men's tea at 5pm after which they are free for the evening.

Later

I am afraid that you will not get this for some time to come as strict orders have been issued with regard to censorship. The only things which will get thro' in reasonable time are telegrams & postcards. However I will continue this in the hope that most of it will arrive some time or other. We have been having very pleasant weather, cool & cloudy & so far practically no one has been seasick. We had a very pleasant Xmas yesterday & ended up with a smoke concert at night. In the morning there was a church parade at which our band made its first appearance in public & played one hymn thro' quite creditably. We did no work all day except to attend to the horses & had a real good loaf. We had our Xmas dinner in the evening & they gave us a great spread. I tried to get a copy of the menu to send to you but there were only one or two copies available & they were all bespoken. I don't know why it is but we are all terribly sleepy & spend nearly all our spare time in our bunks. Time does not hang very heavily as we are kept pretty well occupied all day and we turn in very early at night. I am still collecting things which you put on board for me. I have got nearly everything now except for the knife & fork & mug. I think they must have been mislaid somehow or another but they are very minor items after all. My batman is turning out a treasure & does all my washing. What is troubling him now is that he has not got an iron but I will fix that up at the first port we call at if I can manage to get ashore, which seems doubtful.

It is a perfect day and I am enjoying a loaf in my chair. It being Sunday we get a bit of time to spare. On other days there seems to be something doing all day long. I hope to post this tomorrow so will leave all other news till my next. I will send you a wire tomorrow if I can get one away. With love to you all

Your loving son,

Tom.

[12-01-1915]

My dear Mother

I am writing this the day after my birthday & we expect to get
to our second port of call tomorrow so you will have some idea
of where we are. I heard just on leaving Australia that I had been
promoted to Major so you will have to put that title on all future
letters. I find it rather hard to write just now as our medico who
is nothing if not thorough & who does not know much about
horses is learning all about his saddle by means of a text book.
As his method is to read aloud & ask questions whenever he is at
fault & that is frequently, you can imagine that my progress is not
considerable.

I am glad to say that the parcel from McCarthy's & the knife &
fork turned up at long last about a week ago. I thought that they
had gone astray but the chief steward found them somewhere &
brought them to me.

We have been exceptionally lucky in the weather we have had so
far. It has been beautifully calm all the way and except for two days
there has been a nice fresh breeze which has kept the temperature
down. Those two days were pretty bad. They would have been
nothing if we had been able to stay on deck doing nothing but we
had to work below among the horses & with bad ventilation you
can imagine what it was like. The men took off all their clothes
except a pair of trousers -- the only way they could possibly do the
work. It is really a good thing we have the horses on board. They
take up practically all our time but otherwise I think we would

find the voyage very irksome. Every second day we take every horse out of his stall & walk him round the deck for half an hour or so. It is wonderful how quiet they get on board ship we take them round corners and all sorts of places that no self respecting horse would dream of looking at on land and they seem rather to enjoy it. It does them a lot of good and so far we have only lost two.

I am rather sorry now that I did not bring my stretcher with me. Everyone is using them for sleeping on deck & we get quite a lot of fun out of it. All the stretchers are alike & just as you are dropping off to sleep you are awakened to a fierce altercation. You listen and find out presently that someone has gone to sleep in another man's bed & the rightful owner coming along later objects in no measured terms. Then we generally have a shower during the night & there is a tremendous scurry to get under shelter. I am faring not too badly as I bring my mattress up & sleep on it. By the way the deck chair you got me was not much good. It lasted about a week & then went to pieces. However there are plenty of seats available so it does not much matter.

Next Morning.

One of the P. & O.[5] boats passed us this morning so there is a chance of us getting some mail when we get into port. We should get in late this evening but it seems a toss up or not whether we won't have to lie off till next morning.

I forgot to tell you that our boat proved too slow for the rest of the convoy so they went on ahead & left us to our own devices. I

---

5   Peninsular & Oriental Steam Navigation Co.

think some of them may have got in last night & the others will get in today.

Great excitement land has just been sighted. Of course everyone declared that they had been watching it for the last five minutes but no one said anything till the captain pointed it out. It is nearly breakfast time and I am looking forward to it with great eagerness. I am very well, having just got over a cold. We have all had it and I think working in the stuffy horse decks had something to do with them. It is my turn to exercise horses today so I won't have too much time to spare and then I have to initial all the letters written by the men in the squadron. Each of them seem to have about 20 relatives and they send a line to each one so you can imagine that it is somewhat of a task. We have a splendid lot of men and it's remarkable how quickly they settled down to the routine of ship life. Young Zouch[6] is getting on very well and his officers think a lot of him. Breakfast has just come so no more for the present.

Later

We have been running along the coast all morning & I am just adding a few lines after lunch before closing this up. We have been quite close in to the shore & have been able to see the coconut trees easily with our glasses. Every few minutes we nearly run down one of the native fishing boats but they do not seem to take much notice & just paddle out of our way quite calmly. I must stop now as I have all the squadron letters to initial. I got most of my horses exercised this morning and will finish the rest

---

6   Lt. Essington Lowther Zouch, 7th LH, DOW 17-11-17.

this afternoon. There is just a chance that I may be able to get ashore when we arrive about 5 o'clock & if I do I am going to try & get a small camera. I could get a lot of interesting snaps & send them on to you as opportunity offers. With lots of love

Your loving son,
Tom.

[18-1-1915]

My dear Mother

We are nearing our journey's end now and are due to arrive in port about midday tomorrow. I don't know if we are disembarking there but I think that it is most probable. We heard by wireless yesterday that the Arabs had been sniping the Canal but I don't think it will last long as there should be plenty of troops available to protect it. Right thro' we have had a splendid voyage and have not had a day on which it was at all rough. I wrote to you at the last port but we only anchored there for three hours and then went on again and there was no opportunity to get the letters away, so I suppose it will be posted the same time as this one and they should both arrive together.

We lost another horse last night making the fourth for the trip so far. I don't think we will lose any more before landing and are feeling very pleased with ourselves as we expected to lose 10 to 15. Everyone is wondering where we are going and all sorts of unlikely places are being discussed but I think we will go where originally planned and put in at least a couple of months training before going to the front anywhere. The horses will need at least a month's preparation before they are fit for any serious work.

I am afraid that I will not be able to make this much of a letter as we are busy preparing to disembark. There are such a lot of things to pack up &c.

I am rather sorry I brought all those old clothes with me now. I have worn nothing on board the ship except a shirt and pair of trousers.

The weather has been just warm enough to make it pleasant going about without a coat. I managed to get a stretcher at Colombo and since then I have not slept for a single night in my cabin.

I am continuing this at night. Our sports ended yesterday and we ended up tonight with a concert and the prize giving. Everything went off very well tho' the singing was not of a very high order. A song which took best of all was a parody on Tipperary. The refrain went something like this:

> It's a long way to Riverina
> It's a long way to go.
> It's a long way to Riverina
> To the sweetest girl I know.
> Goodbye Wagga Wagga
> Farewell dear old Hay.
> It's a long way to Riverina
> But I'll come back some day.

Just as the concert ended a violent storm came up and there was also a little bit of rain which I think must be something of a rarity where we are at present. I am getting quite used to being called Major now and my figure is beginning to look the part but I expect to lose all that as soon as we land and I can get a bit of decent exercise again. We got some war news by wireless last night and as far as we can judge matters seem to be much the same as when we left. There was also a brief account of aeroplanes dropping bombs on Yarmouth and of a naval fight in the North Sea during which the Blucher was sunk. I have some papers to sort and as it is getting pretty late I will stop for tonight.

Next morning

It turned quite cold last night and for the first time since leaving Albany I feel quite glad to have a coat on. I will write to you again and tell you what is doing as soon as I get a chance. With love

Your loving son,
Tom.

Ma'adi Camp
Cairo, Egypt
[8-2-1915]

My dear Mother

We are getting pretty well settled down now and are beginning to look shipshape. I can tell you a little more than I could on the voyage but our mail is still censored.

We arrived here about 2 o'clock in the morning after about 8 hours train trip from Alexandria where we landed. Fortunately all our tents were ready pitched for us so that was so much done. We have had to bury a sand bag behind each horse to picket him to. We are camped right in the desert but about 100 yards away there is the suburb of Ma'adi and it consists of very fine houses and gardens, in fact it is a purely residential suburb and as far as I can make out the houses are all leased by wealthy people who come to Egypt for the winter. They are very good and always organising entertainment for the men. Today Gen. Birdwood[7] came and held an inspection. He said a few words to me and was quite pleasant. We had rather an exciting time coming thro' the Canal. The Turks were quite close to the Canal and in fact some of the last ships saw a skirmish between 1000 of our men and the Turks. They have been having skirmishes since then and yesterday about 400 were captured. No one thinks that they can possibly get across the Canal as there are plenty of troops to meet them. We will not see anything of them for a bit as we have to put in at least two months training here first. I managed to get ashore at

---

7   Field Marshal Lord Birdwood. [see Appendix]

Port Said for a couple of hours and sent you a cable which I hope arrived safely. So far practically no one has received any letters from home and I am afraid that some of our bags must have gone astray.

9-2-15

The mail home closes tomorrow so I must finish this and get it posted tonight. I am writing now after lunch and have only a few minutes. The people living near are very kind. I have already met several and they have all given me the freedom of their bathrooms which I very much appreciate. The dust here is fearful and it is impossible to keep anything clean. We are just on the edge of the desert and as other troops were camped here for a couple of months they have the whole place ploughed up about 6 inches deep. Just where we are is a very fertile spot and only needs water to grow anything. In fact there are irrigation channels all through the camp site and I expect that as soon as we leave they will turn the water on and cut it up into farms. I have not been away from camp yet except in Ma'adi, but I have got pretty settled now and hope to get off for half a day tomorrow.

Last night one of the local residents took us to see the festivities in connection with a native wedding. The bride was not visible at all except to the ladies of the party who were allowed to see her. The bridegroom did not seem to be at all an important part of the show and we only saw him once when he came and shook hands all round. I believe the festivities last three days. Last night in addition to a continuous performance of native music on queer pipes and reeds there was an Arab horse who went thro' a most intricate dance.

10-2-1915

I was called away here and am continuing next day. I found out yesterday that I had missed this mail as it closed yesterday at 4 o'clock in Cairo. I will send you a cable this weekend to say that everything is well. I am very sorry about missing it but I will post this tonight to make sure.

I went yesterday afternoon with the Colonel [Arnott] and Major Onslow to call on some of the local residents and we met with a very warm reception. It seems that people can't do enough to make us feel at home. Our mail arrangements here are very bad I have had two letters since I landed from Fuzzie[8] and Cherie Gordon both of which I should have got in <u>Albany</u>. We know that there are stacks of letters here for us but they seem to have got the better of the people dealing with them. I have had no letters from you yet but last night got an Australasian[9] dated Jan 9th and spent a very enjoyable evening reading it in bed. I do not know if I have told you that it is almost as cold here at night as it is at home. The days are warm and fairly windy and about 4 o'clock it begins to get chilly and by the time we get up in the morning every one is very glad to put on their overcoats till breakfast time. Some of the officers got letters dated Jan 12th and I expect mine will come along in the course of a day or two.

The Turkish attack on the Canal has failed and in this morning's paper they are stated to be in full retreat. It is pay day today and we will have some money to go to Cairo on. The joint exchequer was pretty well exhausted. I am sending you and the Girl a belated

---

8   Monica M. Spencer [1894-1970], known as 'Fuzzie'. [see Appendix]
9   The *Australasian* was a weekly newspaper published by the *Argus*.

Xmas present as soon as I can get hold of something suitable. The Australasian I got was addressed Major so I suppose you have heard of my promotion. With love to you all

Your loving son,
Tom.

Mail arrived this evening and received your letter dated 10th January. T.F.R

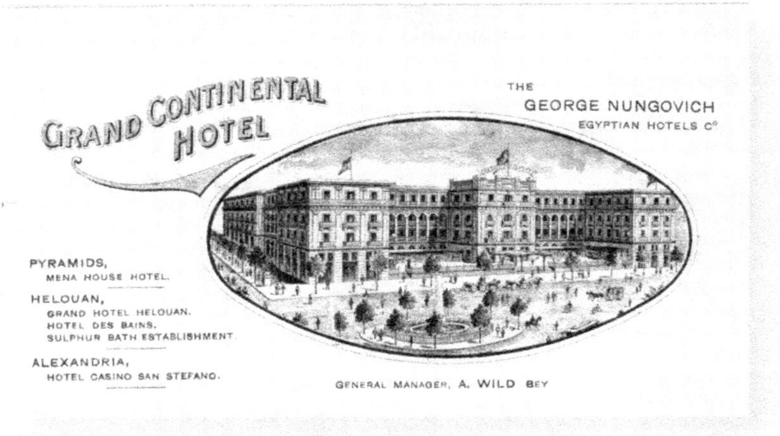

Letterhead from the Grand Continental Hotel Cairo.

Maadi Camp
Cairo, Egypt
15-2-1915

My dear Mother,

The Australian Mail closes tomorrow and I do not want to miss this mail. We are getting on very well here & now very comfortable. I have been purchasing a folding table & chair which make it very much easier to write. You have no idea how hard it is to do some writing when there is not a table available within miles. There is a branch of the English Ordnance Department here which sells us anything at cost price & my table & chair which are really excellent cost me just on £1. I have also bought a woollen sleeping bag & now spend my nights in comfort tho' it has been a little warmer the last night or two. Since I last wrote to you I have been in Cairo two or three times & have seen a good deal.

So far I must say that the hardships of campaigning are not very great. Officers can get leave practically any evening they like about 5 o'clock and spend the whole evening away. There is a train to Cairo every hour & it only takes about twenty minutes to go in. A fair sample evening is as follows:- Catch train at 5-58. Land at Continental Hotel[10] about 6-30 have a hot bath which costs 5 piastres $1 \cdot 0^{1}/_{2}$ [one shilling and a halfpenny] but which is well worth the money. Dine in the restaurant if funds are good otherwise in Grill Room. After dinner go to a music hall or else take a drive round one of

---

10   Grand Continental Hotel.

the bazaars or on Saturday night dance at the Continental or Shepheard's[11] both of which run one on that night. Finally arrive back in camp by 12-30 train. Only it does not do too often as lack of sleep does not help for work next day. Cairo is really quite gay as there are a good many relatives of officers here including quite a few Australians,

I was called away here & am continuing after Dinner. I have just received the wire you sent me to Albany. It must have come along with the convoy & has only just been sorted out.

On Sunday we had a very big church parade at which Gen. Birdwood was present. After the parade was over the General inspected the troops & it was 12 o'clock before it was over instead of 10-30 the usual time. Our padre who is a Presbyterian preached a very fine sermon. As soon as the parade was over I & a mate went into Cairo, had lunch at the Continental & rushed off to see the pyramids. It was a bad day as the place was simply swarming with soldiers & they looked just like ants going up the largest & coming down again. They are most remarkable works but I think you want to see them when there is no crowd about to appreciate them properly. We contented ourselves with a glimpse at the sphinx & a look into a temple just beneath the sphinx & a ride round the largest pyramid per donkey back. The temple was rather a remarkable place. You approached it by a passage which gradually led downwards till well below the surface. Inside there are 16 columns of solid granite of a reddish colour which are very like red marble. They are a tremendous size

---

11   Shepheard's Hotel, Cairo, named after its founder Samuel Shepheard.

and goodness knows how they were ever put in place. I believe
they were brought from a place 800 miles up the Nile. Inside
the temple there are six rooms in each of which was buried
a high priest. We returned to the Continental had a bath &
then dinner. At dinner there were two ladies sitting at a table
close by. I thought I knew their faces & half way thro' dinner
it suddenly dawned on me that they were Mrs Rabett[12] and
Bins[13]. I went up & spoke to them & Mrs Rabett said that she
would write to you & say that she had seen me.

A couple of days before I was in to dinner & who should I run
up against but Arthur Champion[14] and we had dinner together.
He had just been in hospital for five days with influenza, which
is rather prevalent, but he had quite recovered & was looking
very well. I also saw Joe McKay[15] last week. He came out to
find Billy[16] & was quite surprised to find that he had not been
able to come. He was looking very well. I have had glimpses
of Bertram[17] twice but each time he was on guard and I have
not been able to have a word with him. However I expect to
do so soon. I don't think that there is much more for me to say
but I think you will probably understand my letters better if I

12 Madeline, née Lee, wife of Percy A Rabett, of Fullerton St., Woollahra, real
estate agent with Raine and Horne, [*ADB Supplement.333*],

13 Her daughter Alison

14 Lt. Arthur Champion, 1st Bttn, s. of Rev Arthur Henry Champion, rector of
Bungendore; RTA 9-9-16.

15 Pte. Joseph Lewis McKay, 1st LH, KIA 7-8-15. [See G. Ellis, *Our Soldiers*]

16 Joe's brother, Pte. William McKay, Gidleigh, Bungendore, groom, 7th LH,
DOD, 16-8-15 at Lemnos. [See G. Ellis, *Our Soldiers*]

17 Tom's cousin (Harry) Bertram (Ber) Chisholm, Dame Alice Chisholm's 3rd
son. Sgt 6th LH, RTA 15-1-18.

explain about the hotels here about which all our amusements seem to hinge. The two chief ones are the Continental and Shepheard's both of which put the Australia in the shade. Shepheard's is not nearly so popular as the Continental chiefly because Gen. Birdwood has his headquarters there & so the juniors naturally keep away from it. They are both pretty expensive & an ordinary dinner for two costs well over £1. Still most of us are drawing good pay & we only dine there on an average of once a week. Everything is very late according to our ideas. Dinner does not begin till 8 & most of the best music halls & picture shows do not begin till 10-30.

From an architectural standpoint Cairo is a disappointing city. There are a few good buildings but most of them are very mediocre & as soon as you get into the native quarter there is nothing but a succession of flimsy looking buildings made of stones set in mud while the streets are so narrow that in many cases you cannot drive thro' them.

There are all sorts of rumours flying about as to our final destination. It seems to be a toss up between Syria & France & I rather think it will be the former. Still I don't think we will make a move for two months yet & in the meantime tho' we are working hard during parade hours we are trying to see as much as possible when work is over.

Our men are shaping very well with a few exceptions whom you are bound to get in any large body of men. If I get a chance at all I will send you a cable when we are leaving here & as I don't suppose the censor would pass a straight out one I will embody in the cable the word <u>quite</u>. So you will know if you get a cable with <u>quite</u> in it that we are on the eve of moving on somewhere or other. It is nearly bedtime now so I must stop. Love to all

Your loving son,

Tom.

Please give my best respects to the new Miss Gordon[18] when next you see her.

---

18   Philippa Gordon, elder d. of James Henry Forbes & Gladys Noel Lydia Gordon of Werriwa, Bungendore

7th Light Horse
Meadi Camp
Cairo, Egypt
20-2-1915

My dear Mother,

I discovered this week that our information about the mails has been wrong so I am sending you a few lines to catch this one. I find that to be certain of catching the mail I have to post here on Sunday afternoon. I am writing this on Saturday night and will post tomorrow. And now for news. We had a half day off & as the two proceeding nights I had not got to bed till after one I thought that I would have a good sleep. However the Gods decreed otherwise and it was not till half past three that I was able to get rid of some work that suddenly cropped up. I got in an hour & a half but should have done much better. After five I went and called on a lady (I forget her name for the time being) who very kindly gave me a lot of flower seedlings to plant round my tent. It happened in this wise. One day during the week my batman informed me that a lady had been thro' the camp & had told him that she would let me have pots of seedlings if she could have some empty ones in exchange which were left by our predecessors. I naturally agreed & next day a native gardener arrived with about 20 pots which he & my batman together planted out. This afternoon was the first chance I had of thanking her so I went along & had afternoon tea & a look around her garden. All the gardens here are sunk & they are watered by making an opening in a drain outside the fence & flooding the beds. It is rather early for flowers here yet but in another six weeks the gardens will be very good. At present there are a few roses, stocks &c and the fruit trees are just coming out. I spent a very pleasant hour & have been invited to dinner some night.

I don't know if I told you about my batman's man but it will bear repetition. First I must explain that there are always a lot of natives about the camp we have got so that we take no notice of them. I was surprised the other day when my batman remarked 'I wonder where that man of mine has got to'. I naturally made enquiries into his statement and found out that he had one of these natives employed carrying water for him in fact doing any odd jobs. The rate of pay is one piastre a day ($2^1/_2$ d.). I was interrupted here last night by Oatley[19] coming in he kept me so late that I had no time for more. This morning I have not had a chance to get to it & it is now time to post so I must send it on. Mrs Harry Chisholm [20] & Sheila[21] are here but I have not seen them yet. I expect to do so in a few days. I will send a supplementary as there is just a chance that I will catch the mail tomorrow.

With love

Your loving son,

Tom.

---

19   Maj. Frederick Dudley Weedon Oatley, 6th LH, grazier of Umeralla, NSW, RTA, 31-7-18.

20   Margaret Chisholm, née Mackellar, late of Wollogorang nr Goulburn [sold in 1912].

21   (Margaret) Sheila Mackellar Chisholm, her daughter. [see Appendix]

7th Light Horse
Meadi Camp
Cairo, Egypt
24-2-1915

My dear Mother,

There was great excitement in Camp tonight owing to the Arrival of the Australian Mail. I got your letters dated 17th & 24th January also a Sydney mail and two Australasians which I have not looked at yet but which will prove quite acceptable when I have a spare minute which is not often. Camp is pretty quiet tonight (I am writing about 9 p.m.). Today was pay day and as many men & officers as could get leave have gone to Cairo. I did not want to go as I attended a French Class which a lady is running in Ma'adi in aid of the French Red Cross. We pay 4/- a lesson & get conversation for an hour. If we only stay here long enough I expect to become quite proficient. I cannot understand why you have not yet got my letter from Albany. We stayed there three days and the censor certainly had plenty of time to pass it before we left but most probably it was brought on here and you will get it about the same time as this.

It seems rather a pity that the Girl did not go to Tirranna[22]. I am sure she would have enjoyed the races once she got there & then it's about the only chance she has of meeting people from the surrounding districts. I am glad to hear that the country is looking

---

22   Tirranna Picnic Race Meeting was a major social event in the Goulburn district

so well round Goulburn, I hope it is the same at home tho' you do
not say so. I expect you will be glad to have Cousin Amy[23] with you
& I am sure that she will help to entertain Gran[24]. Our letters are
not being censored just at present but orders have been issued that
we are not to say anything about the troops &c except in a general
way & you feel a little difficulty in saying enough & yet not too
much. The first force ran rather wild on their arrival but they are
more disciplined now & ever since we have been here they have
been behaving very well. Our men were rather warned by their
example and we have had nothing to complain of. Of course there
have been a few who have kicked over the traces but the proportion
has not been great and you must expect some bad eggs in any large
body of men. We did hear at Colombo that the New Zealanders
had played up there but nothing definite and you probably know
more than we do. The climate here is wonderful tho' it is rapidly
warming up. There seems to be something in the air that preserves
things & wood seems to last nearly as long as stone even if it does
not finally turn into it. At present the nights are cold & the days
warm but this last week it has been getting noticeably hotter. We
have all got very fat, I amongst them but I think we will all lose it
again as soon as the hot weather comes.

I think I will take to sending you a postcard as well as a weekly
letter. The former seem to be delivered with much more
regularity, and it will make more certain news for you tho' it
seems that just now there is only a fortnightly mail. The fighting
on the Canal was a good deal more serious than the papers have

---

23   Amy, née Ritchie, wife of Thomas Forster Knox
24   Mary Andrews, née Longuehage (d.1919), second wife of Richard John
      Morphy (m.1878) and Jean's stepmother.

led us to suppose. Major Onslow was there on Sunday and he said that they were still burying dead Turks. However the attack failed and there does not seem to be much fear that it will be repeated.

I expect that Max[25] will finally come. He was very restless when I came away and I thought then that it would not be long before he came after us. We hear that people are taking recruiting much more seriously with you now & it looks as if they will be needed. Most people seem to think that the Germans will collapse suddenly but there are no signs of it happening yet.

I am glad to hear that you have got Gladys Masters[26] back. It seems to be too much for one to do all the work, the place is too scattered.

You should come here to see what dust can really be like. It is very fine & penetrates everywhere & makes writing a difficulty as fountain pens clog up & the ink dries up in ordinary wells almost before you put it in. I am going to bed now & will continue later.

I am continuing this letter in pencil on different paper & in bed. The reason is that I am laid up with an attack of influenza. It came on me yesterday & I am taking things quietly today & tomorrow in the hopes of being well on Monday.

I was blocked in here by visitors & continuing on Sunday. I am feeling a good deal better today & think I will be pretty well again by tomorrow. Things have been pretty humdrum this week & we have been doing nothing much except work.

On Thursday night I & Major Onslow dined with a Mrs Bennett

25   William Maxwell Chisholm, Dame Alice Chisholm's 2nd son, m Harriet Christina, d Abram Orpen Moriarty [*ADB 5.289*] in 1913.
26   Gladys A Masters, b 1896 in the Queanbeyan district, d of Charles and Mary Ann Masters, Brooks Creek, Gundaroo.

& had a very pleasant evening. Mrs B. has promised to take me thro' the bazaar some day soon & holds out hopes of getting some genuine antiques in brass. I don't quite know when it will be but I must try & arrange for it soon. I do not think that we will be here more than a few weeks longer. Rumours are thick that we are to move somewhere or other shortly but where no one seems to know. The only certainty is that some of the troops left yesterday & that there are a large number of transports collecting at Alexandria. Our most probable destination at the present time seems to be the Dardanelles. We have received news this morning that the allied fleet have silenced the outer forts and is busy bombarding the inner ones. But after all it is all guess work & if every rumour was true we would have been all over the world several times by this.

I went to see Mrs Harry Chisholm last week but she was not in. However I saw Sheila & had afternoon tea with her. I am going to dine with them some night this week.

We have been doing light mounted work all this week & it felt quite homelike to be on a horse again. The horses were very fresh when we first got on them & men were falling off in all directions. Fortunately the desert is very soft just round camp and no one was hurt at all. The first time I tried to get on one of my horses she started to buck when I was half way on with the result that we parted company. However I caught her & got on & she proved quite quiet. I must stop now & send my batman with this to the post. It is no use worrying about my slight indisposition. By the time this reaches you I shall probably have left Egypt. With love

Your loving son,
Tom.

7th Light Horse
Meadi Camp
Cairo, Egypt
22—3—1915

My dear Girl,

I was very glad to get your letter dated Feb 14th & hear all your news. I am glad to hear that the pony Alf broke in for you is turning out well but I expect you will ride the tail off him & that he will break down in a couple of years. My little chestnut horse is doing well, in fact he is the only one I have got just at present. I have tried two or three others but none of them were any good. However we are getting a few more today & I may get something out of them. I should like to see the Garraway's pugs driving about with motor goggles on. I expect that you will be getting a pair for your pony next.

Mum tells me that one of the little fig trees has 36 figs on it and I expect you are all taken every day to see how they are getting on. Fancy the excitement there will be if one of them happens to ripen before the frost comes on and cuts it. I was in the bazaar on Saturday and bought you a silver puff box which I hope you will like. I expect that you will get it some time or other unless it is stolen in the post. Ruth Knox is going round with me next Saturday & we are going to look at some silk things & I may get something if the finances will stand it. While I was in the bazaar I saw a lot of brass things being made. They are all engraved by hand & some of them are inlaid with silver. The man makes a lot of little holes in the brass, then he gets some silver wire and hammers it into the holes and it seems to stick all right. All the different things are kept in separate places, for instance there is the brass bazaar, amber bazaar, scent bazaar etc. I was very surprised to hear that Tommy Cunningham had gone into Prince Alfred Hospital and fancy Mary going to England to learn massage. The district will be absolutely denuded of girls shortly & probably soon will be easier to get men than girls for dances. How are the Miss Finches getting on you don't mention having seen them lately.

How is Joan Champion. If you see her you might tell her that I see Arthur fairly often and that he is looking well. I see Bertram occasionally & he is generally without a coat and very dusty. I am getting a lot of letters written today as I am Field Officer which means that I have to stay in camp in case there is something to do. It very rarely happens that there is anything so I have a nice easy time. With love

Your loving brother,
T. F. Rutledge

7th Light Horse
Meadi Camp
Cairo, Egypt
22-3-1915

My dear Mother,

I have only time for a line this week to say that I am well. There is not much news to tell you. The chief event of the week is the arrival of Sir Ian Hamilton[27]. He came on Saturday & the general opinion is that he is to take charge of operations in the Dardanelles. I don't think that he is likely to waste much time & we will probably get our marching orders shortly. The weather is getting warm now tho' still pleasant but I think that by the time another month is up it will be quite hot enough. On Saturday afternoon Ruth Knox[28] took me to the bazaar and we got a sort of kimono affair, which the Bedouins wear, for the Girl. It is supposed to be good silk & Ruth says that they come in very handy for evening cloaks. I am sending it by this mail. With love

Your loving son,
Tom.

---

27   Gen. Sir Ian Standish Monteith Hamilton, GCB, GCMG, DSO, C in C Mediterranean Expeditionary Force at Gallipoli.

28   Daughter of George Knox, barrister, eldest s. of Sir Edward Knox.

7th Light Horse
Meadi Camp
Cairo, Egypt
2-4-1915

My dear Mother

There was no mail this week as the Orient boats do not run regularly. I sent you a wire today to say that all was well. I have got a bit of a cold but I am taking quinine and I don't think it is going to be very much. Today is Good Friday and we have had a rest. I went to church in Cairo this morning with Major Windeyer[29] and we afterwards had lunch at Shepheard's and spent a quiet afternoon in the garden there. We came back early as I had to go on duty at 6-30 this evening. I have had a good week.

Our work is slackening off a little & we get more time to ourselves. On Tuesday I had dinner in Cairo with a Mrs Gunn who has been very kind to us all & afterwards played cut throat bridge with Mr Gunn & a Belgian whose name I can't spell. Anyway he is manager of the Railways in the Fayum district & most interesting to talk to. Last night four of us went to Helwan[30] (a health resort with a sulphur spring) & had dinner at the Kewfik Palace Hotel. It is the nicest place I have been to yet & think if I ever came here as a tourist I would stay there. It is quieter than the places in Cairo & more comfortable.

---

29 Maj. Edward Windeyer, 7th LH; commission agent of Koorora, Raymond Terrace, RTA 2-9-16.

30 Also known as Helouan & Kewfik Palace Hotel.

I am ashamed to say that I missed the mail with this letter & will try to salve my conscience with a cable on Saturday.

I am continuing on Tuesday 6th March [April]

Since I began this letter we have had rather stirring times. To begin with there was a row in Cairo on Friday night which at one time assumed a rather serious aspect and it was not put down until some of the guards opened fire and wounded several of the men. It appears to have begun by some of the New Zealanders wrecking a shop in the bazaar. There were a lot of men on leave & they all joined in. Some of the Territorials were called out to quell the disturbance but they only made matters worse and it was not till they got our own men that matters quietened down. It is an awful pity as up till now the behaviour has been improving. I believe that the New Zealanders were the ringleaders right thro' but of course our men were in it (tho' I am glad to say none from this Regiment) and I think that we will get most of the blame. A good deal of the trouble here has been caused by the New Zealanders but people do not discriminate & blame it all onto the Australians.

On Friday I went to Church in Cairo with Major Windeyer & we struck a very pretty church & a nice service. On Sunday I went quail shooting up the Nile with two mates & tho' we only got 36 birds we had a very good day. They are much harder to hit than at home as no dogs are used but a long line of native beaters & you never know where the birds are going to get up.

On Saturday all the Colonial Infantry started leaving presumably for the Dardanelles & by the end of this week they will all have left. The Light Horse are not moving yet & the opinion seems to be that they will not go on till the infantry have secured a landing. However I expect that before a month is out we shall really be on the way.

The Australian Mail arrived today and I got two letters from you & two from the Girl all written from Cronulla.

I am very sorry indeed to hear about Pat' accident but I can see that you have been worrying yourself needlessly. After all (tho' it is bad enough) there are worse things than losing the little finger of the left hand.

Wednesday evening

Someone came in to talk here and I was not able to continue but am now going on. The Australasians arrived all right for the first month we were here but I have had none since then & suppose that they stopped them because they were insufficiently stamped. However I expect they will come along all right & someone always gets papers every week so that we know a little of what is going on. I only write on one side of the paper now because I am expecting every minute that our letters will be censored and they can then cut out the parts they want to instead of destroying the lot as may happen if there is writing on both sides of the paper. It is very good of everyone to take so much interest in what I am doing. I will try & write to the Aunts,[31] Aunt Jane[32] & Cousin Fanny Knox[33] as soon as I can but I never seem to get much time to write & I owe quite a lot of letters to people who have written

31   The Misses Ada Charlotte, Cherry Amy & Augusta Maria Powell of Turalla.
32   His father's sister Jane Eva Rutledge m. Charles Southcote King
33   Daughter of Sir Edward Knox.

to me & the worst of it is I never seem to get any forrader with them. Our reinforcements turned up on Monday, among them Billy [McKay]. I have appointed him my groom for the present but I expect to be able to promote him later on. He is looking very well & cheerful.

I will leave this letter open for a while yet but I don't know if I will have much more to say, anyway I will make sure & post it in good time. Nothing more to add.

Love
Tom

7th Light Horse
Meadi Camp
Cairo, Egypt
Tues 20 April

My dear Mother,

The Australian Mail arrived today & I got letters from you & the Girl. Also the Australasian dated March 6th and a Sydney Mail from Cousin Ned.[34] This is the first Australasian for about 6 weeks. I suppose the others were stopped owing to insufficient postage. I am glad to hear that my first letters from Egypt had reached you. From then on you should get one at least once a fortnight & sometimes once a week. It just depends whether there is an Orient boat or not.

I am sorry to say that I had to leave off here & have not had an opportunity to finish. I can just add a few words now before it is time to post. I was very glad hear that Pat was going on well & I expect that by the time you get this he will have recovered the use of his hand again. There is not much to tell you of our doings. We have been going on in the same old way. I have managed to get four days leave next week and am going to Luxor on Thursday for the time with two others. It is supposed to be the most interesting place in Egypt & anyway two or three days away from Camp will be quite pleasant. From what I know of the Mort[35] girls I don't think you could have found time hang very heavily on your hands while

---

34   Edward Lloyd Rutledge (d.1915), bank manager, s. Lloyd Rutledge of Port Fairy, Vic.

35   Jane, Mildred & Olive Mort, daughters of Arthur E. L. Mort & Constance, née Chisholm.

they were with you. Wherever they are there is generally something doing. I can just imagine the time that you & Hopperton[36] had at the Goulburn show. Must post this now as there is someone going into Cairo straight away. With love

Your loving son,
Tom.

---

36   John Chapman Hopperton, gardener at Gidleigh

7th Light Horse
Maadi Camp
Cairo, Egypt
Wed 28 4-15

My dear Mother,

I did not send you much of a letter last week and I am afraid that it won't be much better this week. I am going to Luxor tomorrow & won't get back till Monday morning too late to catch the mail so I must do my best now. The worst of it is that there is so little news. We hear vague reports about the doings in the Dardanelles but you will get just as much and probably more news in the papers than we get here.

Although we are still training we have slackened off a good bit and not working nearly as hard as at first. For one thing the weather is warming up and the horses would not stand too much. The men are getting a bit impatient now and want to be up and doing. There is a story going round among them called Kitchener's Dream which is worth repeating. Time 1920. Kitchener asleep dreams that he is paying a visit to Egypt and comes out to Maadi. There he finds the 2nd L.H. Brigade grey-headed & still in camp. 'Good heavens' says K. 'I forgot all about them'. Next week we are going to the Barrage[37] a squadron at a time. We march down one day, spend the next in giving our horses a swim and return on the third day. It will be more like a holiday than anything else and will be a welcome change for our men.

---

37   A dam on the Nile.

Billy McKay is getting on well. He is my groom just at present but I hope to be able to promote him later on. There is nothing to tell you & it is nearly bed time. You will hear about the Luxor trip in the next. With love to all

Your loving son,
Tom.

Maadi Camp
Cairo, Egypt
5-5-1915

My dear Mother,

I received two letters from you this week one dated March 28th the other April 4th. You seem to have been having quite gay times at home with the Morts & I am very glad to hear of all the doings. The more I see of the things here the more I am convinced that moping does a lot more harm than good. It is wonderful to see the way everyone cheers up when the mail arrives & it always seems more like home when we hear that things are going on just as usual. Here tho' we are only a couple of days sail from the Dardanelles everyone is trying to carry on just as if there was no war & I am sure that it all has a very good effect on the spirit of the troops.

I can't tell you how shocked I was to hear of Cousin Ned's death. He has always seemed to be so hale and hearty & I thought he was good for years yet. The Sydney Mail he has been sending has been arriving regularly every week including this week. I wrote some time ago to thank him for sending them but I don't know if he ever got the letter or not. I am writing by this mail to Cousin Annie.[38] We are just getting news now about the landing at the Dardanelles altho' there is nothing official yet. Still the wounded have been coming in for the last five days & from them we get descriptions that, tho' necessarily limited are very vivid.

---

38   (Hester) Annie Denne m Edward (Ned) L. Rutledge in 1889 in Sydney.

I cannot give you details as our letters are being censored but from all we can hear our men acquitted themselves splendidly and the landing will probably live as one of the great feats of history. A good many that I know have been killed or wounded but you are sure to have the complete list published long before this arrives. I am wondering what the effect will be when the list is published. I fancy that it will bring home to Australia as never before what the war really means & should bring about renewed activity in recruiting.

Now about the trip to Luxor. Capt Richardson,[39] Lt Bice[40] and myself set off on Thursday afternoon & we are all agreed that we would not have missed the trip for a good deal. Our train left Cairo at 8 p.m. I arrived at Luxor at 9-15 a.m. next morning. Not bad going for over 400 miles. We had the train pretty well to ourselves & were able to sleep nearly as well as if we were in bed. It was fairly warm up there so we rested all day & did our sightseeing in the evening & early morning. I can't very well describe all we saw but I am sending some postcards showing some of the sights & I can only say that the photographs do not do the subjects justice. Perhaps the finest thing was an obelisk at the Temple of Karnak 98 feet high and carved all over consisting of a solid block of granite. How it was quarried & erected passes understanding. The tombs of the Kings & Queens were also wonderful but a great part of their interest is due to the paintings on the walls which are as fresh today as when they were first done. They are the sort of things that can't be described and must be seen to be appreciated. We had three very pleasant days there & returned

---

39   Lt. Col. John Dalziel Richardson, 7th LH, RTA 20-6-19.

40   Maj. Luke Bice, 7th LH, RTA 23-9-1916.

on Monday morning like giants refreshed. I bought a camera up there second hand for £2 and it seems to be a pretty good one. I do not figure much in the snaps I took as I had to be the operator but I am sending some samples which may be of interest.

Now for your letters. I had not heard that the Craces were to leave Gungahleen[41] [sic] & I know how cut up they will be about it. Of course I knew they had got notice but I did not think that the Government would have enough money to pay for it & I am very afraid they will have a good while to wait before they are paid in full. I suppose that the house will be left tenantless except for a lot of idle caretakers. The College[42] certainly seem to be paying you a great deal of attention lately. The Morts are a great attraction wherever they go & always have crowds of admirers. It just goes to show how much naturalness is appreciated when you get the real thing which is not as often as it might be. I was very sorry to hear of Captain Gale's[43] accident & know what a shock it must have been to you. It is a funny thing that a horse who is perfectly quiet with anyone who knows how to handle it will play up with an indifferent rider. However he was lucky to get off as he did. Our horses are in very good fettle and hardly a day passes but some of the men come off, but they never seem to get hurt. It was a great relief to me to hear that you had had good rain & with any decent weather at all there should be good grass for the winter especially as there was some old grass left.

---

41   Gungahlin station was owned by Everard Crace. It was in the ACT. Resumptions for the Federal Capital began in 1913. Gungahleen was an alternative spelling.

42   Royal Military College, Duntroon.

43   Wilfred Ernest Gale, compositor, s. of John Gale [*ADB 4.227*], proprietor of the *Queanbeyan Age*.

I had heard dire reports of the drought in other parts & knew that it must be getting pretty dry at home. 'The Colonial'[44] told me yesterday that they had had only 50 points at Michelago but now the weather has broken there will probably be more. Fancy water being laid onto the garden at Turalla. I don't think that anything could give the Aunts more pleasure & they should have as good a garden as any in the district from this time on. Please give them my love when next you see them. I am always trying to write to them but there is not very much spare time & as a rule I go to bed fairly early. I think that the Easter Monday sports[45] will turn out better than you expect. Mrs Lundie is always prophesying disaster but somehow they generally turn out well in the end.

I am wondering if the wool has been sold yet & what sort of price it brought. Mind you let me know. As far as I can tell we should have had a pretty good year. Tell Pat to let me know how things are going occasionally, I like to have some idea of what is doing. By the way you might get me an unlined rabbit-skin rug & send it on by next winter. I don't want it now & it would only be a nuisance but it will come in handy about next November.

There does not seem to be any immediate prospect of our leaving here. They have to keep up a fairly strong garrison & while mounted troops are not wanted at the front they will probably leave us here. So far the weather has not been hot & I believe this has been the coolest spring for years. As soon as the hot weather comes in we are going to do all our work in the early morning &

---

44   Probably a family nick name for Granville Ryrie.

45   The Easter Monday Sports were a regular event in Bungendore which continued until after the 1950's.

Colonel Granville Ryrie, Officer Commanding 2nd Light Horse, European War, 1914. The Ryrie and Rutledge families were close friends.

take it easy for the rest of the day. I have had no news of Arthur Champion tho' I have made enquiries. At any rate tho' I think he is all right I would not say anything as there is too much risk of a mistake at this stage.

Sunday.

Events have moved since I wrote the foregoing. Some of the Light Horse left last night dismounted and we expect word to go any minute. All our machine guns leave today & I don't think it will be long before the rest of us go. I am not particularly keen on being dismounted but it is getting very wearisome here & we all feel that we should be up and doing. What our work will be I don't know but I fancy that as soon as there is room to move a little, our horses will be sent on after us. I sent you a cable yesterday just to let you know that I was still here & if I get a chance I will send one just before we go.

This foot business has rather upset my arrangements for clothes &c. I had got two saddle bags & was going to take them on my spare horse and they would have taken everything I wanted. Now we have to pack everything in a valise and put it on the wagons. It is all right so long as the wagons keep up but I am afraid that they very often won't. However it is summer now and I can manage a change of underclothes and socks with me so I won't be too badly off. I am not going out very much now, the strangeness of Cairo soon wears off & there is really nothing to do in there. The flies are getting very bad now so we spend most of our spare time sleeping under mosquito nets. With love to all

Your loving son,

Tom.

Ma'adi Camp
Cairo, Egypt
Wed 12-5-1915

My dear Mother,

Your letter of 11th April arrived today and I was very glad to hear that all was well and that you had had good rain.

I can't tell you how cut up I am about Cousin Ned. I can hardly realise that he is gone. It is only when something like it happens that one realises how far away one really is. I am very much afraid for Cousin Annie. She has never had any resources within herself to fall back upon & I am very much afraid that she will go to pieces altogether. I had no ink when I started this but have managed to get some now. I don't think that you need worry about your shares but if you like you could have Pat or someone else appointed. Anyway talk it over with Mr Cunningham[46] if you see him. The Morts certainly seem to have created a stir in the district especially with regard to the College.

You had not mentioned in any of you previous letters about Elma going away for painting lessons for three months. The only part about it is that I don't care for the idea of your being alone but I hope you will get someone to stay with you for most of the time. I think it will do the Girl the world of good to be away on her own for a bit & after living for three months with Jane Mort she should find herself. I know exactly how it is with her as I am built in much the same way myself. I have never been able to assert myself sufficiently & am much too prone to taking a back seat & I think it is the same with her.

---

46   James Cunningham of Tuggeranong and Lanyon in the ACT.[see Jennifer Horsfield, *Mary Cunningham – An Australian Life*]

I am afraid that Selwyn Miller[47] will be some time before he is suited. He is nice enough in his way but very colourless.

We have received our marching orders and are off on Saturday minus our horses. It seems an awful pity to have to break up the brigade (that is as a mounted one) after all the time & trouble we have spent in training but I suppose that those in charge know best & we must go with as good grace as possible. Anyway the long stay here was beginning to get on everybody's nerves. It is just about six months since most of us started & if you remember I said it would take about that time for us to get fit. Still I never expected that we should finally go away as the dismounted foot. Personally I am allowed to take one horse but I don't think I will use him very much except on long marches.

The Colonel got a wire today wishing him good luck so it appears that some rumour of our going has reached you.

Now Mums don't you worry about me. I feel sure that I am going to come back all right & anyway worrying won't do a bit of good. An order has come out saying that we are not allowed to take white handkerchiefs with us. Some bright wit discovered that Condy's Crystals make a beautiful khaki dye with the result that the Medical Officer refuses to part with any more and khaki handkerchiefs of various shades are drying all over camp. Today is Thursday and you will understand that we are all pretty busy. I will write as often as I get a chance but don't expect letters too regularly. Love to all

Your loving son,
Tom.

---

47   Selwyn Miller, b 1892 at Parramatta.

Chapter Two
Gallipoli

[c25-5-1915]

My dear Mother,

We are getting quite old hands at the game by this. We have been here now for a week and at present are in trenches about 500 yds from the enemy where we have been for the last 3 days. I am lying in my little dugout and the only thing that worries me is a battery of our own which occasionally fires a shot & shakes part of the roof down over me. Just at present it is quiet and the only sound that breaks the silence is an occasional rifle shot, the whistle of a bullet overhead or the boom of a gun far away. These sounds have become so familiar that nobody now takes any notice of them. About the situation here I know nothing & could not tell you if I did.

I have not had a wash for three days & have no idea when I will get one but no one worries very much about such things. As far as I can see a trench is the safest spot one can be in. Men sometimes get hit outside the trenches at the rear but scarcely ever in them. In fact since I have been here I have not heard of a single man being hit & we have certainly not had one of our own. A dug out is a bit limited for space but you soon get used to that & then you have everything to hand. Mine at present consists of a niche in the side of a communication trench just long & wide enough for me to sleep comfortably.

We are living on the best of fare including fresh meat, bully beef, bacon, cheese, jam, & biscuit & it is rumoured that we are soon to get bread. Tobacco is plentiful but the only thing that is hard to come by is matches. We get one box of safeties every week & they are as precious as gold. The country here is quite pretty & all over it are dotted patches of scarlet poppies interspersed with grass & patches of low scrub about two feet high. I am getting quite adept at sleeping at odd times as I am never sure when I will get a chance for a sleep. I generally get about 4 hours every night & the rest at any odd time. Billy is at present cooking for me & he makes a very fine bully beef hash. I don't think that there is any more news & I am going to try for forty winks. With love to all

Your loving son

Tom.

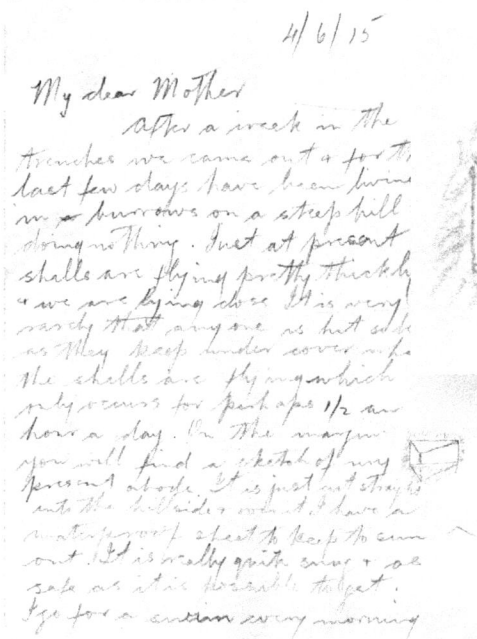

Margin sketch in the letter, dated 4-6-1915.(opposite).

4-6-1915

My dear Mother,

After a week in the trenches we came out & for the last few days have been living in burrows on a steep hill side doing nothing. Just at present shells are flying pretty thickly & we are lying close. It is very rarely that anyone is hit so long as they keep under cover when the shells are flying which only occurs for perhaps $^1/_2$ an hour a day. On the margin you will find a sketch of my present abode. It is just cut straight into the hillside & over it I have a waterproof sheet to keep the sun out. It is really quite snug & as safe as it is possible to get.

I go for a swim every morning before sunrise and the rest of the day sleep eat & smoke. Of course we may be moved anywhere at a moment's notice but it is wonderful how quickly you get used to things. We are not a quarter of a mile from the trenches & I don't suppose a minute passes that we don't hear firing but no one takes the slightest notice unless a shell happens to drop in the vicinity when everyone makes for the nearest burrow. You have seen rabbits sitting around a big warren in the evening & substituting men for rabbits the scene is exactly the same here. I can't think of anything else to say except I never felt more fit & well. Love to all

Your loving son,
Tom.

Have plenty of clothes but you might send 2 pair of woolen socks & a coloured handkerchief every month. TFR

6-6-1915

My dear Mother,

I managed to get a cable to you yesterday & I hope it reaches you safely. It can only be posted from here & will be sent on when it reaches a cable station. For the last week we have been out of the trenches and have been doing nothing except eat, sleep & smoke. We are still doing it but of course may be moved anywhere any minute. We are getting to know the sounds of all the different guns now & most of them have nicknames. For instance there is Tucker Time Annie so called because it generally starts shelling us just about meal time. Then there is Whispering Sally whose shell makes a peculiar noise as it is going overhead. We are right on the sea & one generally manages to get a bathe in during the day. The only thing is that if too many get in together a shell generally comes along & then you should see the scatter for cover. One man the other day dashed out and lay down behind an empty biscuit tin much to the amusement of his mates.

We are having the most perfect weather here you could imagine. Warm bright days & the nights just cool enough to make one blanket pleasant although it would be no hardship to go without any at all.

I don't know if I mentioned it before but Billy [McKay] is my henchman just at present & does all my cooking washing &c. When I first arrived here I brought all sorts of useless things but we have sent all spare clothes back to the base & I have just a change of underclothes a couple of pairs of socks a blanket and a waterproof sheet. Even these are a nuisance & will have to go when we move. I have not seen Arthur Champion at all but expect I will run across him shortly. With love to all

Your loving son,
Tom.

Paper is very scarce & I have only a dozen envelopes left. Will have to take to cigarette boxes when they give out. Have had no mail since coming here but it is rumoured that one is to arrive tomorrow.

11-6-1915

My dear Girl

I expect that you would like a letter from me tho' you will probably be back home again by the time this reaches you. There is not much to tell you. I have not been in the trenches for some days now & am camped in a little hole on a steep hill side. I have a waterproof sheet for a roof & in parts can nearly stand up without bending my head. I spend most of the time sitting in the doorway watching the boats of all kinds which are always on the move. We have seen nearly everything in the shape of a warship that there is to be seen & there are also aeroplanes hovering about both belonging to the enemy & ourselves. When one heaves in sight everyone runs for the field glasses to have a look & find out who it belongs to. There are lots of mules here & they are the cunningest things you ever saw. They climb up almost impossible places with two cases on their backs & they almost never stumble although one night one fell into a hole where two men were sleeping & things were quite exciting for a minute or two till they got sorted out again. Nobody was hurt so it did not much matter.

Just now while I am writing things are very quiet & there is only a very occasional rifle shot. It is sometimes difficult to realise that we are at war & that there are thousands of Turks within a mile of where I am at the moment.

I have not seen Andy Cunningham[48] or Arthur Champion

48   Capt. Andrew Twynam Cunningham, MC, 4th MG Squadron, RTA 8-5-19; s of James Cunningham of Lanyon.

since I have been here. Andy was away wounded but I hear he came back a day or two ago. Arthur has also been wounded & is not back yet tho' I hear he is expected soon. How did you get on with your painting lessons? I expect that when I get back you will have the whole of the new room hung with all the colours of the rainbow. Do you go in for Impressionist or Cubist styles? We live absolutely on our rations & cannot eat all we get. With bully beef, fresh beef occasionally, potatoes, onions, dried vegetables, bacon, jam & cheese we don't do too badly. We also get tobacco & practically the only thing that is short is matches. They are very hard to come by & are used with the greatest care. How is your pony coming on? I bet you don't win a prize with him at a show. With love

Your loving brother
Tom.

Sun. 13-6-1915

My dear Mother,

The first mail since we have been here arrived yesterday and I got your letters of Apr 25th & May 2nd. Also the Girl's two, one form the Girl herself & one from Aunt Gus [Powell]. I think the one of yours previous to Apr 25th must have gone astray as I had not heard of poor Cousin Flo's[49] death. I can imagine how cut up Aunt Em[50] & Aunt Fan[51] will have been. I am sorry to hear that Pat's hand has not been progressing as it should but it should be all right now he has got the rest of the shot out. There may be something in what you say about Jeanie Mort & I'll rather hope there is. The Girl seems to be enjoying her time in Sydney & I have no doubt that it will do her a tremendous lot of good but you must miss her very much. From all I can hear Arthur Champion is going on well but we get no definite news & you probably know more about how he is going on than I do. Andy Cunningham has also been wounded but he is back again. Billy saw him yesterday & says he is looking well. Poor little Barbara Ward[52] must have had a bad time, but I expect she is quite well again by now. I should be very pleased to hear that Dr Radford[53]

---

49   Florence Margaret Smart, née Futter 1855-1915 d in London

50   Eliza Martha Rutledge aka Betty, b. Carwoola 1857, d. Sydney 1949.

51   Fanny Garraway, b. Carwoola 1860, m. Arundel Hill Garraway 1886, d. Sydney 1952.

52   Daughter of Marjorie Ward (daughter of Dame Alice Chisholm).

53   Rt Rev, Lewis Bostock Radford, Bishop of Goulburn 1915-1933. [*ADB* 11.322].

had been made Bishop. I always liked him & think he would be the right man in the right place. There is nothing to tell you about our doings here. The only authentic news we get is from the Peninsula Press a copy of which I sent you. Of course there are any amount of rumours flying round but we have got so that we take no notice of them. When you are not in the trenches the only things that break the monotony are an aeroplane flying over or when one of the warships start bombarding a place four or five miles off. Tell Aunt[54] not to worry about Bertram. I saw him some time ago & he was looking particularly well. And don't you worry about me. It will not do the slightest good & you will only make yourself ill. No one knows when the war will end but I think that when it does come it will come suddenly. Italy is in it now & the Greek elections are coming on today & everyone seems to think the result will be in favour of Greece coming in. With love

Your loving son
Tom

---

54   Jean's younger sister Alice Isabel, (later Dame Alice) Chisholm. [*ADB 7.642*].
      Always referred to by Tom simply as 'Aunt'. [see Appendix]

22-6-1915

My dear Mother

Your letter of 10ᵗʰ May arrived this morning also the two you sent on from the Girl and the Australasian. Papers are very welcome; there are times when we have not much to do and every paper is read even to the advertisements.

I am glad to hear you liked the brass things I sent from Egypt. I bought them with much trepidation but I don't think that I paid more than 10% above their value & they were not very expensive, I also sent the Girl a silk kimono arrangement which Ruth Knox helped me to choose & which is really good. I don't know if she will appreciate it or not but I believe they are used for evening wraps. Pat seems to be having a very bad time with his hand. I hope it will go along alright now that he has had it properly fixed.

We are back in the trenches again now & for the last few days have been settling in. Just in this part the enemy's trenches are a good way away & we are digging towards them. It is pretty strenuous work for the men but I think it keeps them healthy. The last three nights we have put out a line of trenches 200 yards nearer the enemy and have just about got it ready for occupying. As far as I can see the trenches are safer than anywhere else. Last time, I was in for a week & did not have a man hit & as soon as we went out two or three were slightly wounded. So far in this position there has hardly been a shot fired at us. My general health is excellent; in fact I have never felt better in my life. The only thing that worries me is that I can see a shortage of tobacco & matches looming up in the near future. Last week I was without a match of any sort for two days but have manage to secure a couple of boxes to go on with. You might ask Pat to send me a pound of Gidleigh Mixture and a couple of dozen matches every month. Parcels seem to be delivered with fair regularity if they are carefully done up & they will come in mighty handy. Everyone you know in this Brigade is well & flourishing. I saw Andy Cunningham yesterday. He was only slightly wounded & is back again. He is looking very well & has grown a flourishing moustache. The Girl writes to me nearly every week and seems to have the knack of making her letters interesting. I am sure that the trip to Sydney will do her the world of good. Writing paper is very nearly exhausted & I am on my last envelope. Henceforth I will have to take to making postcards out of cardboard as the men do. With love to all

Your loving son

Tom

The monitor[55] has just started firing at some spot or other I must go & have a look at her.

---

55   A monitor was a ship with a very low free board with revolving turrets containing great guns

Sun 27-6-1915

My dear Mother

Your letter dated May 16th arrived a couple of days ago, also one
dated Apr 18th. The latter was due to arrive just as we left Egypt
and has been hung up somewhere. I started to write this just after
Church parade this morning but something or other interrupted
me and I am continuing it now about 4 p.m. while sitting in
the firing line. Everything is very quiet just at present tho' they
scattered a good few shells about this morning, fortunately
without doing any damage. Then later on the monitor took a
hand & shelled a road for about half an hour but whether there
was anything on it or not I could not see. In your letter of April
18th you enclosed two photographs of the little fruit trees and I am
amazed to see how they have grown. It only shows what watering
will do if it is applied scientifically. You have only to see Egypt
to see what can be done with water even in the somewhat crude
hands of the natives. How are the grape vines doing? I expect that
you will be getting some grapes off them next year. A couple of
days ago a Turkish aeroplane flew over our lines and dropped a
lot of leaflets advising us to surrender. They promise honourable
treatment and plenty of food for our comfort if we will do so.
Needless to say they were received with great amusement.
Another interlude here while I demonstrated to some of the men
that it was possible to light a pipe by means of a burning glass.
The demonstration was quite successful. The Australasians are
coming along regularly now & are much appreciated. When not
actually in the fire trenches we have very little to do except be

on the spot if we are wanted and any reading matter is eagerly welcomed. Gen Birdwood was round the trenches today having a general look about, in fact nearly every day some general or other comes along just to see if the trenches are still here.

I am afraid that this is not much of a letter but there is really nothing to say. I will leave it open for a day or two as I may be able to find something to add to it. At present I am feeling too drowsy to think properly.

Later

Nothing of interest to add.

Love to all

Tom

30-6-1915

My dear Mother

I have had a touch of influenza and am being sent to Lemnos for a week to recuperate. It is really nothing & the only reason I am going away is that I will get well quicker if away from the trenches. There is not much chance there of keeping quiet & no invalid diet. At present I am on a hospital ship where I will stay till a tender comes along to take us off, probably tomorrow. Now there is no need to worry about me for I will be as right as rain in a day or two. I am getting soup & milk puddings here & plenty of sleep which is all I want & I will be right in no time. In fact I had a long argument with the doctor this morning as to whether I should go to Lemnos or not. I wanted him to let me stay on board here for two or three days which I am sure is all that is required. This is one of the P&O, boats & most comfortable.

I am not quite sure if the date of this is correct but it is somewhere near the mark. I hardly ever know what day of the week it is and time goes tremendously fast. A week hardly seems to have begun before it is finished. It is now over six weeks since we left Egypt and it hardly seems more than a fortnight. I am afraid this is a stupid letter but there is nothing I can tell you of interest. With love

Your loving son
Tom

7-7-1915

My dear Mother

Am quite well again & back at work feeling much better for a week's spell. I managed to get hold of a few cards while I was away & it has relieved the shortage of writing material that was beginning to get serious. The men are using pieces of cardboard boxes, in fact anything they can lay their hands on & that will take a pencil mark. Love

T.F. Rutledge

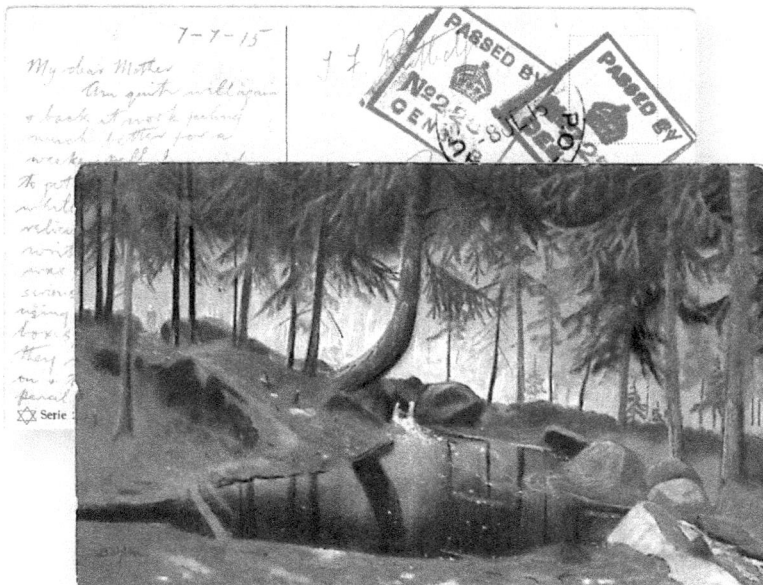

Postcard, 7 July, 1915(above)

10-7-1915

My dear Mother

I received your letter of May 23rd this morning & was very glad to hear the home news. We get our mails here pretty regularly although letters are sometimes delayed a week or so. For instance some letters have arrived dated June 4th. I am glad to hear that Aunt & Doff[56] are going to stay with you for a bit. I don't like the idea of your being alone & yet it seems a pity for the Girl not to finish her course under Rubbo[57]. I think the price the wool brought is very good, in fact far better than I ever expected. Last year all the fleece wool averaged about 11d so that this is a penny a pound better and from what Pat tells me it is not the best of the wool. It has been a long time being sold and I was beginning to wonder what had happened to it. I am very pleased to hear that Dr Radford has been elected Bishop. I think he will be a very good man. He is able & firm which are the two most necessary qualities. Mrs is a bit of a manager & I don't think will be altogether popular. If you happen to see the Bishop, remember me to him. It is just two months today since we left Egypt & the time has passed wonderfully quickly. You seem to have had plenty of rain for the time being & must now be quite safe for the winter. Now I must tell you all my adventures when I was away for a week. I had a touch of influenza & as the trenches are not the

---

56   Dame Alice Chisholm's younger daughter Dorothy, (also occasionally called Belinda).

57   (Antonio Salvatore) Dattilo Rubbo, artist & art teacher. [*ADB 11.473*].

best place in the world to convalesce in the Doctor decided to send me away for a few days. First of all I went onto a hospital ship where I got a mattress on the deck & was fed up with milk & eggs &c. If I could have stayed there a few days I should have come round in no time but it was rather crowded so after being there for two days I was sent on to a hospital on one of the islands to make room for more serious cases. I was pretty well again by this time & the two days rest I had in the hospital where I slept on a real bed with sheets made me quite fit again. After two days there I was passed as fit to return & here my adventures began. With four other officers I set out to return & as a preliminary we went to a ship where some of the staff officers were living. Here we were informed that our boat had left but that they could put us up for the night. I had a cup of tea & was shown into a very nice cabin. I was just preparing for the luxury of a bath when I was informed that another boat was alongside which would take us back, so off I had to bundle.

Next morning when we arrived, all the rest got off into a tug & I was just passing down their bundles when a submarine was reported. Before I could get off, the tug was cut adrift & off we went at our best pace for a harbour in another island. Here I was landed with seven men who had come off shore to unload some stores & it took me a couple of hours to get them fixed up with blankets & food as we had to stay there the night. Next morning we got a boat over & finally managed to land. I may say that during the scare I was separated from all my belongings chiefly a few luxuries that I had managed to get but fortunately I collected them again when I landed.

I have not mentioned the sinking of the Triumph before as I was afraid of it being censored but I see the news has been published in the papers so there can be no harm now in telling you about it. It was when I was in the trenches before and one beautiful calm day I was watching the Triumph & some other ships & destroyers cruising round & occasionally dropping a shell on one of the Turkish positions. Suddenly I saw her fire two or three shots into the water on the seaward side. At first I thought it was one of the Turkish batteries trying to shell the ship but the next minute a great fountain of water rose up alongside the ship & I knew then that the shots had been fired at a torpedo & missed. The water rose nearly as high as the ships masts and then fell all over her. She hauled over straight away & inside a quarter of an hour had turned turtle but she floated bottom up for about half an hour longer. There were a lot of destroyers, trawlers & small tugs about and these immediately went to her assistance, while the larger ships cleared out to sea as quickly as possible. One destroyer was alongside in two minutes & had most of the crew off before she turned over tho' when she did so there were a few men in the water & I was so close that I could see them clearly with the aid of glasses. By this time there was a crowd of boats round & they picked up nearly all the survivors. In the meantime the destroyers were nosing round at full speed for the submarine but unfortunately without success. They looked like nothing so much as a pack of dogs that have been after a rabbit & have just lost the scent. The whole thing was a most awe inspiring spectacle but I never want to see another ship sink. All the men were very much depressed as they looked on the Triumph as their especial property. Her job was to look after the Turkish positions immediately on our front & she did us yeoman service in this regard. It was just like losing an old friend. I started this yesterday but was interrupted so am continuing today (Sunday) after Church parade. Yesterday was more lively than it has been for some time. The guns were going nearly all day. This morning has been very quiet but two shells have just gone over and they may be going to start again.

We have just been making some new trenches and everyone is pretty tired in consequence. I am now going to try & get forty winks before lunch. The flies are awful here but with the aid of a couple of blankets I manage to keep my dugout dark & therefore pretty clear. Bertram is here now busy doing some maps & I see him fairly often. He was a bit seedy but is looking quite well again now. I sent you a cable today to say that we were well & I hope it reaches you fairly quickly. With love

Your loving son
Tom

Tell the Aunts that [Essington] Zouch is well & give them my love.

11-7-1915

My dear Pat

I was beginning to wonder what had happened to the wool
& was therefore very glad to get your letter saying that 143 bales
had been sold for an average of 13⅞ d. Of course I suppose the
expenses of shipping were somewhat heavier than usual this year
but even with that the price seems to be a good deal better than
last year. It will be interesting to see how the scoured wool pans
out. I mean whether it would pay us better to do so every year. Of
course there are many factors to be taken into account that it is
not easy to arrive at an accurate result. I am glad to hear you have
got the rabbits pretty well under. If you let them get away at all it
is the devil's own job to get ahead of them again.

You seem to have done pretty well out of the heifers & I see you
have got some more Red Polled cows & a bull. They are very nice
cattle but I am inclined to think that the black are better[58]. They
are weightier cattle than the red & I think just as good doers.
However as you say it does not much matter what sort of cattle
you keep provided they are all the same & a bad beast always
takes more to feed than a good one. You must have done pretty
well out of the cattle this year & there is no reason why we should
not go on doing so. The only thing is we must be careful not to
get too many breeding cows on. Then if a pinch comes we can
see it through but it will never pay to lose country for cattle. It
seems difficult to tell where stock are going to stop. Next year

58   Tom started an Angus herd after the war. For a long time it was the only one in
the Bungendore district.

breeding ewes should be worth any money. The drought seems to have been worse in many respects than 1902 & with the war as well the outlook must be pretty bad for a good many people. Sorry to hear that your hand is making such slow progress but with time it will probably come round again. I can't give you much news from here. Every day is much the same as every other day & half the time I do not know what day of the week it is. You will get from the papers what progress we are making tho' they are apt to imagine that gains are made which sometimes have not taken place at all. I would not like to have anything to do with this country when we are finished. It is crossed everywhere with trenches at least 6 feet deep & will be bad country to ride over for some time to come.

Your affec. brother,
T. F. Rutledge

14-7-1915

My dear Mother

Since last writing to you I have had three letters. One dated May 30th the others June 5th & 7th respectively. I will answer them in that order. You seem to have had quite a house party with Aunt & Doff and the Wards[59]. I am very glad indeed to hear that the Stipend Fund has been put in a satisfactory footing at last & that John has managed to get £50 out of Mr Maslin[60]. I have always been sure that we could raise the money in Bungendore if only the people could be stirred up properly but it takes almost an earthquake to do that. The Bishop must be a great trial to the Wards & I think it is noble of them to have him. I am glad to hear that Fuzzie has got a patient at last, there should be a good opening for her in Goulburn when she gets really established there.

You need not worry about the mail arrangements. So far I have got all your letters tho' occasionally they come a week late. Provided you put on the Regiment and Brigade they will find me sooner or later.

I do not think that Aunt & Doff will be able to do much good in Egypt[61]. By no means all the wounded go there & probably they

---

59   Marjorie, elder daughter of Dame Alice Chisholm m Ven. John William Ward, Archdeacon of the Monaro, 1913-1921,

60   Mr James Maslin purchased Carwoola from W. F. Rutledge after his mother's death in 1908

61   Tom was wrong. Alice Chisholm became famous for the canteen she established at Kantara, for which she received the DBE [see Janet M Champion, *Lady of Kantara*]

will not see Bertram at all as even if he is wounded he is just as likely to be sent somewhere else. I really can't see how you would be any better off either. You will be away from all your friends & I have no intention of being wounded if I can help it so you would probably be sitting round all day with nothing to keep your mind occupied. Above all don't worry it cannot possibly do any good. I am very pleased to hear that those poor Duntroon officers are at last going to get away. They must have been fretting terribly at being kept doing practically nothing. I am sure you must be delighted at the idea of having the Girl back with you again. I know how you would miss her. I am sending you this as I think it will interest you & paper here is much too precious to waste so have written on the back of it. Please tell the Aunts that young Zouch is well and give them my love.

Your loving son
Tom

The Heroes of Australasia.

IMPRESSIVE SERVICE AT ST. PAUL'S.

THE PRIMATE'S ADDRESS.

An impressive service was held in St. Paul's Cathedral yesterday evening in memory of the men of Australia and New Zealand who have fallen in the war. The Archbishop of Canterbury delivered the address; the Bishop of London pronounced the Blessing, and the Dean of St. Paul's read the lesson. The great church was crowded; and among those present were Lord Kintore (representing the King), Colonel Streatfield (representing Queen Alexandra), Colonel Dalrymple White (Grenadier Guards), the Lord Mayor, who attended in state, and many distinguished Australians and New Zealanders, including

The High Commissioners for Australia, New Zealand, Canada, and South Africa, the Agents-General of the Australian States, Lord Lincolnshire, Sir Edmund and Lady Barton, Brigadier-General J. M. Gordon, Lord and Lady Sydenham, Mrs. Parker, Admiral Sir Lewis Beaumont, Lord and Lady Fraser, Admiral Sir George and Lady King-Hall, General Sir Edward and Lady Hutton, Lord and Lady Lindsay, Lady Birdwood, Lady Petty, Admiral the Hon. Sir Edmund and Lady Fremantle, Admiral Sir Cyprian Bridge, Lady Darnley, Lord Harcourt, Admiral Sir Wilmot Fawkes, Lord Tennyson, Sir William and Lady MacGregor, and Sir Robert Nevinson.

In the nave there were several hundred soldiers, wounded or whole, of the Australian and New Zealand contingents, besides a sprinkling of New Red Cross nurses, and over the choir hung huge banners with the Union Jack and the stars of Australia and New Zealand. Round the base of the pulpit was grouped the band of the Grenadier Guards, splendid in the nave no rare worlds. This band and the organ played during the time that elapsed between the opening of the doors and the first appearance of the long procession of choir and clergy.

There was no processional hymn; but the service opened with "Brief life is here our portion"; and this choice was typical of much in the musical portion of the ceremony. In the short special service arranged for the occasion there were only a few prayers and responses, all directed to the particular intention.

THE SERMON.

The Archbishop of Canterbury, who took for his text St. John xv. 13, "Greater love hath no man than this that a man lay down his life for his friends," said in the course of his sermon:—

We are met to-night for a definite and a very sacred purpose. Here at the centre and hub of the Empire's life we desire to thank God together for the splendid devotion of our brothers from Australia and New Zealand who in the cause wherein we, as a people, have set our land regarded and their lives into the death. Just two centuries ago the Christian philosopher George Berkeley, a singularly clear thinker, was standing, as he tells us, in St. Paul's Cathedral, where he noticed a little fly crawling on one of those great pillars. In it, he thought, is the likeness of each human being as he creeps along. The service which, like some dreadful precipice, interrupts our life may turn out to be nothing but the joining or consent which limits the portion and sections of the complete life into one beautiful and harmonious whole. The dark outlook may be the curse even in the full daylight of a brighter world will be seen to be the inevitable span of some majestic arch.

But in this great gathering to-night we want another intention besides that. We must have the triumphant, for those whose self-sacrifice has earned with New country and to win or honour them. Among the lives laid down could be found, is always, bright example of high leadership; to which we had looked for upholding among their fellows the spirit which was manifested upon the great battle, the fruits of personal loyalty to Christ. For these lives and for the footprints which they have left upon the sands of time we praise God to-day. But it would be unstinted, untrue, to claim for all who thus gave their lives in their country's cause the character of stainless purity, or of the saintliness which we see in our hymns. Some of them, perhaps, many of them, were not saints at all.

They were manly sorts of the greatest Empire in the world. They were brave and buoyant with plenty of the faults and failures which go so often with high spirit. They need, as we shall need, forgiveness and cleansing and new opportunity; and they are in their Father's keeping and He knows and cares.

Blow, trumpets, all your exultations blow!
For never shall their serviled reverence lack:
I see them muster in a gleaming row,
With every mythful brows that nobler show;
We find in our dull road their shining track.

We feel the orient of their spirit glow,
Part of our life's unshaped good.

THE LANDING ON ST. MARK'S DAY.

In these words, seem so high for what we are remembering? The feat of arms which was achieved on the rocky beach and scrub-grown cliffs of the (Gallipoli) Peninsula in the grey dawn of St. Mark's Day, April 25, was a feat we are assured, whose prowess has never been surpassed, whose achievement has scarcely ever been rivalled in military annals. As the open boats under a hail from hidden guns poured out their men in thousands on the beach, before perpendicular cliffs of tangled scrub, the task of breasting and over-topping them, of expert even, a sheer impossibility. But by the dauntless gallantry of brave men the impossible feat was accomplished, and the record of those hours and of the days which followed is now a portion of our Empire's history. Who knows who did it? It was not the product of the long discipline of some veteran corps of soldiers. It was mainly the achievement of men from sleepy stations in the Australian bush or from the fields or townships of New Zealand, of men whose months ago had no dream of warfare as, like other civilians, they went about their ordinary work. Flat the call rang out and the response was ready, and the result is before us all. Those Australasians and New Zealanders are enrolled among the champions whom the Empire, for generations to come, will delight to honour. One of the best traits of all is the generous tribute given by each group to the indomitable valour of the rest. To the Australasian soldier it is the (brave) New Zealander; "the Australasians were magnificent, and deserve every good word that is said of them. And all unite to praise the officers, midshipmen,

and men who formed the beach parties in that eventful landing, each boat, we are reminded, "in charge of a young midshipman, many of whom have come straight from Dartmouth after only a couple of terms." But of necessity it was at fearful cost that these gallant deeds were done, and the great roll of drums under this dome to-night will reverberate our reverent and grateful sympathy to the Empire's farthest bound. This memorable act of abstinent service gives response already to the rallying call of the Poet-Bishop of Australasia—

By all that have died for men,
By Christ who endured the Cross,
count nothing but honour gained,
Count all that is selfish loss.

Take up with a royal heart
The burden upon you laid;
Who fights on the side of God
Needs never be afraid.

Be true to the great good land,
And rear 'neath the southern sun
A race that shall hold its own,
And last till the world be done.

THE SIMPLICITY OF GRANDEUR.

Then came the hymn, "Now the labourer's task is o'er"; and the Blessing brought the service proper to a close. Then the drums of the Grenadier Guards broke into the thrilling prelude to the "Dead March" in Saul, and when at length the last sound of the drums and trumpets had died away, from the far western end of the Cathedral thrilled the call of the bugler crying the "Last Post." Last of all came the National Anthem, played and sung in full.

The service was simple, but with the simplicity of grandeur. It was the expression of deep and common feeling. The brave men whom it commemorated had come from far off to die, far off have come from over which from this central point of the Empire of have given their lives; and last night St. Paul's Cathedral seemed to speak with the single voice of the Empire in love and honour of its heroic children.

R.E. Printing Section, M.E.F.

Newspaper article referred to. (previous page)

22-7-1915

My dear Mother

I don't know if I answered your last letter or not but I think I did. Anyway I don't know where it is now so cannot answer it. I have been having a pretty strenuous time lately but glad to say I got a good sleep last night. We have just been occupying some new trenches we have dug much nearer the Turks & I have just about got things Shipshape. For 72 hours previous to last night I had not more than 12 hours sleep & all the rest of the time I was on my feet getting trenches improved &c. Strange to say it did me good. Before that I was leading a very sedentary life & not getting enough exercise. Today I feel grand, in fact better than I have since landing which is saying a good deal. We are now within 40 or 50 yards of the Turks & I really think it is better for the men as there is more to keep their interest going & they are continually sniping. At night we throw bombs & flares in fact do everything in our power to keep the Turks firing and wasting ammunition.

Bombs or rather hand grenades are rather terrifying at first but they do very little real damage. The Turks threw one into our trench the other day, one of my men fell right on top of it just as the blessed thing went off. He was scratched about a bit but not seriously hurt & will be back for duty again in about a fortnight. Tell Fuzzie that Bice lost a couple of square inches of scalp from a bomb a couple of nights ago but was not seriously hurt. I think in a way it was a lucky thing for him being hit as he was rather run down & will get a fortnight's rest which should just about set him up again.

I have seen a good deal of Bertram lately. He has been making maps for the Brigade. I was able to tell him that Aunt & Doff were on their way to Egypt which he did not know as his letter for that week did not arrive. I am writing to Aunt & asking her to send me some tobacco & small comforts. It takes a good while for the mail from Egypt to get here but they will come along some time or another. If I get too much I can always give it away to the men.

I am enclosing two banknotes with which we were paid the other day they are rather curiosities in their way. As you will see they are English Govt notes & have a superscription in Arabic Characters. You might keep them for me. This is a fine place for saving money. I have spent a couple of pounds on milk &c which we can sometimes obtain, but have drawn no pay since I have been here & my back pay now amounts to close on £100. If we stay here much longer & I don't get wounded which (and there is not much chance of my stopping a bullet here) I will be quite wealthy. Love to all

Your loving son

Tom

English Govt Banknote with Arabic Characters.

29-7-1915

My dear Aunt

I received your letter posted on June 15th today. It was good of you to write to me. As you know Mother rarely says anything about herself in her letters & I am always so glad to hear from someone else how she is & how everything is going on at home.

I have seen Ber fairly often of late since he has been doing the maps for the Brigade. I am sorry to say that he has been wounded slightly in the shoulder but it is not at all serious & may after all be a blessing in disguise. He had not been well for some time & was run down & the rest should just set him up again.

I myself am pretty well now although I had to go away for a week. I got a touch of influenza & if you do get anything wrong with you here it is very difficult to pick up again. However I got away to hospital for a few days and the rest & change of food worked wonders. We have been working very hard lately digging some new trenches and are all just about played out. However we were relieved this morning & have come out of the trenches for a rest for a week or so & will soon pick up again. Just now I am sitting in my dugout high up on a hillside from which there is a most exquisite view. The sea is not 100 yards away and cruising about in the foreground are several trawlers, destroyers & monitors while a white hospital ship is anchored a mile or so out. Farther away there is a battleship with a couple of destroyers in attendance. On the horizon there are two islands one over 5000 feet high & there is just enough haze to soften everything. It is fairly hot in the sun but there is a gentle breeze blowing which makes it very pleasant in the shade. We get most wonderful sunsets here especially when there are a few clouds about. Just at present everything is very quiet and I have not heard a shot fired for the last five minutes.

I wonder if you would occasionally send me a few cigarettes some matches & a little tobacco. They are rather hard to come by here & will be much appreciated only don't send much at a time. It is less likely to reach me & is hard to keep here. I am afraid I have no money just at present but will square up with you some time or other. With love to yourself & Doff.

Yours affectionately
T F Rutledge

Don't worry about Ber there is nothing really the matter with him, he is only run down

29-7-1915

My dear Mother

There is an Australian mail in today and I got a letter from Aunt dated June 15th. But it generally arrives piecemeal so I will probably get one from you this evening or tomorrow. The last one I had from you was dated June 12th & I don't think I have answered it yet. Anyway we had a move today and I can't find it now. As I say we were relieved in the trenches this morning & have come out for a week or so to spell. This was badly needed by the men as they had been working very hard for the last fortnight & were beginning to get played out.

My dug out now is high up on a hill & faces the sea which is not 100 yards away. There are two islands on the horizon and the sunset effects we get just now are very fine. They very nearly approach those at home but I don't think are quite as good and this part of the world is famous for its sunsets.

Bertram got a slight wound in the shoulder the other day and has gone away. It is not at all serious & I think it is a really good thing as he was a bit run down & the change & rest will just set him up again. I have written to Aunt care of Allie Leathes[62] whose address Bertram knew & I hope she gets the letter all right. I have asked her to send me small lots of tobacco & matches occasionally as they are rather hard to get here. I know she won't mind sending them although I have no money here to send to pay for them. She told me in her letter that Gidleigh was looking very well and

62   Alice E Chisholm m Charles Stanger-Leathes in1883

that you were very busy with your new orchard. I suppose that is the one in the bottom of the fowl yard where we had the potato paddock.

By the way how did the potato crop turn out? I am curious to know. I believe that the country here would be very good for fruit. The soil consists of a fairly light loam for about two feet then you come to about two feet of silt with water worn stones in it and below that is a bed of clay. From the maps we find that a good deal of the country near the straits is either orchard or vineyard & there are thousands of olive trees within sight of our position here. How did the willows get on that I planted along the creek? The season should have helped them to get established.

Tell Pat to send me along a Pastoral Review[63] now & again. I get most of the papers you send me & I like to keep in touch with things as far as possible. With love

Your loving son

Tom

---

63   *The Pastoral Review* was a monthly journal covering agricultural affairs Australia wide.

12-8-1915

My dear Mother

I received your letter dated June 26th two days ago and I was very pleased to get some home news. The week there is no mail from Australia seems to make a long break in our mail here & then we get two or three almost on top of one another. I am glad that you were able to see something of Aunt & Doff before they sailed. I do not think there is much chance of my seeing them unless I am wounded but I have written to Aunt & will be able to get in touch with them that way. Thank you very much for sending along the papers & parcels. They generally manage to get here tho' somewhat later than the letters. We do not want much in the way of clothes at present but winter will be here in a couple of months now & I have no doubt that they will prove very acceptable then. Thank you very much indeed for thinking of the rug. I think that in one of my previous letters I asked you to send me one. I am writing to Nell Knox[64] today to thank her for the socks. I am very glad to hear that you & the Girl are going to have a month or so in Sydney & I am sure that it will do you good. It does not do to stick at home too much. By this time it will be getting warmer with you & I expect that the bulbs will be at their best & the shrubs should soon be coming into flower. I take the greatest interest in the new orchard-cum-fowls venture, mind you let me know what progress it makes.

---

64   Helen Edith Knox, b 1888, d of Thomas Forster Knox; lived at Leura, Bellevue Hill, [next door to Rona].

I saw Gen. MacL/n[65] the other day & he expressed a longing to be back again pottering about in his garden.

Yesterday & the day before I had rather a bad time. Our people captured some trenches two or three days before & we were sent along to support them if they were attacked & also to clear up the trenches. They had not had time to bury all the Turks who were killed in the trenches so we had to set to work, & do it & a gruesome business it proved. However we got it finished & got the trench generally cleaned up. I cannot say anything about the taking of the trenches but you will have seen about it & the doings here in the papers long before this reaches you.[66]

I am afraid that there is nothing more to tell you. After spending 48 hours in the trenches I spoke of we came out again & I am occupying a dugout just at present with a fine view & I sit in it & watch the ships all day & admire the sunset in the evening. The Brigadier[67] is looking well. I see him often but not much to speak to except an occasional good morning. Billy has been sick & was sent away to hospital this morning. I don't think that he is seriously ill. With love to all

Your loving son

Tom

---

65   Maj. Gen. Ewan George Sinclair-Maclagan, [*ADB 11.616*], as Lt. Col. Director of Drill at RMC, Duntroon, 1910-14, Served with AIF throughout WWI.

66   Refers to the battle of Lone Pine. See Phoebe Vincent, *My Darling Mick.* p89

67   Maj. Gen. Sir Granville de Laune Ryrie of Micalago, Commander of 2 LH Brigade, [*ADB11.502*].

20-8-1915

My dear Mother

I have received your letter of 29th June & am very sorry to hear that you have been laid up with a cold. However I hope that long before this reaches you, you will be quite well again. Just at present we are doing a good deal of moving about. We are on the job of relieving other people in the trenches & we go all over the place to do it. We do 48 hours in the trenches & then remain outside for the same time before going off somewhere else. The constant moving is not very pleasant as we are never in one place long enough to get settled & have proper dugouts. Just at present I am in a fairly comfortable lot of trenches & am writing this after lunch after having got the men settled in this morning.

George Onslow has been away sick but he arrived back two days ago looking better than he had done since we left home. While in Egypt he saw Aunt & he brought me a letter & a small parcel from her including a bottle of Eau-de-cologne which she said you sent me. It came in very handy as we had just spent 48 hours in some trenches which were decidedly high and I was glad to get something to take the smell out of my nostrils.

Bertram is back again looking much the better for his stay in hospital. He still has the bullet under his skin as they decided not to operate but it does not cause him any inconvenience. The amount collected on Australia Day was cabled over & was received with pride & delight here. It is really wonderful how the money is coming forward.

There is a feeling growing that men are not enlisting as freely as they should. It is a great pity that the Parliaments both Federal & State won't throw themselves wholly into carrying on the war & start a recruiting campaign in real earnest. It is all very well to say what we have done but are we doing all we possibly can & I am afraid that the answer must be no. I myself know a good many in our own district who could have come away but so far I have not heard of them coming. I would like to be home for a month or so to stir them up a bit.

I don't know if I told you in my last letter that Billy McKay has been sent to hospital. I think he has dysentery but is not seriously ill. You will have heard by the time you get this that Joe [McKay] has been killed. I will never forget that he was the first one to leave from home. I am well & in good case. Love to all

Your loving son
Tom

30-8-1915

My dear Mother

I got your letters dated July 5th 10th & 13th all in a heap by the same mail also two Australasians, a Sydney Mail & a Bulletin from you & a Daily Sketch from an unknown source. I have also received all the parcels you have sent me except for the shirt so that altogether I have not done too badly.

I was very glad to get the various addresses you sent me & I have written a line to Aunt Jane just to let her know how I am getting on. I had all the addresses but they are in my writing case which is in my valise but heaven only knows where that is. It was sent back from here when we landed & I will be very much surprised if I ever see it again.

I am very glad to hear about the comforts you are sending over for the men. Tobacco, pipes cigarettes & matches are their chief needs and such things as handkerchiefs shaving soap & fly veils although the latter will not be much use for the winter. They are not very badly off for shirts although of course anything that comes along is appreciated. Still there are issues of clothing & it is more the smaller comforts that they need.

It is very hard now to get any news to tell you. We go into the trenches for a time & come out again & having described our life here there is really nothing else to talk about.

You don't want to take too much notice of the letters from the front appearing in the papers. In the first place it is strictly forbidden by the Regulations to publish the letters & from what we have seen of them here they convey a very false impression. Of course there is no doubt that our men have done wonderfully well & probably, after the regulars (very few of whom are left), they are the equals if not superior to any of the troops—but I am afraid that an impression has been created that they are bearing the brunt of the struggle there whereas, after all there are many more British troops engaged who have had in many ways a harder row to hoe than we have. Where all have done so well it is rather invidious to make distinctions and it is an old saying that comparisons are odious.

I have had two or three letters from Aunt & she sends me some cigarettes and matches so that I am doing pretty well just at present. Tell the Aunts that I have seen Nat Smith[68] who is looking very well & give them my love. With love

Your loving son
Tom

---

68   2Lt Nathaniel Henry Smith MM, labourer, Lake View, Bungendore; 12th LH, MM 1917; commissioned 1919; RTA 28-8-19.

Thurs 30-9-1915

My dear Mother

I am beginning a letter to you now & will finish it within the next couple of days, there is no mail out now till Saturday night so I will have plenty of time. I got your letter about ten days ago but have been pretty busy lately & have not had much time for writing. The papers came along safely but not the parcel consisting of a shirt, & cigarettes &c. However I am not worrying as parcels nearly always take a week or two longer than letters & there has been no mail in since. The next mail should arrive on Sunday or Monday & it will probably come by that. This is the week when there is no Orient[69] boat & so we get no mails for a fortnight. It is a funny thing but there is always a feast or a famine here.

A month ago I had one shirt to my name, now I have got four & don't know what to do with so many. For the last six weeks I have had matches to burn but am just beginning to run short again. Then I have been giving away tobacco as I have had too much & at the same time have not a cigarette to bless myself with. The shortage tho' is not nearly so acute as it was when we first came here. We are getting a few who have been away sick & wounded back again & they always bring supplies. Then Aunt sends me a small parcel nearly every mail. Of course there is never an absolute surplus as you can always give anything over to the men & by arranging for regular supplies from independent sources you are pretty sure to get something by every mail even if some of the parcels do go astray for a while. The great secret seems to

69   Orient Steam Navigation Co.

be not to make the parcels too big & to tie them up very securely. I notice that small parcels arrive much more punctually than big ones but they must be well secured as they are liable to a good deal of knocking about.

I hope Alec Powell[70] manages to get something to do shortly. He is just the sort of man to make a good officer. For trench fighting a good constitution & a disposition to take things as they come are essentials. If a man is inclined to worry or is highly strung the strain seems to tell on him very quickly. I had a letter from Keith not long ago & he told me that Dudley[71] had gone to England to enlist. I think it rather a pity that so many are going to England and enlisting there instead of going with their own people. Most of those who are going are just the type we want & it seems a pity that room cannot be found for them. Of course there are some who have gone (those who do not consider their own Regts class enough) who are perhaps better away. Keith did not mention having moved into Edgecliff Rd tho' I knew of course before I came away that they contemplated leaving Yandooya.[72]

It is beginning to look to us here very much as if conscription would soon be an accomplished fact & I think that the general opinion among the men here is in favour of it. They have a feeling that they are bearing the brunt of the show while those who stay behind reap the benefit.

---

70   Pte. Alick Allman Powell , 1ˢᵗ LH; RTA, 26-12-18; grazier of Eulinga, Bungendore

71   Keith & Dudley were the sons of Prosper Orleans Williams & his wife Florence née Milson

72   Mrs Prosper Williams lived at Yandooya, Cranbrook Road, Rose Bay; probably named after the station Yandooya, near Armidale, NSW.

We have been following the doings at the Liverpool Camp with much interest & in some respects have inside knowledge from our personal experience there. We have had very good news from France & Russia the last few days. We get a wireless message now every day with the principal news in it. It looks as if the advance in France has definitely started & at the same time the Russians seem to have checked the Germans. It is nearly tea time now so I must leave this till tomorrow. Saturday. Am pretty busy today as we have just got some reinforcements and I have been fixing them up. The news from France continues very good but I am afraid that it is rather too close to winter for any decisive progress to be made.

I doubt if there is any understanding between Capt Davies[73] & Tommy C[74]. From what I know of him I fancy that he is rather susceptible but usually his fancies do not last very long.

I am sorry to hear that Cherie Gordon has had appendicitis but I hear from Major Onslow that she is going on well & she will probably be all right again by the time this reaches you. Cousin Tom[75] seems to have had a lucky escape. Blood poisoning is a very nasty thing & it seems to come on so quickly.

I have written to Aunt Jane King & asked her to send me one or two little things that I did not think Aunt could get for me in Egypt.

----

73   Lt-Col Charles Stewart Davies, CMG, DSO, did marry [Griselda] Dorothea 'Tommy' Cunningham in 1916 but Tom was prescient as Davies deserted her in 1921.

74   (Griselda) Dorothea Cunningham, d. of James & Mary Cunningham of Lanyon, known as 'Tommy'.

75   Thomas Forster Knox, [1849-1919], managing director of the Sydney branch [F G] Dalgety & Co. Ltd, 3rd son of Sir Edward Knox, [ADB 5.38].

Will you please thank Nell Knox for the shirt she sent me when you next see her. I will certainly try it & let you know later on if it proves efficacious or not. We do have a certain amount of trouble with vermin & they are sure to get worse when winter comes on & it gets too cold for us to go for a swim. You might also tell her that I am sorry to say that so far I do not think I have killed a Turk or German tho' I have frightened several & am living in hopes of blowing one or two up shortly. Just at present we are playing a little game of mining and countermining with them & it has fallen to my lot to have charge of the operations on our side. So far the honours lie with us we have blown them up a couple of times with success & the only time they tried to do likewise to us they miscalculated somehow & it recoiled very effectively on their own heads.

We are still waiting for our holiday but I don't think it will be delayed much longer now. I have been somewhat run down but have quite recovered now & am as fit as I ever was. Bertram went away sick this week but is not seriously ill. You will have heard before this that poor Billy McKay is dead. I know no details except that it was from illness. With love

Your loving son

Tom

12-10-1915

My dear Mother

I received your letter dated August 24th a week ago & today I got one dated Aug 22nd also a parcel containing a shirt, chocolate, toothbrush & cigarettes. The papers came the week before & I am still reading them. There is another mail in tonight & we should get mail up to 30th Aug by that & that will bring us right up to date. Since writing this I got a parcel of tobacco from Klaisdorff & it was very welcome. There are still some complaints about the mail but I must say that so far as I am concerned I do not know of anything that has gone astray tho' of course letters & parcels are always liable to be delayed a week or so. I got a letter from Jack Wark[76] this mail telling me that he is sending me 15 sheepskin vests for distribution. He collected the money for them from the people on the place & I have written to assure him that they will be most useful. We are all rather dreading the winter here.

From what we can learn it is very cold & wet & things like sheepskin vests are just what will be wanted. So far the weather is delightful but it may change now at any time. I don't think that I ever told you that Dr Flecker[77] left us before we left Egypt & we had a very nice Englishman in his place. The latter has now gone away sick & we have got Dr W. O'Hara[78] from Melbourne in his place. You will know of him. I am glad to hear that you are getting my letters safely. It is very hard to make them interesting now as every week is so very much the

76   John Wark, overseer, Gidleigh.
77   Maj. Hugo Flecker, MB,ChM,1908, FRCS Edin 1912; AAMC, RTA 13-2-17.
78   Capt William Ernest O'Hara, LRCP& S Edin, 1903; Reg. Vic. 1906; AAMC, RTA 17-8-16.

same. I do not mention anything much about the operations as I do not care to risk having them delayed by the Censor. Bertram is still away and I think this time he has probably gone to Egypt or Malta, most likely that latter place. I wrote & told Aunt he had gone so she will probably be able to see something of him before he comes back.

The sheepskin waistcoat & leather breeches have not arrived yet but they are nearly sure to get here in due course. We are suffering from a plague of fleas just now & the insect powder & sulphur will come in handy. I have been wearing a small bag of sulphur round my neck for some time & find that tho' not an absolute preventative, it mitigates the nuisance considerably & the only place I am worried is on the legs. I will try the mercurial tape when it arrives & let you know how it gets on. I have written to Aunt asking her to send the rabbit skin rug over & I expect she will get it to me by someone returning from Egypt. With regard to the comforts for the 6th & 7th Light Horse I should recommend more comforts & less clothes. By this I mean that the authorities provide us with shirts, socks, singlets, & all ordinary articles of apparel & with the exception perhaps of socks the men can always [get] whatever they want. Comforts include such things as sheepskin vests, mufflers, mittens, handkerchiefs &c. Then there are such things as soap, shaving soap, and of course sweets, tobacco cigarettes & matches. Mr Budden[79] who is looking after all the Comfort Funds this side was here not long ago & he will no doubt write over officially. As he is in direct touch with us you can go by what he says & if any sudden want crops up he can always let you know about it. A Field

---

79   Henry Ebenezer Budden, CBE, [1871-1944], a Sydney architect, was appointed First War Chest Commissioner to work on the 'Mediterranean Littoral and Egypt' in July 1915.

Force Canteen has been established here now so we are able to buy all sorts of extras, tinned fruit, fish &c. & I am sure it will make a great difference to our comfort. I think it is a very good idea to send over sweets &c for Xmas. We have not yet received the first lot of comforts that were sent but expect them any time now. I am very sorry to hear that Wynella[80] is to be sold & it will be very hard on Miss de Lauret[81] especially. Of course I know that Austin's[82] affairs were pretty well hopeless but had an idea that Wynella belonged to Miss de Lauret & that it was not encumbered. I had an idea that Mrs Bellasis[83] arranged it when she was last out in Australia.

I am rather surprised to hear that there is an understanding between Tommy Cunningham & Captain Davis. Between you & me I don't think, although he is a nice enough man to meet, that he is any great catch although of course I may be wrong.

I expect you & the Girl will be very glad to get back home again. There should not be much cold weather after you get back & you will be able to see how all the little fruit trees get on. I am very well now & eat enormous meals. I did get fairly thin but am picking up again fast. With Love

Your loving son

Tom

---

80   Resumed by the Government. [See G. N. Griffiths, *Some Southern Homes*], p.63

81   Louise Blanche de Lauret [d.1947] kept house for her brother at Wynella. Her embroideries are now held at Riversdale, Goulburn.

82   Austin Charles de Lauret [d.1936], stock & station agent, Goulburn

83   Marie Sophie Nicholson de Lauret, m. James Campsie Dalglish, inherited his original share in the Broken Hill Proprietory Co., [worth about £40,000 a year] then m. William Joseph Bellasis.

Chapter Three
Malta and Florence

27-10-1915

My dear Mother

I am laid up in Tigné Hospital[84] Malta with bronchitis or a very fair imitation. You are not to worry about me as I have passed the worst & am on the high road towards recovery. I fancy it will be a good while before I am sent back to the front and I may be sent to England later on to recuperate. However I will cable you if I am.

For the present keep on addressing letters as usual. I do not feel up to writing very much now but will send you a better letter in a few days time.

Your loving son

Tom

Australian Imperial Force

Base Records Office, A.I.E.F.

Victoria Barracks

MELBOURNE. 16th December, 1915

Dear Sir

The following is and extract from a Niminal Roll of sick and wounded, received by post, dated 27/10/15 who landed at Malta 24/10/15 from hospital ship "Soudan", Major T.L.F Rutledge, 7th Light Horse Regiment, suffering from influenza.

Any further reports received will be pormptly communicated to you.

Yours faithfully,
J.M. LEAN . Captain.
Officer i/c Base Records.

Mr. H.F. Rutledge
Gidleigh
Bungendore, N.S.W.

---

84   Military Hospital, Tigné, Malta.

20-11-1915

My dear Mother

I am very sorry I have been so long in writing to you but I have not been able to sit up in bed & found it very awkward to write. I have had a pretty bad time but am much better now & hope to be able to get up soon. I arrived here in a delirious condition with a very high temperature. They practically kept me alive for four or five days on beef tea raw eggs & brandy, the only things I could take but I got on well & was just getting up when I got an attack of jaundice which threw me right back & I had to start all over again. However my temperature is normal again now & all I have to do is to get strong as quickly as may be.

I am nearly sure to be sent to England to recuperate and they say that it will probably be three months before I get back to the front. I am afraid that this will arrive too late for Xmas but I wish you all a Merry One all the same. With Love

Your loving son
Tom

P.S. Do you realise that there are two ends to a cable.

1st Dec 15

My dear Mother

I am sorry that I have let so long go by without a letter but you do not realise how time goes by. One day is so very much like another. I am making quite satisfactory progress & the Doctor is quite pleased with the way I am going on but I am very much pulled down & it is a slow business. I am allowed to sit up in bed now & hope to get into a chair soon but as yet I am physically unable to walk. I am allowed solid food now & live chiefly on chicken which is really very good & occasionally we get very nice young pigeons. The hospital where I am (Tigné) is really in peace time the officers' quarters of the Royal Artillery who form part of the garrison. It is a very fine building & not at all unsuited to its present purpose. We are very well looked after & the nurses are all very good.

This place is celebrated for its lace & silver filigree work & I hope to send you & the Girl some samples as Xmas presents when I am well enough to get about. Some residents here who come to see us have promised to go shopping with me so I hope not to be taken in with any imitation stuff. I am afraid that this is not a very interesting letter but when I am able to get about I hope to be able to write a better one. With love

Your loving son
Tom

15-12-15

My dear Mother

I am afraid that I have been a very bad correspondent while in hospital but there is so little to write about and at first I was really too weak & ill to write. I am getting on very well now. I sit out in the sun whenever there is any & am able to walk a little tho' my legs get pretty wobbly if I stand too long. As far as I can tell I will not get back to the Regt till March or thereabouts but where I am going to spend the intervening time is more than I can tell. I will go to England if I can possibly manage it tho' the climate is not the best at this time of year.

It is lucky in a way that I got sick when I did. The weather has turned very cold at the Dardanelles & there are a good many cases of frostbite coming in from there.

There is really no news. I have not been out of the grounds yet so can tell you nothing about Malta but I hope to do so in my next. With love.

Your loving son
Tom

Friday 31-12-1915

My dear Mother

I am getting on very well now and expect to be sent to a convalescent camp in Sicily in a week or two. All this week I have been going about seeing the island tho' I have not been to any of the regular sights as yet. Tomorrow night I am going to the Opera so you can see that I am coming on well.

I hear that the Regiment is in Egypt & I am naturally anxious to get back to them but I am afraid that will not be for 6 weeks yet.

This place has a tremendous population & every square inch that is not built over has a crop of some sort. All the hills are terraced with stone walls & the island should be looking quite green now but the fields are so small that the walls shut most of the green out of sight & give the landscape a very grey appearance. I am not very taken with the place & will be glad when I am moved on somewhere else. We get very little war news but from what we can gather things seem to be at a standstill nearly everywhere.

Have just found out that by posting now I can catch a mail. With love

Your loving son
Tom

Tigné Hospital
Malta
Jan 9th '16

My dear Mother

I am afraid that I have not much news for you this week. I am getting on very well but see no prospect of getting away for some time yet. I hear the Regt. Is back in Egypt & I am naturally anxious to get back to it but they won't let me go till I am quite fit. I am feeling quite well now but I was pretty low & it seems to take a long time to completely recover. I go about & can do pretty well as I like but find that I cannot go up a hill or upstairs fast. If I do, it knocks me up. I don't think there is much chance of my getting back till well on in February. I think I will be sent to Italy or Sicily first. I shan't be sorry as there is very little to do here. I have driven over most of the island & seen the show places & there does not seem much left.

Besides the apologies they have for cabs are most uncomfortable things to ride in & the man I have been going about with is leaving tomorrow. He is a Scotchman & we got on very well together. There is no one else I have met that I care very much about. Most of them are town men who do not care for the country & we have not very much in common. The English Colony here is very good & they are always asking me out to afternoon tea but you know how much I care for that sort of thing. I went to an afternoon tea yesterday and was the only man there amid something like a dozen women. It took me about an hour to get my tea as I was kept so busy handing things round.

I don't want you to think I am growling or low in spirits because I am not & I can generally manage to make myself at home. It is not having anything to do that is so strange. I have never been idle for very long at a time & it comes rather strange to me now. The submarines are still showing some activity here & they got the *Persia* the other day but I don't think it will be long before they are caught. The Navy has a way of their own of dealing with them that is proving very effective. One never hears anything of what they are doing but they do not let the grass grow under their feet & probably the secrecy that is maintained helps them considerably. I got your cable on New Year's Day & was pleased to hear that everything was well.

Nearly all my letters are going to London but two from the Girl have managed to get here but both were very old. I have now written to have all my letters sent back to Egypt, & I will have a regular orgy when I do get them. I am afraid to have them sent here as I may be moved out at any minute & then I would probably lose them altogether.

The weather here is splendid. Except for one heavy storm here I have not seen any rain worth speaking of since I left Australia & am beginning to forget what it is like. I see by the papers that you are having rain at home & the price of wool is soaring so you should have a good year. With love to all

Your loving son

Tom

Le Balze[85]
Fiesole
Florence
25-1-16

My dear Mother

It is a good while since I have written to you but there was really nothing to write about in Malta and I was sent off here at a moments notice.

We left Malta at 7 in the morning in a small Red Cross steam yacht which has been lent by Lord Dunraven[86]. The sea was not rough but the yacht was a bit lively & most of the 25 officers on board were pretty sorry for themselves. I was not among the number & quite enjoyed the trip. We arrived at Syracuse about 5 p.m. & spent the night in an hotel there. There was no time for sightseeing as we left there by train at 10 the next morning for Messina. There are one or two sights worth seeing there & I may put in a day on my way back. The journey to Messina was most interesting. All the way we were travelling through orange & lemon groves with the fruit just ripe still on the trees. We got a splendid view of Etna which was in sight nearly the whole way. The line runs along the coast & the scenery is splendid although the number of tunnels we passed thro' interfered somewhat at times. At Messina our train was carried bodily over the straits in a ferry & we continued travelling all night. We arrived in Rome about 10 o'clock next morning. We had to wait three hours there

---

85   Villa Le Balze, built in 1911 for Charles Augustus Strong. Since gifted to Georgetown University. [See Katie Campbell, *Paradise of Exiles*, ch 14, p132].

86   Col the Earl of Dunraven and Mount-Earl, DSO, Commandant Lines of Communications 1915

but by the time we had some breakfast & a bath there was no time left for sightseeing. We had not been able to get sleepers the night before so you can imagine that a bath was a necessity. We arrived here finally about 10 o'clock at night tired out & were glad enough to get to bed. Fiesole is about four miles from Florence & so far I have done no sightseeing. Sunday, there was a fog all day & yesterday I had to call on the Doctor just to let him see how I was. I have to go again before I leave & he then sees the change that has taken place. Now I must explain how we came to be here at all.

As you know there is a large English & American colony living here & Lady Sybil Cutting[87] who seems to be a sort of leader arranged with several of them to put up convalescent officers.

(I was stopped here & am continuing next day hence change in ink).

About 20 are sent over from Malta at a time & they generally get about a month here. The scheme was started about June but unfortunately they had some of the wrong sort here who had no idea how to behave & in consequence people have cooled off a little. Still they give us a very good time & for my own part I am rather glad that there are not too many social entertainments as I much prefer poking about with a mate.

I am staying with five others in a villa belonging to a Mr Strong[88] who is rather a recluse. Mrs Strong was a daughter of Rockefeller the American millionaire but she is dead & Mr Strong & his

---

87   Lady Sybil Marjorie Cutting (Née Cuffe), daughter of 5th Earl of Desart, m William Baynard Cutting of USA (d.1910), m 2ndly the writer, Geoffrey Scott. She purchased Villa Medici at Fiesoli in 1911 and was the mother of Iris Origo. [See Caroline Moorehead, *Iris Origo*, p58]

88   Charles Strong, an American philosopher

daughter are in England at present so we have had the place to ourselves with three servants to look after our needs. The villa itself is rather peculiar. There are one or two old pieces of tapestry on the walls but no attempt has otherwise been made at decoration & the effect is rather severe. In other ways it is most luxurious. The house is heated throughout with steam for warmth and in addition there are wood fires for looks. Each bedroom has its own bathroom which is awfully nice. The floors are a sort of green mosaic.

Every night when I go to bed I find that it has been warmed while my pyjamas repose gracefully on top of the radiator. I get a cup of tea in bed & the housekeeper always takes away my clothes & brushes & presses them while I am having my bath. No room for any more in this letter but will continue to write a bit daily. Love to all

Tom

Le Balze
Fiesole
12-2-16

My dear Mother

I am very sorry that I have not written for nearly a fortnight, but I find it hard to settle down to writing. I have been having a very good time here & enjoying myself in a quiet way.

My day is generally as follows: I go down to Florence some time between 10 & 11. The journey down in the tram takes about an hour & then I make for a tea room where all the English people seem to gather. I stay there talking and drinking coffee till lunch time. I generally go to some Italian restaurant for lunch and as I can't read a word of Italian & the waiters as a rule speak no English I get many surprising dishes but in the end get a very good meal. After lunch I go sightseeing for an hour or so & then come back home. I have been round most of the best things now but I am afraid that I do not really appreciate them. There are just one or two statues which I like very much but for the rest I feel that I do not understand what the sculptor was driving at. Some of the churches are rather nice but most of them appear much too florid for my taste.

I have seen most of the pictures including some very famous ones but here I also do not understand anything about it & masterpieces & ordinary ones look just the same to me. Of course there are some that I like better than others but I generally seem to pick the wrong ones to admire.

Five of us hired a car last week & went to Pisa. It was a very nice day but we had a most adventurous journey & only had time just to glance at the most famous sights. First of all the road from Florence to Pisa is said to be the worst in Italy & I can quite believe it. Nearly all the way it was just a sea of mud where it was not fresh blue metal. Our driver was very poor especially where the road was at all bad & he used to nearly stop whenever we passed a vehicle which was about once a minute on the average. The consequence was that it took us $4^{1}/_{4}$ hours to do 56 miles. The only adventure on the outward journey was the sudden collapse of the wind screen which covered us with glass fortunately without hurting anyone.

We came back by a slightly longer way & as the car would not pull it was dark long before we got home. Then the lamps refused to burn & we charged heaps of blue metal that nearly upset us & finally about 2 miles from Fiesole the engine absolutely refused to pull so we ended up on shank's pony. The return journey lasted 6 hours for not more than 75 miles & it was after nine when we finally got back. Still I quite enjoyed the trip. In parts the scenery was very fine & we saw the country in a way we never could have done from the train. There is a censorship here so I can give you no impressions of how the war is going here & I will have to leave it till later. I have had no letters but hope to get them all when I get back to Egypt.

I am getting on well now & think that I will be able to get there before long. The climate here is rather like our own in winter tho' not quite so cold & I am sure it is a much better place to convalesce in than Malta. With love

Your loving son

Tom

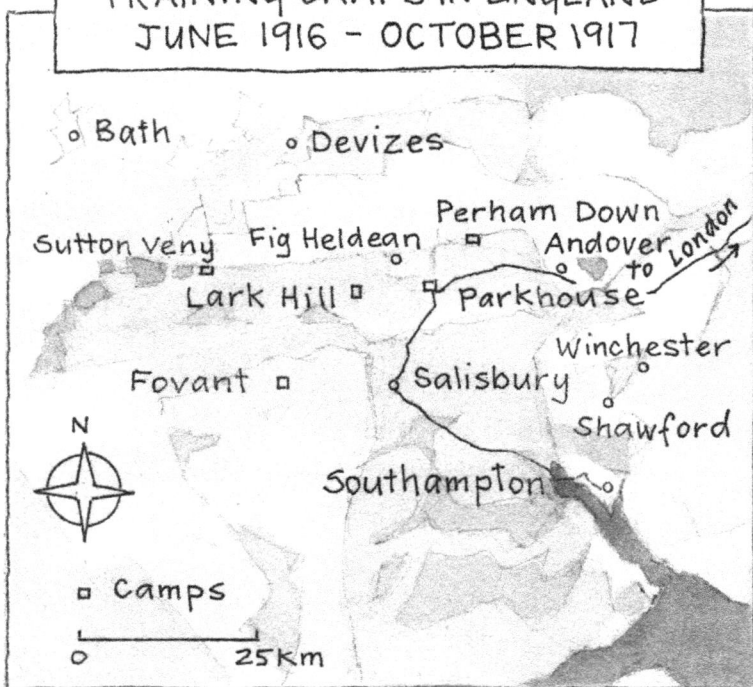

TRAINING CAMPS IN ENGLAND
JUNE 1916 – OCTOBER 1917

Bath · Devizes · Sutton Veny · Fig Heldean · Perham Down · Andover · to London · Lark Hill · Parkhouse · Fovant · Salisbury · Winchester · Shawford · Southampton

N

□ Camps

0   25 Km

Map by Catherine Gordon.

Chapter Four
Training Camps in England

Perham Downs Camp
Sun 18-6-1916

My dear Mother

I wrote you a letter just before we reached Gib & I hope you receive it safely but I am rather doubtful as three other letters that I wrote at the same time were mislaid somehow or other and were returned to me on our arrival here. We had a splendid trip all the way over and did not see a single submarine although on two occasions we received word by wireless that there were some close to us. We arrived at Gib early in the morning & sailed again the same evening so I did not get a chance to get ashore but I do not think that there was very much of interest that could not be seen from the ship. The boat we came over on was a captured N.D.L.[89] liner the *Derfflinger* which has been renamed *Huntsgreen*. I had a three berth cabin to myself and was very comfortable. We arrived at Plymouth late on Sunday night & landed first thing on Monday morning. The weather for the last three days of the trip was very cold & when we landed we found that they were having the coldest June for years. It is a little warmer now but nothing to boast about yet although yesterday was a beautiful day.

The trip from Plymouth here took practically all day & I never imagined that anything could be so beautiful. We are stationed on Salisbury Plain & the whole trip was wonderful. We came along the coast for a good part of the way & then cut across country thro' the heart of Devon.

---

89   Norrdeutsche Lloyd, German shipping line

Now that I am here I am out of a job again & don't know what is to become of me. I may be sent back to Egypt but rather hope not. Still I do not much mind where I am so long as I can get a permanent job. Anyway I managed to raise two days leave & paid a flying visit to London. Of course it would have been much better if I had had a mate, still I managed to enjoy every minute I was there. I stayed at Morley's Hotel in Trafalgar Square a very comfortable place & very central. It is rather old fashioned & fairly quiet & suited me down to the ground. I saw three theatres including Romance which is very good, quite one of the best things I have ever seen. The rest of my time I wandered round the streets finding my way about & if I got lost I just took a taxi back to the hotel & made a fresh start. I did not see any of the sights as I was too pushed for time but I know where they are now & if I get up there again I will be able to go straight ahead. I have not written to anyone I know yet as I may be shifted any minute, but as soon as I can get some permanent address I will try & get into communication with everyone I know, that is if I stay in England for any time. Ink has run out in my pen so I must continue this in pencil.

In this camp we are in huts & we really are in the lap of luxury. I have a room to myself & it is fitted with electric light & a stove & is quite commodious. The camp is very well laid out with baths, canteen & the men have very comfortable huts with special buildings for having their meals in. Altogether we have fallen on our feet tho' I believe it is a pretty cold spot in winter. I must finish this off now as I have to post it tonight to catch a mail via America tomorrow. It is now nine o'clock in the evening & still quite light. Of course the daylight saving scheme has put the clocks on an hour still it will stay fairly light for another hour yet. I am feeling splendid now & fit for anything. Nearly all the other officers have had colds &c. but so far I have escaped. With love

Your loving son

Tom

Perham Down Camp
Mon. 26th June 1916

My dear Mother

I don't know that I have very much news for you this week but I will see what I can scrape up. The mail for Australia leaves on the 29th and I will post this tomorrow to make sure of being in time. I am still pottering about without any definite job but I think that something will turn up soon. If not I will apply for leave as I have practically nothing to do here & am only a nuisance. I have been getting myself into condition by doing a good deal of walking lately. After dinner at night there are still two or three hours of daylight & I generally get a mate & we explore the country round. I know it all pretty well now & am getting quite an expert walker. I think nothing of 6 or 8 miles after dinner. On Saturday all the Australian troops on Salisbury Plain were reviewed by Mr. Hughes[90]. It meant an 18 mile march for us there and back & I returned pretty footsore but otherwise well. Unfortunately it was not as good a day as it might have been. It was showery all day & we all got wet to the skin. Just as we were formed up & everyone had their coats off for the inspection a heavy shower came on & wet everyone so that after that it did not much matter what happened.

However everything went off successfully & we will have to get used to rain here tho' so far it has been remarkably fine & it was the first rain we had had for a fortnight. Yesterday afternoon four of us hired a motor car & went for a run to Salisbury & Stonehenge. It was a very pretty drive chiefly thro' lanes with high

---

90   Rt. Hon. William Morris Hughes, Prime Minister of Australia 1915-1923 [*ADB 9.393*].

hedges on each side. We saw the outside of Salisbury Cathedral but did not go inside as there was a service going on. Stonehenge is not very much to look at. Just a few weather worn stones on top of a small grassy hill & after what I have seen in Egypt there did not seem to be anything very remarkable about them. Still it was a very nice trip & only cost us 8/- each which I thought was very reasonable. It is raining again this afternoon but we must not expect too much from this climate. I have been so long in Egypt that I have got quite out of the way of ever expecting it to rain. I have had no letters since I left Egypt over a month ago so am not very well up in what is going on at home.

We see by the 'Times' this morning that Mr Hughes has bought 15 ships and is going to establish a Commonwealth Line. I suppose it will be another failure like nearly all Government ventures. From what I can hear Pat should be nearly here by this. He will be camped not very far away and as soon as he arrives I will go & see him.

How is the Girl getting on with her motor car. One of the things I noticed in London was the number of women driving cars in the streets and generally quite alone. In fact I think that there are almost as many women chauffeurs as men in England now. I am afraid that this is not much of a letter but I will try and do better next time. Ted Rutledge[91] is here. I saw him a few days ago but not for long. I am hoping to get up to London with him for a week end soon. With love to all

Your loving son

Tom

---

91   Major Edward Hamilton Rutledge, MB, ChM, 1908, AMC; s of Edward Knox Rutledge

Perham Down Camp
Andover Hants
12-7-1916

My dear Mother

I have received no letters from you since I left Egypt over a month ago and I am beginning to wonder what has become of them. Still they will probably turn up shortly. I got a letter last night from Egypt which was written to me from Cairo about a week before I ever left Egypt so there is hope yet. I hear that some of Pat's unit have arrived in camp about twelve miles from here. He is probably with them & I am going over as soon as I possibly can to try & see him.

I myself seem to be permanently fixed here for some time to come. Just now I am President of a Court of Inquiry which will probably take a fortnight or three weeks and then I know of several other jobs that are waiting for me.

The great trouble about this place is the difficulty in getting about. Camps are spread all over the Salisbury Plains there are no trains & motors are fairly scarce. I am thinking seriously of getting a motorbike. I can get a good second hand one for about £25 and although I have never altogether liked them it would certainly be a great convenience. With daylight lasting until 10 o'clock I could often get a run in after an early tea. I do not like hanging about camp always. You get stale & a spin of twenty miles or so would be just the thing to blow away the cobwebs. I have not been able to get leave since my first trip to London but I am living in hopes. Of course I can nearly always get week-end leave but that means I do not get to London till about 6 o'clock on Saturday evening & I have to be back in camp on Sunday night so that it is scarcely worth the while.

I am sorry to say that I have lost nearly all the addresses of people I know in England but I hope to get hold of them by degrees. I have managed to get hold of the Gilchrists'[92] & am writing to them. They will be able to put me on to a good many people I know. Then I am also writing to Mrs James & Mrs Debenham[93] both of whom wrote to me when I was sick. There are quite a collection of Rutledges scattered about Salisbury Plains now.

Ted [Rutledge] & Noel[94] are in a camp not far from here & Cyril[95] is also near here. He came and saw me the other day & is looking very well tho' he had a very bad time with enteric. Noel I have not yet seen. My trouble in finding Pat will be that I do not know his number or what Battery he is in. All I know is that he is in the artillery. I am going to try and find Capt (or Lt Col I believe he is now) James[96] & he will probably be able to put me onto him. I am still attached to an Infantry Training Battalion but I have nothing to do with it really & am simply living with it. I like the C.O. very much. He is a Victorian named Major Clarke[97] &

---

92   William Oswald, eldest son of John Gilchrist [*ADB 1.442*], founder of the shipping firm, Gilchrist, Watt & Co. married Clara Elizabeth, eldest d. of Sir Edward Knox & Martha, née Rutledge.

93   Helen Styles m George Padley Debenham, of the Forbes district, in 1880.

94   Lt Noel Beresford Forster Rutledge, 3rd Div Arty; s of Thomas Forster Rutledge of Werronggurt, Warrnambool, KIA 3-6-17.

95   Pte Cyril Percy Rutledge, 1st Div Train, Disch. 4-3-19.

96   Lt Col Tristram Bernard Wordsworth James, DSO, 7th FAB, 3rd Div Arty. [see Appendix]

97   Maj [Cyril Wilbeforce] St John Clarke, 4th LH, from Cobham, Vic . RTA 27-7-17.

is a very fine chap & we have rather palled up together. We went to Salisbury on Saturday night & had dinner there just to break the monotony a little.

I have practically given up hope of rejoining the Regiment again & have made up my mind to take the first permanent job that comes along whether it is infantry or anything else. I feel that I must be doing something & I would have to wait months in all probability to get back to the Regt again. You probably know Capt Forsyth who is on the Court of Inquiry with me. You will remember he is the man whose wife was drowned in New Zealand about three years ago.

Please tell the Girl that I am very sorry that I have not written to her for so long but she shall have a letter by the very next mail. The mails now only seem to go about once a fortnight except an odd mail via America & you never seem to know when that is going until it is too late to catch it. With love to all

Your loving son
Tom

Tom in London, 1916.

Morley's Hotel
Trafalgar Square
London W. C.
24-7-16

My dear Mother

I am writing this in London. I have put in for four days leave and I am just waiting now for a wire to say whether it has been granted or not. I had to come up today on duty and when I came away my application had not come through so if I don't get a wire within an hour or so I will have to go back tonight. I am going in a few minutes to have afternoon tea with Mrs Wesche[98]. She sent me a line asking me to lunch or tea & as I could not get to lunch I am going to tea instead.

I got a letter from you a few days ago which was addressed to me at the Commercial Bank[99] also one written on Easter Monday which was forwarded to Egypt. What has happened to the ones in between I don't know. I think you had better send all my letters to the Commercial Bank for the present. I do not think there is much chance of my being moved from here for some time to come, in fact I have been half promised the command of a Training Battalion which will probably mean that I will be stationed on Salisbury Plain for two or three months.

I forgot to tell you that I was up here for two days last week in connection with the Court of Inquiry I was on. While I was up I met Mr & Mrs Dave Dickson[100] who are staying in Kensington.

---

98   Phoebe Ellen Wesche, née Twynum, [*ADB 12.445*].

99   Commercial Banking Co. of Sydney.

100   David Peter Dickson, land and income tax adjuster; m. Alice Christina Blomfield at Denham Court in 1882.

Mrs Dickson said that she would write you a line & tell you that I was looking well.

27 – 7 – 16

Well I have managed to get my four days leave & am very busy looking up people I know. On Tuesday I went to see the Willie Gilchrists & found them fairly well. Mrs Gilchrist has been ill but she was up for the first time & said she was decidedly better. I am to dine with them tonight. Yesterday I went & saw Dr & Mrs Chisholm[101] who were both well. Airlie[102] was away but is expected back on Friday. I also called on Mrs Pat[103] & Mrs Harry[104] Osborne but they were both out. Mrs Harry wanted me to lunch with her today but I am going down to Essex to see Mrs Debenham. I have also seen Mrs Wesche & Tommy Davies [née Cunningham] so you can see that I have been kept on the go pretty well. I received your letter of June 10th yesterday & a very doleful letter it was. That was a black week when you wrote it but things are much brighter looking now & worrying never did any good. Pat & I are both well & not likely to be sent to France for a while yet so there is no need for you to bother yourself. No more just now I have to post this to catch the mail. With love

Your loving son

Tom

---

101   William Chisholm, (brother of Harry Chisholm), BA, Syd, 1875; MD (AEG), 1887; m Emma Isabel, née Mitchell. The parents of Lt. William Chisholm, the first Australian killed in World War I.

102   [Helen Isabel] Airlie, their daughter.

103   Elizabeth Jane (Jeanie) Atkinson, m Pat Hill Osborne, [*ADB 5.376*], of Currandooley, Bungendore.

104   Daisie Madden m. Harry Osborne of Currandooley. Her sister, Ruby, m. Pat Hamilton Osborne of Willeroo, Tarago.

No 3 Camp
Parkhouse
Salisbury
3-8-1916

My dear Mother,

I received your letter of June 10th while I was in London last week. I am very sorry indeed to hear that you have been worrying about me, quite without cause. I think I explained to you that I got Aunt to send the telegram for me as I was ordered away from Egypt at a moment's notice & did not have time to send it myself. My health was never better than it is at the present time and I hope that by the time you get this you will have heard from several people in England who have seen me & perhaps they will be able to set your mind at rest. I was just on my way from Egypt when we got the news of the Jutland battle and the death of Kitchener & I can quite imagine that you were rather upset by the first news.

I had a very busy time while in London & spent most of it flying round trying to see people I knew. Among others I saw the Gilchrists (Mrs. Gilchrist had not been at all well but was better & they were all going to the seaside for a change) Dr. & Mrs. Chisholm, Mrs. Harry Osborne, had dinner & went to the theatre with Helen James & her people & also managed to get down to Essex one afternoon & see the Debenhams. I also called on Mrs. Pat Osborne but she was out & I did not manage to see her. You can tell from the above list that I was kept moving and as I also went to the theatre whenever I was not engaged for the evening you can see that I did not have much time spare.

On Saturday I went to see the presentation of colours to the A.I.F. by the Princess Royal[105]. It took place on the Guards parade at Wellington Barracks & was a most successful affair. Unfortunately however very few people seemed to know that it was taking place and there were very few Australian officers there after the ceremony all the Australians present were presented to the Princess. We all then adjourned to a house in Buckingham Gate nearby where we were entertained to afternoon tea by a Col. & Mrs. Chaloner who have something to do with the British Empire League. I forgot to say that Miss Chamberlain[106] made a very fine speech during the presentation of the Colors [sic] & afterwards at afternoon tea I met her & we had quite a long conversation. She was most interesting to talk to & speaks very well. Gen. Ryrie who is over on leave was there also & I had a few words with him. He was looking very well. That morning he had been to Buckingham Palace to receive his C.M.G.

You will see by my address that I have been moved again & am now in command of the Pioneer Training Battalion. I have hopes that this is a more permanent job but I shall know for certain next week & I will let you know then. In the meantime I am pretty busy getting the hang of things in general.

I see by the papers that 6 o'clock closing was carried in New South Wales but we have no details. I got one Australasian this week that was sent c/o Commercial Bank but that is the

---

105   Princess Mary, d of King George V, later married the Earl of Harewood.

106   Beatrice Chamberlain (1862-1918), eldest d. of Joseph Chamberlain, sister of Austen & Neville.[See Oxford DNB]

first since I have been in England. None of my mail has so far come along from Egypt but I hope to get it some day. Please continue sending letters to Commercial Bank. I have seen nothing of Pat lately but will try & look him up this week end. With love to all

Your loving son
Tom

No 3 Camp
Parkhouse
16-8-1916

My dear Mother

I received a letter from you yesterday dated June 25th and was very pleased to hear that everything was well at home. I am very sorry however to hear that you have not been well. You must take things easily and try & not do too much.

Pat came over on Sunday and spent the afternoon. He has been promised his commission and is now only waiting for it to be gazetted. In the meanwhile he is working very hard at the school but he looks very well on it. He was stuck for some uniform but I managed to fit him up with some old stuff of mine that will do him till he can get some made. At last we have had a break in the weather and the last day or two it has been showery with an occasional thunderstorm. It was beginning to get quite dried up here but the rain has freshened things up wonderfully.

I don't expect that we will get more than an occasional warm day now. It is the middle of August & next month we will probably start getting frosts. I had a letter from Aunt yesterday, the first I have had since coming to England. She was just opening a tea room for soldiers at Port Said and seemed to be very busy.

I am having a fairly busy time myself just at present but am getting things pretty straight now & will not be kept so hard at it for the future.

I am afraid that this is not much of a letter but there is a mail via America tomorrow & I wanted to send a line by it. The American mail these times is a good deal the quickest. With love

Your loving son

Tom

No 4 Camp
Perham Down
Andover Hants.
12-9-1916

My dear Mother

Just a line to let you know that I am quite well. I am writing this in a fearful hurry as there is just a chance of catching an American mail. As you see I have changed camp again but think that we are settled for a while now. I have been very busy this last week changing & there have been a good many reinforcements coming in. Lord French[107] is coming to inspect today so you can imagine that I have not much time to spare. I have not seen Pat lately. Last time I heard from him he was going away on a week's leave to Oakhampton & I think he only got back a day or two ago. Ted Rutledge is in this camp near me now & I see him sometimes.

It has been quite chilly the last day or two & I think the best of the summer is over now. I am very sorry this is such a poor letter but I hope to send a long one next mail. With love

Your loving son
Tom

---

107   FM Earl of Ypres, KP, Commander of British Home Forces 1915-18

No 4 Camp
Perham Down
Andover Hants.
12-9-16

My dear Mother

I am very sorry that I sent you such a sketchy letter this morning but I had only a minute to drop you a line to catch the mail. I am very busy indeed just at present and hardly ever seem to get a minute to myself. However I am very glad to have something definite to do again and I think that the job I have now will be more or less permanent. Of course I may be sent out to France later on but I do not think that is particularly likely just at present as my Regt is not there & I do not think it likely that I will be sent to Egypt. You will have heard that George Onslow was wounded but I have heard nothing about his condition.

We moved over here from Parkhouse last Wednesday & have been busily settling down. Since arrival here a lot of reinforcements have come in & some of them have been put in tents for a week or so until other men move out to France & make room for them. At present I have 1300 men under my command so you can realise that there is a good deal to do. While at Parkhouse I was in command of the whole show for a week & had about 4000.

This camp is not quite so convenient as Parkhouse but the situation is better & does not seem so lonely. I notice that the woods are just beginning to change colour & I don't think it will be long now before winter is on us.

I have not had any papers for some time & do not know much of what is going on but from what I hear it seems to have been a mild and wet winter. Wool seems to be keeping up in price. At sales in

London last week it advanced if anything & I think that there is no doubt that the price will hold for a good while to come. We are getting quite hardened to inspections now and hardly take any notice of them. There are generally some Parliamentarians round & last week we had Gen. Sclater[108] who is in command of this district while today we had Lord French. It is rumoured that the King will shortly be coming round, they say that he generally follows Lord French.

19th It has come up very cold since I last wrote & it really looks as if winter was setting in. Since writing the above I have had letters dated Aug 1st & Aug 8th & also two Australasians. The first I have had for months. With regard to Hopperton's[109] proposal to lease a part of the Sugarloaf I think that he has chosen a good spot & I can see no objection to the site. It is in a corner of the paddock & will not interfere with it in any way. I went to Lark Hill on Sunday to see Pat & get his ideas about it but he was out riding. He has now been posted to 23rd Howitzer Brigade & had only gone there on Sunday morning.

Have had a very busy day today & must post this tonight. My adjutant has gone sick & so far I have no one to replace him. I did not even get time for a smoke before lunch so you can see I was kept going. Have 1100 men now & they take a bit of looking after. Feeling very fit & enjoying myself. Love to all

Your loving son

Tom

---

108   General Sir Henry Crichton Sclater, GCB, GBE, General Officer Commanding Southern Command 1916-1919

109   J.C.Hopperton leased an area on Gidleigh to establish an orchard. The remains of it can still be seen.

No 4 Camp
Perham Down
Andover Hants.
[29-9-1916]

My dear Mother,

I am just seizing the opportunity to write a few lines while I have nothing else to do. Since I last wrote you I have been on the go continually but as you know I am always best pleased when I have plenty to do. On Wednesday we were reviewed by the King[110] and you can imagine that we were pretty busy for a few days preparing for the event. Everything went off very successfully & I believe His Majesty was pleased but of course it rained both before & after the review so that we returned soaked. Still it was fine for the actual review & might have been a lot worse. After the actual review Commanding Officers of units were presented & among them was myself. We marched up in line shook hands wriggled away somehow or other without turning our backs & went away again. All the troops meanwhile lined the road & cheered as he went away. It was really a most impressive sight. I think I saw Pat there but am not sure. Of course I did not get a chance to go looking for him. Then yesterday we had some sports for all troops at Perham Down Camp.

2/10/16

I was on the committee & had a good deal of work to do. We had a most successful day & I am pleased to say that my battalion did very well, in fact I think we won more prizes than anyone.

---

110   King George V

On Sunday I took the day off & went into Andover to see Mrs F W Osborne[111] & Valentine. They have been living there all the summer to be near the Colonel but are going back to London this week and are going to share a flat with the David Dicksons. I spent a very pleasant afternoon with them & enjoyed being away from camp for a while. I have a horse here but do not get very much chance to go out on him. I am going to try & get some leave soon & am going to see the Mackays[112] & get a little partridge shooting.

We are getting some wet weather now & today it has rained steadily all day. I am afraid that this place will be pretty rotten in the winter but we won't be working at quite such high pressure then & we may be able to get away a little more. I am sorry to say that as usual I am writing against time but someday I hope to be able to settle down for an hour or so & write a really nice gossipy letter. This has to be posted tonight and I have seized the opportunity of a few minutes before mess to write. Today has been a fair average day & I will just give you a sample to show what I do.

9 a.m. Went to office signed a lot of papers went thro' mail & told adjutant several things I wanted done.

10 a.m. Went to Camp Headquarters to a 'confab' which lasted an hour.

11-12.30 Office signing more papers & attending to fresh correspondence that had collected.

---

111   Mabel Susan Osborne (nèe Blomfield), m. Lt Col F.W. Osborne in 1891, sister of Mrs David Dickson.

112   Jessie, 2nd d of Sir Edward Knox m Eric Henry Mackay. [see Appendix]

12-30 to 1 Held orderly & sentenced about 15 men to various punishments

1-2 p.m. Lunch

2-3 p.m. Held orderly room for another battalion whose C.O. was away.

3 p.m. Went in motor car with Staff Officer to Headquarters to discuss several matters connected with training. Arrived back 4-30 p.m.

4-30 to 5-30 p.m. Office signing documents & letters of various sorts, attended to several matters which had cropped up, read thro' orders which had arrived & picked out parts to go into our own orders, fixed letter up & then started writing this.

I should also have inspected the huts & cookhouses to see that they were clean & tidy, a job that always takes an hour, & left one or two other less urgent matters stand over. Still I am interested in the job & feel fit for a good deal more. It takes a tremendous lot of organisation & am just beginning to get things going. Had to stop here to fix up some English officers who are doing a school here and are attached for messing. I am sending this by San Francisco. There is a mail by Suez in a couple of days & I will send a line by it if I can. Love to all

Your loving son
Tom

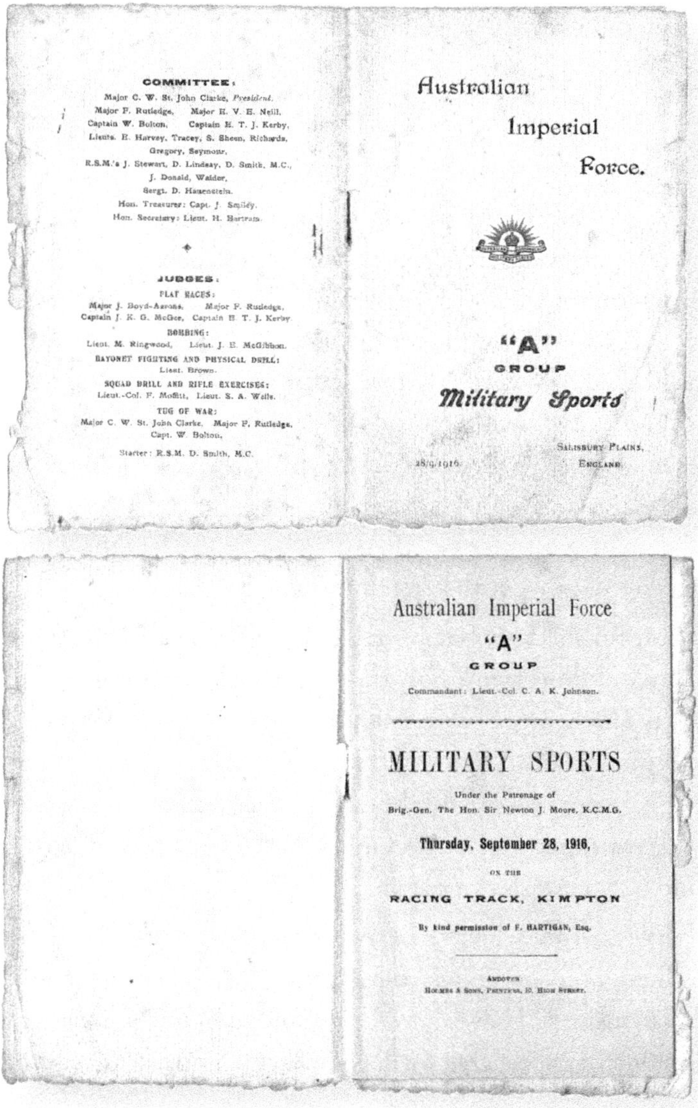

COMMITTEE:

Major C. W. St. John Clarke, *President.*
Major F. Rutledge, Major H. V. E. Neill,
Captain W. Bolton, Captain H. T. J. Kerby,
Lieuts. E. Harvey, Tracey, S. Sheen, Richards,
Gregory, Seymour,
R.S.M.'s J. Stewart, D. Lindsay, D. Smith, M.C.,
J. Donald, Walder,
Sergt. D. Hauenstein.
Hon. Treasurer: Capt. J. Smiley.
Hon. Secretary: Lieut. H. Bartram.

JUDGES:

FLAT RACES:
Major J. Boyd-Aarons, Major F. Rutledge,
Captain J. K. G. McGee, Captain H. T. J. Kerby.
BOMBING:
Lieut. M. Ringwood, Lieut. J. E. McGibbon.
BAYONET FIGHTING AND PHYSICAL DRILL:
Lieut. Brown.
SQUAD DRILL AND RIFLE EXERCISES:
Lieut.-Col. F. Moffitt, Lieut. S. A. Wells.
TUG OF WAR:
Major C. W. St. John Clarke, Major F. Rutledge,
Capt. W. Bolton,

Starter: R.S.M. D. Smith, M.C.

Australian
Imperial
Force.

"A"
GROUP
Military Sports

28/9/1916.

Salisbury Plains,
England.

Australian Imperial Force
"A"
GROUP

Commandant: Lieut.-Col. C. A. K. Johnson.

MILITARY SPORTS

Under the Patronage of
Brig.-Gen. The Hon. Sir Newton J. Moore, K.C.M.G.

Thursday, September 28, 1916,

ON THE

RACING TRACK, KIMPTON

By kind permission of F. HARTIGAN, Esq.

Andover
Holmes & Sons, Printers, 10, High Street.

Part of the program for the sports day.

Camp 4
Perham Down
Andover Hants.
17-10-1916

My dear Mother

I have had three letters from you in the last week & I think they all came by different routes. The last was dated Sept 3rd & told of frosts but you had plenty of rain & a little fine weather should not hurt especially for the lambs. I have been going very hard lately and although winter seems to be setting in now & we get rain every second day I do not seem to notice it. On Saturday last (this is Tuesday) we had a visit from Gen Birdwood & as the Commandant of the Camp was away I had to take charge of the whole parade, & lead them in a march past. Then on Monday we had the voting on the referendum[113], & that kept me going pretty well.

It is not finished yet but we are to take the rest of the votes on Thursday. I don't know how the voting has been going so far but there is a little more opposition to it than I expected. I think the trouble is that the scheme has not been explained properly to the men. We knew very little about the scheme here till the last few days and I think that a good many of the men feared that there would be no exemptions at all.

In between times I have been kept fairly busy as I have been President of a Court Martial & that is always a fairly long & tedious business. I have signed my name so much of late that I am beginning to expect that I will get writer's cramp or something of the sort.

The officers I have at present with some exceptions are not of the best & I have been having trouble with a few of them especially

---

113   The Australian Government held a referendum on conscription on 28th October.

one. He seems to have rather had the idea that because I gave him every chance I would continue to do so indefinitely. However I have brought him up with a round turn now & I don't think that I will have much trouble with him for the future & I also think that I have inspired a very healthy respect in the remainder. Ted Rutledge has just been sent down to a place called Wool to a new camp there & I will not see very much of him for some time. I had a letter from Pat this morning. He was riding over to see me last Sunday but was caught in a shower & got wet through. He says he is coming over next Sunday weather permitting. There are rumours that the 3rd Division are leaving for France within a month & I am rather inclined to think that it is true but you can never really tell what is going to happen until it has actually happened. We are busy now organizing entertainments for the men for the winter months. We have a fair amount of talent in the Battalion & they run quite a good concert every week. Then we have a boxing contest every week & with an odd concert party visiting us, don't do too badly. Then we have football matches on Saturday afternoons & taking it all round, the men don't do too badly. I am sorry to hear that Dalgety & Co. have behaved so badly about the car. I know what is wrong with it but am afraid that it must have been carelessness that caused it in the first place. If it had been properly looked after there is no reason why it should have worn at all. Anyway put them off till Mr. Yarwood[114] comes back & set him onto them & I think he will soon settle their hash. The rug he sent me has arrived & is a great comfort. With love

Your loving son

Tom

---

114   Frank Nelson Yarwood, FCPA, the Rutledge's family accountant. [see Appendix]

Pat Rutledge at the time of his enlistment.

Perham Down
Andover Hants.
22-10-16

My dear Mother

There is an extra mail out tomorrow via America & I want to send a line by it. Yesterday afternoon one of the officers here who has a car motored me over to Shawford to see Cousin Jessie MacKay. We found them in and had afternoon tea. Both she and Clara were looking well, also Cousin Eric & they were very nice. They want me to go over soon & have a few days partridge shooting. The difficulty is to fix a time as I never quite know when I will be able to get away. We got back home without adventure although the man who drove me is rather reckless and I do not think would suit you as a chauffeur.

Today I hired a car, took another officer with me & went over to Lark Hill. There we picked Pat up & then went on to Marlborough for lunch. After lunch we came back by Devizes to Salisbury where we had afternoon tea. Then our troubles began. We had a puncture early in the day at Marlborough but that did not matter much as we were carrying a spare wheel. But it was dark after leaving Salisbury & we had not been going very long when we got another puncture. This was a much more serious business as we had to put in a new tube in the dark on a wet road. (It had been raining but I am getting used to the climate now & hardly notice whether it is wet or fine). However we finally got it fixed, took Pat back to camp & came on here. It was a pleasant trip although it was rather cold. Pat was looking very well & has got very fat. If he goes on at the same rate he will hardly be able to see out of his eyes. (I know the Girl will be amused to hear this).

He is now a stone heavier than I am & I myself am heavier than I have ever been so you can see that the military life is agreeing with both of us. I am not quite so hard worked as I was. I have got an adjutant now who has his head screwed on the right way & he takes a good deal of work off my hands. Although he has lived in Australia for some years he is very Scotch & has a most marked accent. When he is on parade the R's simply fly round in all directions & I sometimes have difficulty in understanding what he says.

Pat had had a letter from Uncle[115] with the result of the crutching sales & also reporting the sale of a lot of sheep. The prices seem excellent & it looks as if we are in for another good year. There is no sign of wool dropping here, the tendency is rather the other way. Of course there is the Super Tax[116] but I am inclined to think that it will not hurt us very much & one must be prepared to sacrifice something these times. I must stop now as it is time I was in bed. With love to all

Your loving son

Tom

Please excuse the awful crest, I am getting some other paper as soon as I can.

---

115   Jean's brother, Harry Morphy.

116   A federal income tax ranging from 3d to 5/- in the £ was introduced as a war time measure. People in the armed services were exempt. It was the first time that the Commonwealth Government taxed income. [See WF Whyte, *William Morris Hughes, His Life and Times*, pp 176-7]

Camp 4
Perham Down
Andover Hants.
25-10-16

My dear Mother

I have had four letters from you lately, dated Aug 27th, 30th & Sept 3rd & 10th. I find that I get my letters thro' the Bank about one post before the regular Australian Mail is delivered. I have been going thro' all my letters tonight burning old ones & generally tidying things up. I have been invited to go & see the Mackays on Sunday & have a day's partridge shooting on Monday & have put in for leave as I feel that a day away from work would do me good. I have been having a pretty heavy time lately & am very busy this week as I have 500 men going to France at the end of the week. That will reduce my numbers a bit but I think that there will soon be more coming in. A good many of them are sick just at present. Nothing serious, mostly colds & influenza.

As far as I can see I am stuck in this job anyway till the end of January & probably longer but I intend to make a great effort then to get away. Meanwhile it is splendid experience but very strenuous & does not lead to anything. In fact it is all kicks & no halfpence. However I have no chance of getting a move for three months at least & meanwhile I am learning that there is more in soldiering than I ever dreamed of before & I think I am getting on as well as most. For some time past I have been next senior officer in Camp to the Commandant & as he is often away the command of the whole Camp has devolved on me a couple of times. This has meant nothing except that I have had to take charge of a couple of ceremonial parades. It is rather a big step from a troop two years ago to a brigade today. On Saturday week we had Gen Birdwood to inspect us & last Saturday Sir Newton Moore[117] had a parade to present a medal to a man who won it in France. My chief trouble is that I have rather an inexperienced lot of officers & though they do their best, with one or two exceptions it is not as good as it might be. Still they are getting better every day & in about three months I should just have them working nicely. Col Fred Osborne[118] & Major Magee[119] (a great friend of the Leura[120] people) are in this camp but the man I like best is a Major Clarke from Victoria. I was attached to his battalion for some time (in fact I brought it over from Egypt) & we have become rather pally.

The next mail does not go till Nov 2nd but there is a chance it will be the Xmas mail so I am getting a good start on. The only trouble about writing every week without bothering about when the mail goes is that many of the mails are via America & unless the envelopes are specially marked they will not send them that way.

We had the Referendum on conscription here last week & tho' I don't know the result I am afraid that there were a great many noes. The whole thing was very badly organized & no information was available as to what were the exact proposals. Then there seems to have been a pretty strong organization in opposition tho' I have only my opinion and nothing definite to go on. The men's

117   Maj Gen Sir Newton James Moore, KCMG, [*ADB 10.567*], Brig General commanding AIF troops in England as well as camps & depot.
118   Lt Col Frederick William Osborne, 36th HAG [RTA 7-2-19].
119   Maj. Jasper Kenneth Magee, MC, 6th Battn [Disch 20-11-17]
120   T. F, Knox & family lived at Leura, Bellevue Hill, Sydney.

attitude seemed to be (that is those of them who have been to the front) that they did not want their relations compelled to go thro' what they had. Our only hope now is that the women's vote will carry the day. I don't like to think of what would happen if the verdict was against conscription. You will probably know in a week or so, long before you get this[121].

In your last letter you told me that Hopperton has decided on the piece of ground in the Sugarloaf. I wrote some time ago that I quite approved & I discussed the matter with Pat on Sunday & he is quite agreeable.

I am very sorry to hear that Mr. Cunningham has not been looking well. He has never really been right for a long time and it must be a great wrench for him to part with Tuggeranong[122]. The leather waistcoat you are sending me will be much appreciated. I was thinking about getting one made but now I will not bother. I still have some clothes in Egypt and I am collecting a lot here but most of them are useless. I will try & find some charity & give them away. It is no use sending them out to Australia, it would cost more than they are worth & there is nothing that I value at all. In spite of being in England I am not spending much money & I think I will send my savings out to Mr. Yarwood to invest. He should be back before very long now & I might just as well be drawing some interest. Beyond a few clothes & my mess bill I hardly spend anything except when I get a motor & go for a run. I am not going to post this now but will wait a few days & I may be able to add to it.

---

121 The referendum was defeated 1,687,557 votes to 1,160,033 [Whyte *op cit* p 303]

122 Tuggeranong station was resumed for the Federal Capital.

I hope that your trip to Albury will set you up. Don't try to do too much. Let the Girl run the housekeeping it will relieve you & do her good.

27-10-16

I am continuing this tonight as I have some other letters to write for the Xmas mail and I may not get another chance. I have got my leave and am going over to Shawford on Sunday to stay with the Mackays & have a day's shooting. I will be glad to get away. This has been a bad week & somehow or other everything seems to have gone wrong, but next week I intend to stir things up generally. Every now & again I find that I have to regularly go for the whole crowd from top to bottom & then for a while things improve but unless you are continually on the go they soon backslide. Tonight we had a concert for the men & some of the items were quite good. We have quite a lot of talent in the battalion including a ventriloquist & a couple of acrobats. One man smeared himself over with some white paint and gave us some living statuary. A notice was put up to tell us what each pose was supposed to represent & included Bacchus spelt BACCUS. Still I think that on the whole everyone enjoyed themselves. I have a big draft ready to go away now. They expected to go tonight but did not & now they are rather a disturbing element until they have gone. I am sorry to say that I won't be able to get any Xmas presents away by this mail but I will try & get some the next time I go to London and you will understand why they are late.

31-10-16

This has to be posted tomorrow so I must finish up tonight. I had a very pleasant trip over to Shawford except that the weather was vile and I did not get any partridge shooting. It poured nearly all Sunday & again on Monday morning till the shooting was put off, when it cleared up. Cousin Eric & I went out to see what we could get and managed a couple of pheasants & hare & some rabbits. We also got wet thro' as it came on to rain again before we got home but I enjoyed being away from Camp for a day. They want me to go over for a days shooting on Saturday & I will if I can manage it. Wishing you all a Happy Xmas & with lots of love

Your loving son

Tom

No 4 Camp
Perham Down
Andover
Tues 14-11-16

My dear Mother

I have your two letters of Sept 17th & 24th. I think that this mail will reach you just in time for Xmas although to make sure I sent by the last mail. In fact we were told that the last mail was the Xmas mail but I rather think that that was done to try & avoid some of the rush for this mail. On Saturday week I went over to Shawford & had a day's shooting with Cousin Eric Mackay. We did not do very well but I enjoyed the day very much. They are very kind & have given me a general invitation to go over whenever I feel inclined. If I only knew that I was settled here for some time I would buy a small motor so that I could run about the country a bit but I do not think that I will be here for more than three months at the longest. I am not feeling very bright today. I have a beastly cold & yesterday & the day before I stayed in bed all day. I am better today but feeling a bit heavy still. Today it has been foggy all day but considering everything the weather is very mild. The leaves on the trees have been beautiful this last week but they are beginning to fall now & I think the best is over. I am writing to Chris Champion[123] but I am afraid that there is not much chance of my seeing him. I am tied down here pretty much & it will be worse shortly as I am losing a good many more officers whom I have more or less broken in. Still he will probably be coming to this camp sooner or later & I will see him then. You

---

123   Lieut Christopher Henry Champion, 30th battn, KIA 14-4-18; son of Rev A H Champion, See G. Ellis, *Our Soldiers*.

ask me what I think about your coming over & I am afraid that it is rather a difficult question to decide. There are a good many points for & against it & I will try & set them out. We would both love to have you & the Girl over here as we are at present, but then we do not know how long we are going to stay where we are. It is rumoured that the third Division are leaving for France shortly & as I said before I do not think that I shall be here a great while longer. Then you must remember that at home you have other interests to keep you from worrying but if you were here you would see scarcely anything of us (if we were in France we would get four days leave every six months) & I am afraid that you would worry a great deal more. Then again there is the risk of getting here. The submarines are very active just at present (the Arabia was sunk only last week). In fact for the last fortnight the Channel has not been safe & some of our drafts have been held up in consequence. On the whole I think it would perhaps be better if you did not come. I know how much you want to see us & I would love to have you here & if there was any likelihood of either of us being here for some time I would say come, but our movements are very uncertain & if we were in France I know that you are much better off at home.

The last letter you wrote was sent from Albury. I am very glad that you went up there. I am sure that the change would do you good and it was just the right time of year to go. I am glad to hear that Charles & Aunt Fan[124] are so popular but I think that they would get on anywhere. I am glad to hear that you got the tea set

---

124   Probably a slip for Aunt Jane who m. Charles King; Aunt Fan m. Arundel Garroway.

I sent you from Malta, safely. The sugar basin is not lost. I missed putting it in somehow or other and I have it with me but I am rather afraid to send it by post unless I can get a strong box to pack it in.

I have not had an opportunity to get any Xmas presents but I will send something as soon as I go up to London again. The leather waistcoat you are sending will be a great boon. It has not arrived yet but I expect will do so shortly. It generally takes parcels a week to a fortnight longer than ordinary letters. With love to all & wishing you a Happy Xmas

Your loving son
Tom

Camp 4
Perham Down
Andover
29-11-16

My dear Mother

There is an American mail out on the 1ˢᵗ & I am just sending you a line by it. I have just this minute received word that the Pioneers are to move to Lark Hill on the 4ᵗʰ & 5ᵗʰ so I will be pretty busy between now & then. It is a nuisance but we shall have more room at Lark Hill and I think will be more comfortable, although I am sorry to leave here. I got on very well with my present Commandant here & all the staff & it means getting to know a new lot of men. We have had two fine frosty days lately but today it is misting again. I forgot to tell you that the leather waistcoat arrived safely about a week ago and contrary to expectation it arrived in a parcel addressed to myself. There was only one waistcoat in the parcel so I suppose that Pat got his own all right. I do not think that Pat has gone to France yet & I will be able to see something of him over there. No more news. With love

Your loving son
Tom

Camp 26
Lark Hill
Salisbury Plain
12-12-16

My dear Mother

The mail leaves on the 14th so I must post this tomorrow. Since writing to you last I have changed my address & have been very busy. We suddenly got orders to leave Perham Down & come here & you can imagine that it is rather a business when you have been settled into camp for some months to suddenly have to transfer lock stock & barrel to a new place about twelve miles away. However we arrived here safely & are just beginning to get settled down. I do not like the situation so well as at Perham Down & it is a good deal more muddy but we have more room & are not so cramped for quarters. We are not a mile from Stonehenge & you can clearly see the stones sticking up from almost anywhere in the Camp. Pat is only about half a mile away but we are both of us too busy to see very much of one another.

Today at lunch time I received your letter dated Oct 29th & I cannot tell you how shocked I was to hear of Bob Osborne's[125] death. I looked upon him as being good for years. It must have been terrible for poor Mrs Bob[126] having no one in the house with her. I am sure the Aunts must be terribly cut up about it. I am sending a line to Mrs Bob tonight. I suppose they will sell

---

125   Robert T Osborne of Foxlow, Bungendore.
126   Charlotte, née Powell; sister of the Aunts at Turalla.

Foxlow[127] if they can but I do not think that it will prove a very easy place to sell. A lot of it is good but there is a good deal of poor land on it which rather frightens people.

I thought I had told you before that I was in Command of the Pioneer Training Battalion. I am not in love with the job but I hope to be relieved some time in early February. I was supposed to be appointed for six months & my time will be up at the end of January. The Pioneer Training Battalion is composed of reinforcements for the Pioneer Battalions. They are trained here for a time & then sent on to France. Where I will go when I leave here I do not know but the first thing to do is to get relieved & then I will probably either get something in France or be sent back to my regiment in Egypt. We are getting real English winter weather now. Foggy dull days with occasional rain & light falls of snow. The ground is sodden & I suppose will remain so till the spring.

I have had a cold but am on the mend now & otherwise perfectly well. There has been great excitement here lately with regard to the Parliament. Everyone seems very pleased with the change & it really seems as if under Lloyd George[128] something will be done at last. Anyway it was high time that Asquith[129] was removed & I think that any change should be for the better. You will have

---

127   Foxlow was sold after the war to F B S Falkiner owner of Haddon Rig, the well known merino stud. In 2014, it was sold by his grandson, B S Falkiner for $15 million.

128   David Lloyd George, 1st Earl Lloyd George of Dwyfor, Prime Minister of Britain, 1916-1922.

129   Herbert Henry Asquith, 1st Earl of Oxford and Asquith, Prime Minister of Britain, 1908-1916.

seen by the papers that the food question here has been causing anxiety. It is not that there is any real scarcity but the question of shipping to bring the food here is the chief trouble more especially now that the American wheat crop is short & they will have to import more from Australia. And there is no doubt that there is a great deal too much money being spent on luxuries. However they are now limiting the meals in the hotels to a maximum of three full courses, dessert & soup counting as half courses which is as much as any reasonable person can want. The coal question is also getting serious & every day there are appeals in the papers for people to travel by train as little as possible.

I don't think there is any cause for anxiety in this, it rather seems to me to be taking precautions in good time & I think will do good if only to make people realize that the war is a serious business. I am glad to see that the coal strike is over in Australia. It seems pretty certain that the British Govt. are going to take over the Australian wool clip but the terms they are offering seem to me almost unduly generous (55% above 1914 prices & I think we should be quite contented with them. Must stop now. Love to all

Your loving son

Tom

I sent you & the Girl birthday presents the other day, I hope you will like them.

Camp 26
Lark Hill
Salisbury Plain
17th Dec

My dear Mother

I am beginning a letter to you now as I have a little time to spare & I expect to be very busy next week. All this last week we have had most peculiar weather. It has been freezing day & night with the exception of one day for about an hour. The ground is like a rock and the water is frozen everywhere. Then all the time day & night there has been a fog which has varied from light to very thick. One day about sunset I started to walk from my office to the mess (about 100 yds.). I thought it was taking me a long time getting there when I suddenly found I was back at the office again. At times I could not see a hut 12 yards away. On the whole except for the fog it has been pleasant. Before the frost came the ground was inches deep in mud & by evening you had to dig to find your bootlaces but now it is as dry underfoot as if no such thing as mud ever existed. I have not felt the cold so far & think that now we have had a fair sample of the winter. Of course there are the east winds in March to come yet, but we have already had a sample of east winds & they did not prove as black as they were painted. The men felt it in the beginning a good deal & a lot of them were sick but they are getting more used to it now. I am busy now preparing a Xmas dinner for them & often wish that I had a Goulburn Cookery Book[130] with me both for the men & the officers' mess.

---

130   The *Goulburn Cookery Book* was written by his mother.

I have never seen troops better fed than these are here & for less than it costs at home. Of course we are all learning as we go along & waste less. For Xmas the men are getting poultry & plum pudding so they won't be too badly off. We are planning a great Xmas dinner in the mess but I do not know the exact program. Yesterday I saw Ned Twynam[131] who informed me that Mary Cunningham[132] is engaged to young Kennedy[133] who was a cadet at Duntroon. They have written out asking for their parents' consent but have fixed the wedding so as to allow just enough time to get a cable & Ned says that they intend to get married whatever happens. I think it is rather a pity. He is a nice young fellow but I should say is no older than she is & I don't think it would do either of them any harm if they waited a year or two.

Ned was as flourishing as ever. Of course he has bought a motor car (a second hand Ford for which he gave £40) & travels round the country like a lord with a fur collar on his coat and a blanket for a rug & a petrol tin full of water for a foot warmer & a soldier to wait on him. There is no doubt the Twynams are a wonderful family. Cousin Jessie Mackay has asked me over for Xmas but I can't go & leave the camp tho' I am going to try & go over some other day.

I have not seen Pat for the last fortnight. He is as busy as I am. We had arranged to meet today but at the last minute he

---

131   Major Edward Twynam,14th Battn, [RTA 4-8-17]; brother of (Alice) Joan Twynam, Sister AANS, [RTA 27-2-17] & Mary, w. of John Cunningham.

132   Mary Paule Cunningham [Tommy's sister].

133   Her Uncle Ned seemed to have been misinformed as Maj Dunlop in fact married her sister, Mary Cunningham, 4th LH & a graduate of RMC, Duntroon, [RTA 13-4-19].

had to prepare for some shooting tomorrow and could not come. The news from Verdun the last day or two has been very good & is a good answer to the German talk of peace. Everyone here seems to think that the offer is only bluff & that they are beginning to feel the pinch. As far as you can make out they are in a pretty bad way for food especially fat & it really looks as if there might be a chance of them collapsing next year but I would not build too much on it till we see what the winter brings forth. The situation in Greece is bad but they seem to have taken time by the forelock there & got a move on before any damage was done. This week I have had quite an orgy of papers. A Herald & Telegraph with an account of the IWW[134] trial & three Australasians the last one only a week older than your last letter. I do not think that they send papers except by P & O & Orient mails. Still I am always glad to get them as they keep me more or less in touch with things. The London wool sales for December have just opened and prices are keeping up. I am wondering if you will have got any of our wool in for sale before Xmas. As it seems to have been pretty wet I rather doubt it. Anyway even if the Government take it over we will get far more for it than before the war & it will only go in excess profits tax anyway. Still the war has to be paid for & Pat & I are living on our own screw at present so it does not matter much. As a matter of fact I have a credit balance here of something over £400 & am thinking of sending most of it out to invest in War Loan. When the wool money comes in we should be pretty well clear of debt altogether

134   Industrial Workers of the World.

which will be a great thing when the war is over as a period of depression is bound to ensue for a while & that is always a bad time to owe money. I am going to have some supper now & then to bed. I will finish this later on.

31ˢᵗ Dec

I am sorry to say that I missed the mail with the first part of this & the Times has now ceased to publish Australian mails so I will send a weekly letter & chance when it goes. I spent a pretty busy Christmas as I had a draft placed under orders & was busy getting them ready. They left last night & I have now time to look round again. I spent Christmas evening with my commandant tho' I would much rather have been in the mess here. We had a real good spread arranged & I am sure that I would have been much merrier in the mess. However it could not be helped. On the following two days I was in bed with a cold but am better now. I have had catarrh in the ear & it has given me some trouble but it is quite right again now and I think I have shaken off the cold at last. Pat also spent Xmas day in bed but I think it was as much laziness as anything. He had had a few days leave in London & only returned early that morning. He came down and saw me the night before last & we had a couple of hours together. He is looking very well now & has put on a good deal of weight.

He left for France this morning & was very pleased to have finished the weary training. It is just about a year now since he enlisted & he was beginning to think that he would never get to the front. From all I hear he is doing very well & is the mainstay of his battery. Major James came & saw me for a few minutes the other day & had a talk but they were all very busy. Jimmy [James] was looking well after his illness & was full of Mary Cunningham's wedding which he attended as did Pat. I can't help thinking however that it was rather a mistake their being so precipitate and although he is a nice enough fellow he is very young and I don't think he has anything. One can't help feeling that both the Cunningham girls might have done better for themselves. We are getting now a splendid sample of English winter. It is either freezing hard or raining. Christmas day was a fine sample. When we woke there was a light covering of snow on the ground & it looked threatening. By midday all the snow had melted & it was brilliantly fine. At four o'clock it was raining hard & at 10 o'clock at night the stars were shining & it was freezing.

Yesterday I received two letters from you written on Nov 12th & 13th & today I got one from Uncle Hadge. What a wet season you seem to be having. I don't really know what Gidleigh looks like when it is really wet. It looks to me as if the lake will be full again especially if you get a wet winter again. I could not get away for Xmas as very few of the men could get away & I was busy giving them as good a time as I could.

The parcel you sent me has not yet arrived but they always take longer than letters. The Australasians come in batches. For a month I get nothing & then three or four come all together. The only thing I want is tobacco. I cannot get any that I like here & what there is, is very dear. I am sorry to hear that Mr Cunningham is so ill. He has been a very good friend to us. I know he must be terribly cut up about leaving Tuggeranong. I can't think of anything more to say just at present. I think I told you that I am C.O. of the Pioneer Training Battalion & that my job is to train reinforcements as they arrive from Australia. I don't know how much longer it is going to last but I have hopes of getting away shortly. Now don't you worry about Pat. Howitzers are about the best thing he can be with. With love

Your loving son

Tom

I am enclosing a recent snapshot taken just outside my quarters.

Camp 26
Lark Hill
Salisbury Plain
6-1-17

My dear Girl,

I was very pleased to get your letter dated Nov 13th short & sweet as it was. Pat went off to France last Sunday. He was very pleased to think that at last he was going to get to the front. He has got very fat since he has been in England and his cheeks were beginning to bulge. I think if he had stayed here much longer he would have been broader than he is long & his easiest mode of progression would have been to lie down & roll. Jimmy [James] also went. He had been sick & was afraid that he might not be able to get away.

You seem to be living at the College just now to judge by Mothers letters. Please remember me to all the old ones next time you are up there. The book you sent me for Xmas arrived quite safely & I like it very much. Last Xmas I got the Sentimental Bloke[135] so I am well set up now. I hope you like the present I sent you as a combined Xmas & Birthday present. It should reach you just about your birthday if you are lucky, that is to say just about now. I have rather a good horse to ride now but he is a terror to pull & besides he does not get enough work & so is pretty lively. When Gen Birdwood was inspecting today, first of all he tried to bolt with me, then he tried to buck & finally he refused to keep still for a minute. Gen Moore asked me where I got him & when I said he was issued he said trust a Light Horse man to pick a good one. Gen

---

135   *The Songs of a Sentimental Bloke* by C J Dennis was published in 1915.

MacLagan was also with him & I had a word or two with him. The horse is a dark grey & he is a good sort but a little bit on the common side. I don't think he is as good as either Crispan or Chester. By the way how are they, you have not told me anything about them?

Tomorrow if it is fine I am going out for a ride simply to give the grey a bit of exercise. I do not like this camp nearly so well as Perham Down. The surroundings are not so nice & it is much more muddy. In fact the only time it is nice underfoot is when the ground is frozen hard. Have you seen the Twinfants[136] lately? I have not heard of or from them for a long time now. I don't know whether I owe them a letter or not. I really don't think it is much good Snowy[137] enlisting. Even if he gets away from Australia I don't think that he will ever be passed here. I have not had any leave for a long time now and am going to try for some shortly. But it is not very easy to get it now. They are trying to stop people travelling on the railways as much as possible & are cutting down leave in consequence.

You seem to have been having a tremendous lot of rain at home. I expect that if it keeps on much longer the lake will be full again. Can you drive your little car all by yourself yet. If not it is high time that you learnt. You should be able to drive Uncle about wherever he wants to go & make yourself useful for once. I expect you will have heard all about Mary Cunningham's wedding long before you get this. Pat & Jimmy

---

136 Marjorie Granville 'Da' & Gwendolyn Granville 'Dee' twin daughters of Granville Ryrie.

137 Pte Maurice Parish, grazier, Bungendore; 2nd Mob. Vet. Section, 2nd AVC, disch, 5-11-18.

[James] were both there & I believe that it was a very jolly affair. They all say that Mary was looking very well. I can't think of anything more to tell you this time & it is time I had some supper & went to bed. With love

Your affect. brother,

Tom

Camp 26
Lark Hill
Salisbury Plain
6-1-17

My dear Mother

I think I told you in my last letter that the date of departure of mails are no longer being published. Why they have done so, I cannot understand. However I am now going to write a weekly letter & post it & it must just catch the first mail that goes. Christmas & New Year are now over & I am rather glad of it. They have a rather unsettling effect on the men & it takes a week or so to get things running smoothly again.

Gen Birdwood was here today inspecting & with him was Gen MacLagan. Everything went off very well & he seemed satisfied. I am so used to inspections now that I take them quite in the ordinary course of events. I did not get a chance to speak to Gen MacLagan but there is a rumour that he is going to take command here shortly & expect that I will see something of him then. I hear that he was at Mary Cunningham's wedding & I think that they rather look to him to appease Mr. Cunningham's wrath if he should be annoyed. Since writing I have received the two books you & the Girl sent me & I enjoyed them very much. The comforter has not come yet but we have got word that part of the mail by the Mongolia has been delayed so it should turn up all right. I also got an Australasian so I have been well off. A good many people seem to think that the war will finish this year but I must confess that I am not very hopeful. It is clear that Germany would like to make peace but on her own terms & I think she will have to be thoroughly beaten before she will accept the mildest terms we could offer. Fortunately the New Govt. seems determined to go on till Germany is beaten & there is no doubt that she is beginning to feel the pinch. I really believe that this year will see a great change & bring the end well in sight. The experience that has been gained has been invaluable & when our next offensive begins it should produce better results than before. Pat went off last Sunday very pleased to have at last got away. I see that George Onslow has got the D.S.O. & I think he deserves it.

I don't know when I will get away from here but I am going to agitate at the end of this month. I will have had a fair spell by that time & will be glad to let someone else have a turn. The worst of this job is that it is all hard work & very little credit. There is really very little news. One week is very much like another. Sometimes on a Sunday afternoon if the weather is fine I go out for a ride & see some of the country round but otherwise do not leave camp very much. The last week the weather has been quite mild, just like spring & all the papers are talking about it but I rather expect we shall pay for it later. When all is said & done I don't notice it any colder here than we have it at home. The only thing is that there is more of it & not nearly so much sun. You should have a good crop of apples & peaches this year. When you last wrote, there had been no late frosts & it was getting rather late for them. Has the little apple tree that we transplanted into the fowl yard ever had any fruit? If not it is about time that it was rooted out and something else put in. I expect that all the trees in the fowl yards are now doing well & this wet year should help the nuttery along. You seem to be having a very wet year. Every week we hear of floods in some part of Australia or the other & there are rumours that the wheat crop has been to a large extent spoiled.

It seems there is a great probability of a shortage of wheat this year and all sorts of economy measures are being tried but to my idea they are more or less playing with the thing. The so-called standard bread even now does not contain enough of the wheat, & the limiting of courses for meals really leads to more food being consumed. Now people have joints & two helpings at that, whereas before, as you know, in a six course dinner trimmings made up more than half the dinner but with it limited to three courses about half as much meat again is consumed. Still it does look as if the new Govt. is going to really do something. Whatever happens they can't be worse than the Asquith Govt. & it looks as if they will be a great deal better. I don't know quite what has happened with regard to wool, & whether the British Government has taken over the whole of the Australian clip or only part of it[138], but the wool sales are still being held here & the price is still going steadily up. I don't like to think what our wool would have brought here today but it would be something over 2/- per lb. Still, even if the Govt. have taken over the clip the price will pay us very well & by the end of this financial year (March) we should be quite clear of debt.

I am very sorry to hear that Mrs. Gordon[139] is so ill. She is a wonderful woman & I know how upset the girls will be. I had a letter from Cousin Clara Gilchrist a few days ago saying she had heard from you & asking me to go & see them again.

---

138   In November 1916 the British Government agreed to buy the entire Australian & New Zealand wool clips for 1916-17 at a guaranteed price. [see B D Graham, *The Formation of the Australian Country Parties*, p 98]

139   Beatrice Deuchar Gordon, wife of William Forbes Gordon of Manar, Braidwood. d at Woollahra, Sydney, in 1917.

Unfortunately leave is not very easy to get these times but I intend to try shortly. I have now got a Captain here whom I can leave in charge with a quiet mind when I am away. I expect that you will shortly be thinking of a trip to the seaside for a month or so. Remember that if you are short of money any time if you will let Mr. Yarwood know Pat & I will fix it up. We are both easily managing on our pay and really I feel quite a millionaire. I know how the cost of living is going up here & it must be quite as bad in Australia. I am going next chance I get to Salisbury to lay in a supply of socks before they become prohibitive. I have a draft going away tomorrow so I don't expect that I shall get the ride I usually take on Sunday afternoon if the weather is fine.

I love poking about the lanes & seeing the villages. There are lots of Tudor buildings & even earlier round here & last Sunday I saw the traditional Chestnut tree beneath which the Village Smithy stood. There is certainly a chestnut tree & a smithy beneath it. The village is called Figheldean but how you pronounce it I don't know. It is a quaint old place and quite picturesque. The Avon River (one of the many) is quite close & the road running alongside has many pretty little bits. All the scenery here is more or less pretty but so far I have seen no views on a larger scale that can touch Australia. It is bedtime now & I can't think of anything more to say. Generally in the evening after mess & I retire to my room & sit over the fire & read the Times right through. It is about 9 o'clock before I finish & I then have supper & to bed. With love

Your loving son
Tom

Camp 26
Lark Hill
Salisbury Plain
14-1-17

My dear Mother

Last week I received your letter of Nov 24th and also three Australasians. The latter are coming better now but I generally get two or three together & then perhaps a week later another earlier one. We have been having vile weather lately. On most days it snows just enough to cover the ground, then it turns to rain & sleet & you can imagine what the ground is like underfoot. The only time it is at all decent is when it is frozen hard but we have not had very much of that lately. I have not yet heard from Pat. Your letter is full of the coal strike but I am glad to say that that is over long ago. You certainly seem to be having an extraordinarily wet season & it must have been a fearful nuisance not being able to get on with shearing. Since your letter too we have had cables telling of the floods in Queensland. The drought seems to have really broken at last and I should not be surprised if we are in for a spell of wet years. They are just about due.

There is very little to tell this week. I am very busy on some Court Martials just at present & will be kept going on them all next week. Keith is over from France on leave & has wired to me to try & meet him but I am afraid that it is impossible. The papers here are all making a lot of fuss about food economy & they have made a lot of regulations which may do some good but it is very hard to make a lot of people realise that they will have to economise. The efforts to grow more home grown

food I don't think are going to do much good. They have
started too late in the season to do much for the next crop
& the labour question will be a big difficulty. People seem to
think that the only thing necessary is to plough every available
acre but the first thing is to get it done & the next is to get
it sown. Then again they have fixed the prices & as regards
potatoes (one of the most necessary things) I think they have
fixed the price too low. Of course a lot of town councils are
going to do great strokes cultivating vacant allotments, &c.
but I think that in the end these small patches will not affect
the food supply very much and they will find that the cost will
be more than the benefits obtained.

Of course by next year probably the efforts as a whole will
do good but what they want now is not little patches but to
get decent areas of the large amount of vacant land available
under crop & in this I don't think there is time to do much
before next harvest. To my mind the authorities are paying
too much attention to small areas & not enough to the larger
ones. The papers become very excited that some Duke or
other is ploughing up a few acres of his park to grow wheat
or someone else is planting spuds on their front lawn while
they don't seem to bother so much about the thousands of
acres that are at present practically idle. All over the plain
here there is any amount of land at present practically out of
use which would grow good crops. Still it all shows a desire
in the right direction & by next year there should be a very
big increase, but I don't think it will have much effect this
year.

Of course all the trouble is caused by the shortage in America & the number of ships the submarines are sinking. It will do Australia a good turn if enough ships can be got. They will simply have to import as much wheat as they can from there. The submarines are worse now than they have been & nothing is more certain than that they will go on sinking ships till the end of the war. They are worse now than they have ever been & although the navy catch a tremendous lot of them they can never stop them altogether & considering everything it is remarkable that the submarines have done as little damage as they have up to the present. The shortage of food in Germany seems to be becoming more acute & it looks as if they will be very badly off in the spring. I don't think that the war will end before next winter, if then, but I do think that we are going to make considerable progress this year & in the autumn the end should be clearly in sight & only a matter of time.

The photographs Mr. Windeyer took arrived safely & I was most interested in them. The strawberries in the fowl yard certainly look very well & the young trees also. The banksia roses must have been very good.

I am rather amused at the Snowy [Parish], Sel Miller affair & to see the Girl handling it must be rather amusing. I will probably see John Ward when he arrives but that won't be for a month or six weeks yet. I am glad that he is coming. We want good men badly & I am sorry to say that some of those who have come away are not altogether suitable for the job. We have a good one here now, a man named Gordon from Tasmania. We have made him mess secretary just to keep him out of mischief as we tell him. I expect shortly to get a trip over to France not to stay there but more or less a sort of Cooks tour. It will be a pleasant change after the monotony here. I don't know when I am going to get out of this job but I hope it will be before long. I am beginning to feel that it is time I let someone else have a turn at 'a nice soft base job'. Once I get out of it they will never catch me again if I can help it. I have just heard a rumour that a mail goes out tomorrow so I will get this posted bright & early in the hope of catching it. With love

Your loving son

Tom

Camp 26
Lark Hill
Salisbury Plain
22-1-17

My dear Mother

I missed writing to you yesterday, Sunday, as I was very busy but I must get this posted tomorrow as there is a mail out the next day. Your letter of Dec 3rd arrived last week. You seem to be having a very wet time & judging by the papers it is still continuing. I wonder if you will get shearing over before Xmas. I can once remember the men being paid off on Xmas day. The place must have been a sight with all the grass. I have seen little patches good but with all the rain it must have been splendid everywhere. We are having poisonous weather here. For the last fortnight it has been threatening snow & the ground has been just covered once or twice but that is all. At other times we get an odd flake now & again. It still continues & shows no signs of clearing up. Generally it thaws in the middle of the day for an hour or two but for the last two days it has been freezing hard all day. I think we really prefer it that way as then there is no mud. I do not feel the cold very much & do not think that it is any colder than it is at home though of course there is a good deal more of it. I don't think there has been an hours sunlight in the last three weeks. But it is fairly dry & not nearly so much sickness among the men as there was a month ago.

The days are beginning to get a little longer but we still have to put the lights on about half past three on a dull afternoon. You seem to have had rather an experience on your trip to Cooma. I am afraid that you would not care for motoring on the slippery roads here. The cars skid a lot & I have seen them when they could not get up a little hill the surface was so slippery. As for riding you can't take a horse out of the stables unless he has frost nails & they are very difficult to get. I knew about the British Government having commandeered the wool clip but even with that we will get what in other times would appear a splendid price, & it is war time now. if only people would realise what this war really means & what would happen if we were beaten I think they would not worry so much over what are after all petty considerations. Even over here there are a big lot of people who still do not consider anything except themselves. It seems as if the German advance in Rumania has been checked at last & I should not be surprised if they shot their last bolt. Of course they will continue to have minor successes but I do not think it likely that they will ever be able to make another big advance.

Germany seems to be feeling the blockade now worse & worse & although you have to discount a lot of what is said about the food shortage there it really seems that things are getting in a pretty bad way. I think too that they will shortly find a good deal of difficulty in keeping their supply of munitions up to requirements. On the other hand we will be able to exert practically our full force next spring & tho' I am not among those who think that the war will be over this year I do think that we shall have it won to all intents and purposes by next Xmas. I hope to see John Ward when he comes over. He is nearly sure to be here for a while before he is sent to France.

I think that I am going to France next week not permanently but for a trip (what we call a Cooks Tour). Periodically a party of officers are sent over just to look round & see what they can. It helps to keep the training here in touch with the actual conditions. I am looking forward to it & should get away unless anything unforeseen occurs. At present I am pretty busy. I have six Court-Martial cases to dispose of & also a Court of Inquiry so I do not expect to have much spare time on my hands for the rest of the week. I went into Salisbury on Saturday to make a few necessary purchases. I find a great trouble in getting decent socks. There are plenty available but they are very poor quality as a rule. I think it is up to the Girl. If she starts now she ought to get a pair finished in time for next winter. With love

Your loving son

Tom

Camp 26
Lark Hill
Salisbury Plain
28-1-1917

My dear Mother,

At last we have managed to get hold of some paper in the Mess which is at least respectable to write on. You have no idea how hard it is here to get decent paper except at an exorbitant price. England may have been a cheap place to live in before the war but it is certainly not so now & I believe Australia is now better off in that respect. I received your letter of Dec 9th last week. It looks as if you would never get the shearing done. The grass must have been a sight. I can remember once a very long time ago when the yard was a foot high but that must have been in the early 90's. I expect that 15^d will be as much as we will get for the wool but that is a very good price compared with pre-war years & if we get that I don't think we have any cause to grumble.

It is an awful pity about the wheat but I don't think you people in Australia realise what the transport question really is. You had only to move about the Mediterranean to see the enormous number of ships required for the comparatively few ships there & I should not be at all surprised to see some restriction imposed on people travelling by sea very shortly. That is to say I think that people unless they have urgent business reasons will be discouraged from travelling as much as possible, & the number of passenger steamers considerably reduced. I am not very much impressed with the efforts to increase the amount of home grown food here so far. They are making great efforts but it seems to me rather in the wrong direction. There is any amount of pasture land suitable for agriculture but they seem to be rather neglecting that in favour of backyards parks &c & I doubt if their efforts will increase the supply very much. Of course I am speaking only of the coming season. By next year their organization should be good & they will have this year's mistakes to go on. There is no doubt in my mind that England can enormously add to her home grown food supplies but it will take time & that is exactly the thing most people here do not yet seem to realise. Standard bread seems to be a very good idea especially now that another 5% of the wheat is being added but even that percentage I think could be increased without seriously harming anyone.

Then there is the question of prohibition. An enormous amount of necessary food is at present being consumed in brewing. Unfortunately the temperance cranks have rather seized on the opportunity to advocate total prohibition which has naturally aroused a lot of opposition & has rather tied the Govt.'s hands. If they had left the thing alone the Govt. would have been able to bring in prohibition as a war measure without a quarter the opposition they will have now if they try to do it. We have been having vile weather here the last week. There has been a black frost all the time day & night & a cold north-east wind blowing. Up to yesterday the sun did not appear at all. But yesterday & today were sunny although it continued to freeze hard all day. The funny part is that the ground was wet when it started to freeze but it is now quite dry & the dust is beginning to fly. The wind is rather like our westerlies & dried up the ground even though it was frozen. It is my first experience of the famous east wind & I have seen quite enough of it. But don't think that I am feeling the cold because I am not. My work keeps me indoors a good part of the day & I don't find it any worse than it is at home in the winter. The muffler you sent me has arrived at last also the socks Fuzzie [Spencer] sent. The muffler is a great comfort & I am wearing the socks at the present moment. I also received a pair of mittens from Mrs Ryrie[140] but unfortunately they are both for the right hand. Someone also sent me a calendar but as they omitted to say who it came from & as it was posted in Sydney I cannot very well write & thank them. Don't worry about the duration of the war. I have never been very sanguine as you know, but every day now I am becoming more confident that the end although still a good way off will soon be in sight. I rather expect that there will be something doing shortly.

I have nothing to go on but there is a general feeling of expectancy in the air & I really believe that Germany has shot her last bolt. In today's paper she has been driven back in Rumania & the attack on Verdun failed miserably. I leave tomorrow morning for a week's tour of the front & when I get back from there I may know a little more of what is going on but things are being kept very dark. I am looking forward to the trip very much. It will be a welcome change after six months solid work. I have been very busy all this week with Courts Martial and a Board of Inquiry & have hardly seen the battalion. When I will get away from here I don't know. Just at present the prospects are not too rosy but intend to keep on trying. It is not that I mind the work so much. There is plenty to do but there is a good deal of scope for using

---

140 Mary Frances Gwendolyn (née McFarland), wife of Sir Granville Ryrie.

your head. The trouble is that one is more or less side-tracked & there is practically no opportunity of getting any recognition no matter how well you do your work. This does not weigh with me however to such an extent that I would try to get away, as I feel that I am doing good work here but there is always the feeling that you are living more or less in comfort while the man at the front is not & he is standing all the hard knocks. If only I could see some service in France I would not mind so much. However I will bide my time & it will be pretty hard if I do not manage it sooner or later.

I expect that Uncle Charlie & Aunt Janie [King] will be back here before long. I don't think that he will ever live away from England if he can help it. I am glad to hear that the little fruit trees are doing so well. This wet year ought to establish them anyway and once they get a start we will have more fruit than we will know what to do with. I am also glad to hear that the willows I have planted are doing well. Some day I hope to get them all along the creek. I am sure that the proper way is to plant good big poles. Then when they do grow it takes so much less time to make trees of them & the stock do not knock them about nearly so much. No more this week I am pretty busy tonight fixing things up so as to be able to getaway tomorrow. I hear there is a mail out on the 30th so this will just catch it. With love

Your loving son

Tom

Camp 26
Lark Hill
Salisbury Plain
11-1-17
[11-2-17]

My dear Mother

Here I am safe & sound after being away nearly a fortnight. I left here only on Monday morning & went to Southampton by train arriving just in time for lunch. After that, I made enquiries & found that the boat did not leave till evening so had to put the time in as best I could. Southampton in not a very interesting place but I managed to spend a few hours comfortably. Went on board about 6 o'clock & found the boat very crowded but managed to get a cabin of sorts & also some dinner. There were 30 in our party altogether & only one other Australian with whom I travelled all the way going & coming. I knew him before & we got on very well.

We arrived at Havre about 6 a.m. on Tuesday morning, had breakfast on board then landed, got our instructions, drew gas helmets & what are known as 'tin hats' (steel helmets) had some lunch & got on a train for Rouen. What with water bottle haversack, gas & tin helmets we looked very like Father Christmas wandering round the streets.

The French trains are now very slow there is so much traffic on the lines & it took us four hours to get to Rouen, about 36 miles. On arrival there we found there was no train on that evening so we had to go to hotels in the town for the night. These were nearly all full up but at last we managed to get a room in a funny old fashioned French place which however was very comfortable & the food was very good & cheap. Spent nearly all next day looking round Rouen which is a most interesting old place but you could not see very much in a day especially as it was difficult to find where the interesting places are. We left Rouen at 4 o'clock on Wednesday afternoon for Amiens & arrived there about 2 o'clock next morning.

We immediately bundled into two old London motor busses painted grey & a char-a-banc & started on the worst journey I have ever had. It was very cold, in fact all the time I have been away it has been freezing hard. The thermometer has never once risen above freezing point while at nights on several occasions it was very close to zero. I was unfortunate enough to get into the char-a-banc for part of the way & as it had no springs, and the roads are worse than anything we have at home you can imagine what sort of journey I had. As a matter of fact my feet were never on the floor for two seconds at a time and several times hit the roof. The roads were once good but the traffic has been so heavy that the surface has been worn into great holes & there is no avoiding them. We finally arrived at our destination a village called Engelbelmer about 7 o'clock & very glad we were.

I then found that I was attached to an English battalion for six days & about 10 o'clock after breakfast I met the colonel & went with him to the headquarters about a mile away. Here I was provided with a dugout containing a stove made from an empty oil drum & was really quite comfortable during my stay. I did not do much during the first day but afterwards I started out soon after breakfast & did not return till six or seven at night. I spent the days going round seeing various parts of the trenches & generally getting what wrinkles I could. During the time I was there minor attacks were in progress which led up

A char-à-banc, typical of the kind in which Tom, '… started on the worst journey I have ever had'.

to the capture of Grandcourt. although we did not actually occupy Grandcourt itself till the day after I left. I got plenty of walking exercise & enjoyed the time I spent there very much. The officers were a very good lot of fellows & treated me with the greatest kindness & hospitality. All the time I was there, there were 3 inches of snow on the ground but the days were bright & clear & as I was walking all the time I did not feel the cold at all but it gave me a good idea of what the troops have to put up with in the trenches. Imagine lying out all night in a shell hole with ice & snow in the bottom of it & the temperature somewhere in the neighbourhood of zero. Some of them got frost bitten while I was there but on the whole they are very cheerful & healthy looking. You can have no idea of the desolation wrought in some of the villages. The pictures that are published give absolutely no idea. I saw the place where

Thiepval[141] once was. I walked thro' the village going up to the trenches & had no idea that there had ever been anything there. Coming back I was told that I was standing in Thiepval & after a patient search I found the remains of a brick wall two feet high still standing. Except for that I do not believe that there are two bricks standing on top of one another in the whole village.

For a radius of a couple of miles round the village the ground is literally covered with shell holes touching one another and you make your way by walking along the edge of the craters which is rarely more than a foot wide. There were once large woods round the village but all that now remains are a few stumps which look as if they have been struck by lightning. I also saw thro' a tank one of the first to be used (HMLS *Crème de Menthe*). You will have seen pictures of them by this time & I cannot add anything to the description. It was most interesting seeing through it but I cannot very well describe it fully. Pozières is only a couple of miles from Thiepval but I did not get to see it. I arrived on Thursday morning & left on Tuesday night about 12 o'clock. I had no very exciting times while I was there. Got shelled a few times but nothing came very near me. The Boche was reserving most of his shells for the trenches & left the roads & railways in the rear almost entirely alone only sending along an occasional shell. The trip back to Amiens in a char-a-banc (with springs this time) was about the coldest I have ever experienced. I am sure the thermometer was below zero. The night before there were 25 degrees of frost & this seemed a lot colder. Halfway the petrol pipe sprang a leak.

---

141 Thiepval was totally destroyed in the Battle of the Somme. It is now the site of a Memorial to the Missing of the Somme which was designed by Sir Edwin Lutyens.

Luckily we had a spare one & managed to get it changed. During the change I did a war dance on the road & managed to get some feeling into my feet which just about carried me through to Amiens. We arrived there about 6 on Wednesday morning and just managed to catch a train, but it took us till half past five that evening to reach Rouen. I was sorry to miss seeing Amiens but each time I only drove thro' & it was pitch dark. At Rouen there was no train on so we had to stay the night & catch a train for Havre about five o'clock the next day. On arriving at Havre we found that the boat was full so that meant staying the night & the next day & catching the boat the following night. We afterwards heard that the boat we could not get on rammed a submarine but do not know if it is true or not. Had a very comfortable passage from Havre and arrived back here from Southampton in time for lunch. Since then I have been sleeping and cleaning up generally. I found two letters from you waiting for me dated Dec 18th & 24th. Also three Australasians & a Pastoral Review.

I am glad to hear that you had at last got shearing over and from what I can make out I think that we will get a very fair price for our wool. It seems to me that we will average somewhere about 15d all round & considering that in 1913-14 we only averaged about 10 pence we will not do so badly, & then there are the 60 extra bales. We should be able to get completely out of debt & have a surplus even with the increased taxation. I am very sorry that I missed seeing the grass. It must have been wonderful. It is a pity that we cannot get cattle to eat it, but it is always a pretty risky proceeding buying store cattle when the price is high & the only things that are at all safe are young cattle. I am glad that you like the Feldhams & are seeing something of them. The district must be very dead now with the Craces leaving. I am very sorry to hear that Mr. Cunningham is so sick. He has had a long spell now & he is not as young as he was. He is bound to feel losing Mary & Tommy too. I hope that you won't think of coming over. The submarines are worse than ever & I am afraid that they will not be a great deal better until the war is over. I read in a paper while in France that no more passports were being issued in Australia for people to come to England & I rather hope that it is true. The food question here, while I don't think it will become acute, is certainly very serious & I really think that people can do their bit better by staying at home & working there. It is now after bedtime so I must stop. With love

Your loving son

Tom

Camp 26
Lark Hill
Salisbury Plain
18-2-17

My dear Mother

I am afraid that I have not much to tell you this week. There has been no Australian mail in & consequently no letter from home. I have been busy practically all the week on a Court of Inquiry which is not finished yet but which I hope will finish sometime next week. The thaw has finally come & the whole place is now inches deep in mud. The frost lasted about three weeks, then it gradually got warmer & finally on Friday night we had a shower of rain which finished it. We are bound to get some cold weather yet but the days are getting appreciably longer & the sun is warmer, & I think that after this month the worst of the weather will be over. The food question here still seems to me to be in a pretty bad way. Of course I do not mean to infer for a minute that it is a question of starvation or anything like it but it does seem as if a great deal more economy will have to be exercised & people will have to do without a great many luxuries that they are now getting. The submarine question is still acute although they have not been getting quite so many ships lately. They have now sunk an American sailing vessel & it does seem as if the United States will be forced to come in. Not that I think she can help very much but there is always the moral effect. Of course financially if she does come in she can do a great deal & I expect that her help will chiefly consist in that & supplying munitions. I see by the papers that there are still a lot of Australian women applying for permission to travel in spite of the prohibition, but when all is said & done they are not wanted here at the present time in addition to the very real danger there is from submarines.

The trouble over here at present is that there are too many more or less idle people & steps are now being taken to get them organized for national work. But there is nothing to show that there are not enough people in the country to do that work if properly organized, and if there are enough why have a single unnecessary person here that can be avoided, having regard to the shortage of food. Of course there is no doubt that it is very hard in individual cases but this is a time when self must be sacrificed for the general good. Of course a large number of the Australians over here are doing very good work in Canteens &c. but after all the work would go on much the same even if there were none of them here. I don't know how it will affect Marjorie [Ward]. Unless she got away in January it looks pretty doubtful if she will be allowed to come. I have heard nothing of John yet but expect he will turn up shortly now. It takes up to 12 weeks by the Cape according to circumstances. I have no more news so must stop. With love

Your loving son

Tom

Camp 26
Lark Hill
Salisbury Plain
26-2-17

My dear Mother

I am afraid that you will not have much of a letter this week as there is very little news. There has been no Australian mail in for three weeks & report says that it is hung up in America owing to the submarine campaign. Whatever the reason is the latest letters we have had were written about Xmas time. I expect that by now you will have been to Cronulla or will be just on the point of going for a few weeks change. The frost here has broken at last & for the past week it has been quite mild with showers most days. The frost played havoc with the roads & at present I have 300 men repairing them. The surface seemed to rise & then the heavy motor lorries broke thro' & last week it was quite a common thing to see them bogged. Imagine this in England. We are practically cut off from the outside world as far as heavy traffic is concerned & last week I had considerable difficulty in getting through to Lidworth in a light ford. However we will get it fixed up before long. The chief items of interest during the week have been the formation of the National Govt. in Australia[142] & Mr. Lloyd George's speech in the House [of Commons] on the food question.

It seems to me rather a good thing that they have agreed to settle their difference in Australia & form a National Govt. There is no doubt that the people here look to Mr. Hughes to represent Australia at the forthcoming conference & no one else would

---

142   Hughes, having lost the support of the majority of the Labor Party, formed a coalition with the right of centre National Party. [Whyte, *op cit*, p 315]

have half the same weight. Then again whatever Mr. Hughes' shortcomings I believe that he is a thorough Imperialist. With regard to the food question here the position seems to be pretty bad but I think it is all to the good that Lloyd George has spoken out & told the people exactly what the position is. I really believe that the mass of the people are at last beginning to realise that there is a war on & I don't think that it will do them the least harm in the world to feel the pinch a bit. The prohibition of the import of apples will hit the fruit growers in Australia pretty hard but that under the present circumstances can't be helped & we must hope that it won't be for more than one season at most. Wool is bringing some tremendous prices here. Last week greasy wool from Victoria was sold for 3/6 a pound which I think must be a record for the last fifty years. New clothes will soon be unobtainable if the price of wool continues to go up much more. It is now bedtime & I must stop. I don't know when this will go as the submarine business has upset everything. They have not been getting nearly so many ships at present tho' that may be partly due to the fact that most of the submarines have gone back to port for supplies. No results of our measures are published but there are various rumours going round & while taking them with a grain of salt there is no doubt that a good many of the submarines that come out never get back. With love

Your loving son

Tom

Camp 26
Lark Hill
Salisbury Plain
10-3-17

My dear Mother

The submarine trouble is playing up terribly with the mails. I have received your letters of Jan 15th & 21st but nothing in between although the Australasian has arrived safely up to Jan 13th & I got a letter from Fuzzie dated Jan 6th. Still one must not grumble & be thankful that some mails are still arriving. I have also had a line from Pat saying that he is well but very busy.

We have had a return of bad weather & on Thursday we had snow rain sleet & sunshine on the same day. Still the days are getting longer & there should not be very much more. Gen MacLagan was here the other day inspecting & he asked to be remembered to you. I am afraid that I have not much news for you this week but things have been going on very much the same as usual. The two topics of the week have been the Food Shortage & the finding of the Dardanelles Commission[143]. The latter you will have seen in the papers so there is no need to go into it. It looks as if no one could have made a greater muddle than was done & beyond taking it as a warning for the future I do not see that much good is done by bringing it up again. The Food Shortage grows more serious every day & I am afraid that before the harvest is in things will be pretty bad. By this I do not mean that I think there is fear of a famine but people will feel the pinch. It looks as if the Army ration will be cut down slightly & I don't think that would be

143   An enquiry set up by the British Government into the failure of the Gallipoli campaign.

done unless the situation was fairly grave. On the whole if it does not become too bad short commons should do a tremendous lot of good in bringing home to a large section of the people the fact that we are at war. The voluntary rationing has been to a great extent a failure & probably very shortly some sort of card system will be adopted. The Govt have managed to bungle the potato question pretty badly but then they were left in a very bad position by their predecessors. Also their efforts to increase the food supply (home grown) I am very much afraid are not going to add greatly to it.

The weather has been all against ploughing, there is a shortage of labour & it looks as if the amateur efforts that are being made will result in a great many cases simply in the waste of valuable seed. I see by orders that John Ward has arrived & has been sent to Wareham. It is some way from here & I doubt if I shall be able to see him but I am writing to him to get into touch.

I am very sorry to hear about Mrs Gordon. She always seemed to enjoy so much whatever was going on & when I came away I thought that she was likely to live a long time. I did not think that Bob Osborne was so well off but I think his father gave them all something a few years ago. Deuchar[144] will have his hands pretty well full but he has a great capacity for work & I don't think he could have got a better executor. I am glad to hear that the Girl is shaping so well as a housekeeper. It will do her a lot of good having to look after things. She is certainly enterprising, riding up to Michelago. When is the Government going to take over

---

144   (William) Deuchar of Manar, Braidwood, s. of William Forbes and Beatrice Deuchar Gordon.

Lanyon? Or are they going to leave the house or any part of the place? I am rather interested to see what the wool will bring this year. I have an idea that the best of it should make about 17^d but of course that is only a guess & you can't really tell until you have seen the wool & can compare it with other clips. As far as one can tell from the papers you seem to have had a wet summer right through & the grass must have kept green pretty well all the year. If you get any rain this month it ought to assure a good winter. Tomorrow if it is at all fine I am going to try & go over to Shawford but it is not very promising just at present blowing & raining. With love

Your loving son

Tom

Camp 4
Fovant
Wilts
25-3-17

My dear Mother

Another move. When I wrote to you last week I thought that I was settled for all time but sudden orders came along & we are now at Fovant. It is a small place about 9 miles from Salisbury near the Dorset border but much better than Lark Hill. We are off the plain here & it is much more sheltered & besides it is not nearly so much at the back of beyond as Lark Hill. We are right in a valley & the surroundings are much more typically English than at Lark Hill. Besides there is an absence of mud which is very pleasing. The men seem more cheerful & I think it will prove a great improvement all round. In about three weeks time the trees should be coming out into leaf & the country will be very pretty.

When I will be able to get away I don't know but I live in hopes. Anyway I am going to try & get leave shortly. I think that it is about due to me but I want to wait until the weather is a little more settled. We have been having a splendid example of the English climate lately. On the same day (1) it rains (2) it is fine (3) it snows (4) is fine & finally blows hard thaws or rains again. This has been going on for the last fortnight or so but it never does the same thing for more than an hour at a time.

Still the days are getting considerably longer & the crocuses are beginning to come out so it won't be long before spring is here. There has been no Australian mail in for some time now so I have not very much to write about. I have not been getting the papers very regularly since I have been here but there was a small paragraph in the Times a day or two ago saying that Mr. Holman's[145] party had been re-elected with a working majority. From all accounts he must have had a good deal harder fight than was expected but it should be an indication of how the Federal Elections will go next month & once they are over there should be a better chance of getting to work on the recruiting problem. I am very much afraid that the war will not be over this year although I think that by the Autumn the end should be in sight. At all events we have a Government here now which will at least try & do something, although the number of controllers they are appointing is getting alarming. Still although they are far from being infallible they are a long way better than their predecessors. The revolution in Russia has created a great stir but the general impression seems to be that it will be a help rather than a hindrance to the prosecution of the war. It looks as tho' there will not be any great push till the end of May or beginning of June. I do not think that the present German retreat on the Somme will have any great bearing on the question. It looks as if America is going to come in at last but while it should make the end more certain I do not think that it can affect operations this year very much.

It must take them a very long time to organize & train any force in sufficient numbers to be effective. Of course the moral effect of their coming in will be considerable and finally they could be of very great assistance. I am afraid that this is a stupid letter but there is really nothing much to tell you. With love

Your loving son

Tom

---

145 William Arthur Holman, Labor Premier of NSW, 1913-1915; National party Premier 1915-1920. [*ADB 9.340*].

14-4-17
Camp 4
Fovant

My dear Mother

Since last time I wrote to you we have been having a perfect example of English spring weather. Nearly every morning on waking up there is anything from one to three inches of snow on the ground. It is probably brilliantly fine & the snow melts quickly. Then before lunch it is blowing a gale & raining in the afternoon the rain stops & later turns to snow & so on. The one thing is that there is no monotony beyond the fact that the weather is generally bad. Everything is very late this year. I have only seen one or two primroses in the hedges & the daffodils are only now just beginning to come out. I have seen a few violets but that is all. There is no sign of green yet in the hedges & I do not think there will be for a fortnight yet. Still the cold has not been really so bad as one would expect. I have felt it quite as cold at home as anything we have had here. Still the days are getting longer & we should get some nice weather shortly. This week I have been very lucky. I have had your letters of Feb 10th, 18th, 25th, also two from the Girl. Previously there had not been any mail for three weeks. I will now set about answering your letters in order.

I am sorry to hear that Gran has not been well but she is a wonderful old lady & it is just like her to summarily dismiss her doctor. I told you a long time ago what I thought of your coming over here & there is nothing very much that I can add. The trouble at home with regard to recruiting is that they do not realise what the war really means. There are a lot here just the same but I rather think that it will be brought home to them shortly. The submarine campaign continues and I think that before very long there will be a real food shortage here. I do not mean starvation but a real pinch & it will probably do a lot of good in bring home to people what they are up against. Otherwise the war news is distinctly encouraging. America has at last come in & tho' except financially she cannot do very much before next year the moral effect must be very great & if the war lasts long enough she has vast reserves to draw upon. The allies should be at their maximum this year but now America has come in this maximum should be the same next year & meanwhile Germany must grow weaker. The recent successes on the Somme & at Arras are a real blow. Of course they do not mean the end but they do show that we have now got the superiority & we should keep it. Next month I think that there will be very good news. We have not really exerted our full strength yet. The Girl seems to have been enjoying herself to the full at Michelago. She is a great person for adventures & always seems to come right side up. To my mind it is a pity that Ev. Crace[146] has enlisted. There should be better work for him to do at home. This war is not for the old, young or middle aged. The men who can stand it best are those from about 22 to 37 & Ev. must be over forty. Of course there are exceptions but they are rare. It is a pity that Selwyn Miller is not enlisting in Australia. Personally I have not very much use for men who come over here looking for jobs. It was a different thing in the beginning but now good men are needed badly for ourselves & it seems to me to be setting a bad example to not to take his chances at home. I am sorry to hear that the weather has been playing up so much with the lambs. Still one can't have everything. The photos arrived safely & I am always very interested in any snapshots like

---

146   Pte Everard Gregory Crace aged 42, grazier, Gungahlin, Federal Territory; 40th Battn. RTA 21-3-19

Billy Byron and his dog, January 1917.

Willows trees planted along Turallo Creek, at Gidleigh.

them. I am very glad indeed to hear that Mr Cunningham is at last getting better. He must feel it a good deal, Tommy & Mary being away & Andy too. Still Twynam[147] should be a great help to him. You enclosed the prices for the wool & they certainly amaze me. I had no idea it would bring anything like the price. It must have improved tremendously since I left home. I am sure Cousin Reg[148] should be very pleased with it. It is chiefly his doing. We should pay off all our debts this year & have a little in hand for a rainy day. I don't think either Pat or I will want to draw anything. Our pay at present is quite sufficient for our needs, indeed I have quite a respectable sum saved. My only expenditure here is my mess bill & occasionally hire of a motor car when I go for a two or three hours run. If it was not for the difficulty of getting petrol I would buy a small car but I am afraid that the petrol trouble cannot be overcome. I am sorry to hear that Fuzzie is not as robust as she should be. I am afraid it must be because she has no one to quarrel with. You need not worry about her future. Pat & I will do all that is needful in the matter should it become necessary in the distant future.

The photos arrived & I am much amused at Billy Byron[149] & his dog. The little willows have certainly made splendid progress. I think it would be a good thing if you got Uncle to put more of them in both up & down the creek. As long as big poles are put in they have a fair chance of growing. It is no use putting small ones in. You will enjoy having Nell Knox with you for a while. She is generally amusing & cheery.

---

147   James Edward Twynam, 2nd s. of James Cunningham.
148   Robert Reginald Futter 1861–1944, s. of John Sedley Futter and his wife Jane, née Styles. [see Appendix]
149   William Byron, senior, Neil's Creek, Bungendore, grazier.

I do hope you haven't written to Gen. Ryrie & asked him to try & get me back. It is most unmilitary. I have not given up hope of getting away & my chance will come sooner or later. Just at present I am very busy preparing for a review by the King which is to take place next Tuesday at Lark Hill. As soon as that is over I am going to try for a week's leave & then make another effort to get away. I am getting very tired of this work. There is a good deal of worry and not much thanks. I may even yet be able to get back to Egypt. I am very glad indeed to hear that Aunt has been mentioned, she certainly deserves it if anyone does. I am most interested to hear all about the little fruit trees. Next year, if the spring is at all propitious you should have more fruit than you know what to do with. John Ward is at present busy in England here & I hope to see him before long. I do hope that you will arrange to go away this year for at least three months (June July & August). You must remember that you cannot stand the cold & you are not justified in staying. You are sure to get sick again if you do.

Also you must remember that Pat & I are spending nothing of our income & so it does not matter if you do spend a little bit extra. We are quite wealthy & there is absolutely no need to count the pennies. Of course I do not advocate extravagance but my definition of extravagance is spending money unwisely not the mere fact of spending. I must stop now as I have some more letters to write & will not have a chance again for a few days. I will tell you all about the review in my next letter. With love

Your loving son
Tom

Camp 4
Fovant
Wilts
21-4-17

My dear Girl

I am afraid that I owe you several letters but I have had very little to write about lately. I have had your letters from Michelago. You seem to be having a most adventurous time there & spend most of your days getting wet. Are you going to take up your abode there permanently or are you sometimes coming home for a visit. Mother sent me a photo the other day of the wonderful Minerva. She does not look very much in the photo. Her wither is too high and she has a bad neck. I have a big grey horse to ride here. When I first got him he was a brute. He would not walk a step & pulled very hard, but I have got him to be quite a decent hack now. He walks well & is a good trotter. All the roads round here are very hard & I have to either walk or trot nearly all the time except when I get on the downs. I must get my camera in working order & send you some snaps. I have taken a few but I have only got one print & do not like to risk sending them by post. Now that the weather is better I should be able to get some good snaps but I do not get much time off.

I am going to get a motor bike to run about here in the evenings so you may expect to hear of some smashes shortly. The only trouble is that I do not know whether I will be able to get enough petrol. It is very hard to get it now over here. We are getting much better weather now & all the last week it has been beautiful but I expect it won't last long. I am afraid that this is not much of a letter but will try to do better next week. With love

Your affect. brother
T. F. Rutledge

Camp 4
Fovant Wilts
23-4-17

My dear Mother

The review last Tuesday was a great success but was rather strenuous. We had to march to Lark Hill on the Monday a distance of about 17 miles & got nicely wet doing so. Then when we arrived we had to more or less picnic as the camps were all pretty full. Tents were up for us but they were very wet so most of the men slept in dining huts & such like places.

We had to make a very early start on the day of the review which meant breakfast before six o'clock. Fortunately the day proved fine but very cold & after we were drawn up for the inspection we had three quarters of an hour to wait facing a very cold wind. I don't think I have ever been colder. However the march past was very good & I hear that His Majesty expressed his appreciation & now everyone is patting everyone else on the back. Gen MacLagan was over here the other day & asked to be remembered to you. He is always very nice & is very popular. The day after the review we marched back here again & were very pleased to get away from Lark Hill although it was a tired Camp that night. Ever since then it has been beautiful weather & it really does seem to have set in fine at last. A green tinge is appearing here & there in the hedges & the primroses are just coming out but all the trees are leafless so far & this is very nearly the first of May.

We have been having some concerts for the men lately getting parties from Salisbury. They usually come into the mess & have supper afterwards & some of the nurses from the hospital which is just next door also come. We usually end up with quite a gay evening & I think it does good, as it makes a break in the daily round. I think I told you before that there are two tennis courts here. We have now got these fixed up & they are not at all bad & as it is daylight now till quite 8 o'clock we manage to get some good games in. We are also installing a billiard table & will then be quite well set up.

All these improvements are being paid for out of the profits & as our daily subscription is only 2/- I don't think we are doing too badly. I have often paid 8/- & 9/- a day in Australia for worse food than we are getting here. Of course by now we have more or less an idea of how to run a mess. I must stop now. I am sorry this is such a poor letter but will try & do better next time.

Your loving son
Tom

Fovant
Wilts
6-5-17

My dear Mother

I have had two letters from you this week dated March 11th & 18th. The result of the wool sales surprised me tremendously. I had no idea that it would bring so much. As you say we should be out of debt now with a bit to spare. I do not think there is any cause to worry over the Super tax. While the war is on it does not really matter how much goes for war purposes & they will always leave a fair balance. Our expenses at the present time are not great & when the war is over we shall be in a very strong position.

I know how glad you must be to have the Girl back again. She always seems to have plenty of friends staying with her & should cheer you all up, it is a good thing she is taking to housekeeping. I think she has plenty of ability & should do it well once she sets her mind to it. We have been having wonderful weather here for the last three weeks. Bright sunny days & almost too hot. The only trouble is that it has been too dry & all the crops are beginning to need some rain. It is not too late yet but will be if there is not some rain within the next fortnight. The change has been wonderful. Last week there was hardly a bud of green showing while now all the trees are half out & the hedges covered in green. The primroses in some of the woods are a perfect sight & the violets are now just about at their best. I expect by this time you will have had your first frosts. Strange to relate I have purchased a motor bike & hope to get some rides round the country in the evening. You will hardly imagine me on such a mount & I would have got a car but for the trouble in getting petrol. Still with a bike I will be able to get away from camp & see some of the country, & they are certainly very handy. Several other officers are getting them and we should have some good trips. I have at last managed to get a week's leave & am starting on Thursday. I am going to London first & afterwards I don't know where. It all depends on how I like London; that is of course unless a court martial which I am on, on Wednesday, does not delay me but I think I can manage it all right. Over here we are meeting a few people who are inclined to be sociable.

One lady has had three tennis courts put in order & has given us the use of them daily while on Saturday & Sunday she provides afternoon tea for the players. I have also met some people near Shaftsbury about 15 miles away who have asked me there on Sundays & I intend to look them up. Then there is Mrs Smiley the wife of a Colonel of an English Battalion who is stationed there. She is a niece of Cousin Janie Knox[150] & we have quite forgathered.

I don't know if I told you before that I have had a letter from Alf Taylor.[151] I answered it but he did not give his unit & as I did not know it I am afraid that if he left the hospital from which he wrote, it will not reach him.

When you are writing again please let me have his address so that I can drop him a line. I don't know if I told you before

---

150   Jane, née Price and wife of George Knox.

151   Sgt Alfred Charles Taylor DCM, motor mechanic, 18th Battalion; [RTA 10-1-18]; See G. Ellis, *Our Soldiers*.

that we have now got our tennis courts going here & have also installed a billiard table both of which are proving great boons. I am sorry to say that most of the socks you have been sending have not been delivered. I received a light coloured pair about a fortnight ago which are just what I wanted. They are not too heavy & come well up the leg which is usually a great fault in most socks one gets. Please send an odd pair occasionally as some of them are sure to come & they are much better than any bought ones. I am sorry to say that I never received the ones Fuzzie sent me with my initials. Please tell her that I [will] write soon but it is very hard to write just now. It is daylight till nearly nine o'clock & the evenings are too fine to stay indoors. The week has been fairly full of happenings. We have just got a new G.O.C. Gen McCay[152] instead of Gen Moore. Then the news came of the *Ballarat* being torpedoed. The men seem to have behaved very well, tho' of course they had plenty of time to get off. The trouble is when a boat sinks in a few minutes.

Today we heard the first results of the elections & by then Mr. Hughes seems to have got a good working majority in both houses. We voted here & as far as I can tell there will be a fair majority for the ministerialists[153] but I]cannot tell definitely as I had to be very careful not to influence the men in any way. The only thing I know is that two officers who are both strong Labourites voted ministerial. Still here politics are more or less sunk tho' we do occasionally get up an argument. I will have to

---

152   Major-General Sir James Whiteside McCay, KCMG, KBE; 2nd Infantry Brigade [RTA 19-4-19] [*ADB 10.224*].

153   Refers to the Coalition formed by Hughes.

finish this pretty quickly now as the light will be going out soon & I can't go on in the dark. Of course Pat & I have no objection to you giving something to the Easter Sports from the Station. The trouble is that this letter will reach you long after they are over. I have been very busy lately planting vegetables in all the spare plots round the camp in an endeavour to increase the food supply. By the Autumn we should have something to show for our efforts. With love to all

Your loving son
Tom

The Royal Overseas Officer Club
At the R.A.C.
Pall Mall
London, S.W.
13-5-1917

My dear Mother,

As you will see from the address I have got my leave all right & am writing this on Sunday morning. Later on I have promised to go to the Park & watch Airlie Chisholm ride. I went to see them on Thursday but found that Mrs. Chisholm was in hospital while the Dr. had been called up & was working at a hospital too, from which he only managed to get away occasionally for dinner. I have also seen Sister Ann who is looking after her Mother. You will have heard that the latter broke her leg I think it was. Yesterday I went to see the Allison's[154] and Mrs Williams. I saw Marjorie & Mr Allison & Mrs Williams but Mrs Allison was out. I think that is about all the people I have seen so far except Mark Beresford[155] who has applied to get a commission in the British Army. He has passed the Doctor safely & sent his application in & is now only waiting to hear the result.

Today I am lunching with the Gilchrists and afterwards am going on to see Mrs Pat Osborne. The latter is a very difficult person to find at home but I wrote to her & she replied saying she would be in this afternoon. On Tuesday afternoon I have to go to Dorothy Plomley's[156] wedding. The first I knew about it was when I got the

154　William Allison, his wife Ellen, née Milson, & their daughter Marjorie, b.1896.

155　Marcus de la Poer Beresford, b1888, Gunning; m Susan Campbell, granddaughter of George Campbell of Duntroon.

156　Sister of Maj Norman Rutledge Plomley, MC*, 4th Battn, RTA 23-9-18.

invitation. We are having a wonderful spell of fine weather just now. For the last three weeks there has not been a drop of rain & in fact hardly a cloud in the sky the whole time. It has been quite hot too, more like August than May. The only trouble is that it is too dry for the crops & if rain does not come soon I am afraid that there will be a partial failure.

The new G.O.C. [Gen McCay] was round last week inspecting. I was away the day he came to the Pioneers but he left a message to say that they were the best battalion he had seen. As a rule he is not given to praise so you can imagine I am quite pleased. There is just a slight chance that I may get away shortly but nothing definite yet & I am not building on it very much. With love

Your loving son

Tom

Camp 4
Fovant
Wilts
10-6-17

My dear Mother,

The weather is continuing to show us what the English summer can really be like when it tries. Day after day it is fine & bright & the growth is wonderful. I am getting quite a vegetable garden going now. I have about an acre in with potatoes that are looking very well indeed. Then I have about 2000 cabbages & 1000 lettuces planted out besides big beds of peas, French beans, turnips & runner beans. Of course they will not go very far towards feeding all the men I have but still it will be something as everyone else is doing the same. I have been lucky in striking a bit of fairly good ground & I have been getting plenty of stable manure to put on it. I think I told you in my last letter that Gen McKay [sic] is very pleased with the Pioneers & says that they are the best unit under his command. Well he was here the other day again and presented a couple of medals. After it was over he congratulated me in front of the parade on the turn out & as he has never been known to do such a thing before it means all the more. Most people do not like him & go in terror but just at present I seem to be his white haired boy.

Gen MacLagan was here the other day & asked to be remembered to you. I don't know what has happened to the Australian mails lately. There has been none in now for nearly a month & I think the last letter I had from you was dated April 1st. Still the submarine trouble is not quite so bad as it was. I think that the entry of America has been a great help in that direction & practically ensures that there will not be any serious shortage of food here. Of course in a military way they will not be able to give much help before next year but then it should prove very valuable. I think I told you some time ago that I have got a motorcycle & I find it a great convenience especially now that it is practically impossible to hire a car to do any long trips. This afternoon three of us went for a run of about 70 miles just touching the New Forest & then on thro' some very pretty country. I have got to know one or two people about here now & sometimes I go out to dinner & bridge afterwards. There is a Mr Combes here on whose farm the camp is built & I generally go there about once a week. He is a cousin of that Mr Combes[157] who lives at Lake Bathurst. I am going to try & get over to Shawford next week end to see Cousin Jessica [Mackay] if I can.

Ted Rutledge is still here at the Command Depot but he expects to be going overseas shortly. I am afraid that this is not much of a letter but I will try & do better next time. With love

Your loving son
Tom

157　Chas B Combes, Grazier, Lake Bathurst

Camp 4
Fovant
Wilts
24-6-17

My dear Girl,

I am afraid I have been a bad brother lately & have not written to you as often as I should but for the future I will answer every letter you write.

I am going to answer now the letters you wrote on April 1st & 22nd. I wish I had seen you giving Rupert a dose of castor oil it must have been very funny & I only wish someone had been by to take a photograph to send me. Castor oil is really very nice if you sip it, you try it yourself next time you want a dose. I told Mother in her letter what it felt like to go up in an aeroplane which I did the other day. The drawing of Crispan is a beauty what I like about it is that it is so true to life.

Mother did not tell me that Sylvia & Arthur[158] were talking to each other all the time they were being married or how the bride had to borrow the groom's hanky. It must have been very funny to see Tom Knox & Rupert racing but there are very few horses about that can trot like Crispan. I am glad to hear that you managed to cure Tom Knox of his cold without having to give him red pepper. He might not have liked it. My old grey charger is very fine now. Not long ago he had worms badly and lost condition but I dosed him & he is well again now. My groom stuffs him with clover all day long & I can see him swelling visibly. I am afraid that I have not many photos to send you but I am enclosing a postcard of a

---

158   Sylvia Crace & Lt Arthur Champion

badge which the pioneers made on a steep hill facing the camp. It is 90 feet across so that will give you some idea of the work there is in it. Generally now on Saturday & Sunday I go out for a ride on my motor bike. So far I have only had one fall & that was because another man ran into me from behind & it was not my fault. Several of the officers have them and generally one of them is undergoing repairs but I think it is their own fault for going too fast. Ted Rutledge has just gone over to France, he left last week. I don't know if I told you that we have a billiard table in the mess now. We have just been having a tournament & I thought I had a chance of winning it but was blown out easily in the third round by the man who afterwards won. Still it is a great acquisition & is nearly always in use—that is after parade hours, I won't let anyone play while parade is on. Nearly every week we have a concert for the men & after the concert is over we get the party to come into the mess & have supper. Last week after supper was over we had a small dance but had to stop at 11 o'clock as the electric light all over the camp goes out then. Still we had quite a merry time for an hour or so. The men have also got a party going among themselves and give quite a good show. They dress up as Pierrots & I believe they have a scheme to get some ladies dresses as well although I am not supposed to know anything about it yet. Now this is really not a bad letter & I hope to send one like it a little oftener in the future.

Your loving brother

Tom

Camp 4
Fovant
Wilts
24-6-17

My dear Mother,

I had four letters from you this week dated April 8th 15th 22nd & 28th also a lot of papers including the Bulletin which I have not opened yet. I have been having a pretty busy time lately. On Tuesday there was an inspection by Sir Francis Howard[159], Inspector of Infantry, yesterday we expected Lord Derby[160] & although he was here he did not come to see the Pioneers, while today I have to go to Hardcott a couple of miles away to meet Mr Holman. I am just writing this before I go but will not be able to finish it so will tell you of the meeting later on. Gen MacLagan was here with Sir Francis Howard & asked to be remembered to you. In fact whenever I see him he always asks after you most kindly. He had just had an account of the Champion Crace wedding. Last Monday I went to Upavon to the Central Flying School where I have some men working putting up a big shed for aeroplanes & after I got the business finished I went for a fly. On the whole I enjoyed the sensation although once or twice when we started doing what are known as stunts I was a bit scared. I think we did everything possible except looping the loop & would probably have done that if the aeroplane had been suitable. The worst sensation was when we shut off the engine & did what is known as a 'nose dive' that is you head straight down & drop. Altogether I was up about 20 minutes.

---

159   Maj Gen Sir Francis Howard, KCB, KCMG, Inspector of Infantry 1914 – 1918 [see Who Was Who, vol III]

160   Earl of Derby, Secretary of State for War 1916-18.

I find my motor bicycle a great acquisition. It is impossible to hire a car now but nearly every Saturday & Sunday afternoon I go for a ride somewhere or other if it is fine. I have managed to get a petrol licence & it just about does me. A couple of other officers have got them too & we generally go out in parties, I have only had one fall so far & in that case I was run into from behind so it was not my fault. I must stop now but will continue this afternoon. It is threatening rain & is too uncertain to go out.

Later

After being kept waiting for an hour Mr Holman turned up shook hands all round & went off again. Still we are quite used to these sorts of affairs by now & they do not worry us.

I think this must be one of the best summers there has been in England for a long time. It has been uniformly fine for the last two months & in fact we are beginning to want rain pretty badly for the crops. Today is the first bad day we have had for a long time; it is cold and windy. Now I must set to work & answer your letters I will take them in order. I think I told you before that I have seen John Ward & that he was looking well & hearty. I have also had a letter from Alf Taylor which I answered but I have not heard from him again & don't know if he ever got my letter.

I am very glad to hear that Easter Monday was such a success, especially after the rain & all. I think it was an awful pity you did not sell Mrs Champion's umbrella. You could have got her another one & it was all in a good cause. I don't know where all the money comes from round Bungendore. I think it would be a very good idea to get a Ford for parish work & I am pretty sure that it would not be any more expensive than a horse. I am very much amused to hear that the Girl was thrown in Bungendore by one of her ponies. I don't think you need worry about the Australian troops being sent back to England to reorganize before the war is over. As for reinforcements; there are enough here in England to last till November at least & by that time something will probably have been done to stir up recruiting. I don't think that I will be much longer here now but one never can tell. Still things seem hopeful that I should get away shortly.

The food shortage seems to be much less acute now than it was and I think that America coming in has made a vast difference. The trouble now seems to be prices, There is a lot of talk in the papers about profiteering & they are going to do great things to keep the prices down but I rather doubt if they will meet with very much success. It seems quite strange to think of quail at home again.

Doff [Chisholm] does seem to have tangled up her matrimonial affairs considerably, but I think it is much better that she has broken off her engagement to Jack Storey[161] if she did not like him enough. He is really not a bad fellow & I think would have made a good husband but... I have not heard very much about Sheila [Loughborough] since I have been here but from the little I have heard I do not think that things are running quite smoothly. Still it may turn out better than we fear. She has a baby now. With love to all

Your loving son

Tom

---

161 Lt Col John Colvin Storey, OBE, MB, Syd; AMC [emb Nov. 1914; RTA, 30-8-18]; s. of Sir David Storey,[*ADB 12.105*].

I enclose a snapshot of myself playing tennis on the court in front of our mess. You will notice our badge[162] in white chalk on the hill in the distance. This was done by some of my men.

The Australian Army badge at Fovant, done by some men under Tom's Command.
Image courtesy of the Fovant Badge Society, Salisbury.

162 Regiments camped at Fovant under the chalk downs, carved their badges into the chalk. These are now cared for by the Fovant Badges Society

Camp 4
Fovant
Wilts
6-7-17

My dear Mother,

I have a few minutes to spare and am starting my usual weekly letter now on Friday as I hope to go over to Shawford to see Cousin Jessie on Sunday if the weather is fine. You will have seen that the Mongolia has been sunk & I am afraid that just about now you will be without letters for some time. The mails now are most irregular. One or two officers have had letters from Australia dated May 23rd but the last most of us have had were written in the end of August [April]. However I think that the worst has been reached and from now on I expect that there will be a gradual improvement. Last Sunday I went for a motor trip to Bournemouth with Mr & Mrs Combes & we had a very pleasant day. We came back through the New Forest which is just about looking its best at present. I am enclosing one or two snapshots taken during the trip which I expect you will like to have. The young lady in the snaps is an heiress whom I have been advised to make up to but I am afraid I am not in the running. On the way back we had three punctures which delayed matters somewhat.

Last Wednesday we had a concert for the men & a tremendous lot of guests. The mess was quite full. Gen Antill[163] was the guest of honour & seemed to enjoy himself very much.

---

163   Brig. Gen, John Macquarie Antill, CB, CMG, 3rd LH, [*ADB 7.8*], [Disch. 24-8-17]

There were also Major & Mrs Anderson.[164] He is from New England (Newstead) Cousin Reg I think knows him also Aunt Em [Rutledge], half a dozen nurses & several local residents. The concert was quite good & afterwards we had a very merry time at supper. I lost a pair of gloves as I bet a nurse that she was not game to put a paper cap she had made on the General's head. She did it after a lot of persuasion although she was very frightened but I think when I told her she was Scotch it did the trick. Tonight we are having some boxing contests which I think are going to be rather good. We had a terrific rainstorm the other day but fortunately not much damage was done. Just imagine in England five inches falling in a night. Since then we have had some steady rain & it has done a lot of good to my vegetables.

I have seven acres under cultivation now, chiefly potatoes, turnips, lettuces & cabbages & they are all looking well especially the potatoes.

Monday

I went over to Shawford on Saturday but found that Cousin Jessie & Clara had gone to Bognor for a change I think Cousin Jessie is coming back in a week's time but Clara means to stay two or three months. The war news is better than it has been for a good while. It really looks as if Russia is going to amount to something this year after all.

The chief topic of interest at present is the Mesopotamia Commission although the last air raid in London has had some

---

164 Colin Alexander Anderson, s. of Mr & Mrs Duncan Anderson late of Newstead North, Inverell, [See G N Griffiths *Some Northern Homes of NSW*]. He married Nina Ogilvie at St Mark's, Darling Point, in 1915.

effect in distracting attention. I am afraid that the raids will continue & I am very doubtful if we will be able to do anything very effective against them for a considerable time. With love

Your loving son
Tom

Camp 4
Fovant
Wilts
15-7-17

My dear Mother,

A pair of sox arrived a few days ago & proved most acceptable. There is nothing so good as hand made socks provided they are properly made & not skimped & if I can get them I won't wear anything else. I think they must have been sent some time in August [April] as so far I have not had any letters since those written on April 28th. I see that all mails up to May 21st have been sunk and it is too soon yet to get any of a later date. On Saturday some of my men were playing cricket against Marlborough School & I went over per motor bike a distance of about 40 miles. I saw our men get a lead on the first innings & then came away after afternoon tea. The cricket ground is a terrace on a hillside overlooking the school & a more beautiful site you can hardly imagine. I was introduced to the Captain of the School who made himself very pleasant & altogether I enjoyed myself tremendously. Coming back I came thro' Savenake Forest which is supposed to be one of the finest in England.

I am getting to know quite a lot of the country round here now that is within a radius of forty miles or so and am thinking of going to Bath next weekend. It is only about 35 miles away & that is not very far. One of the nicest places round is Shaftsbury. It is only nine miles away & is an old world market town which has not been spoilt by a railway. There is a very good hotel there at which I often have a meal. It is set on top of a hill & the view is one of the finest & most extensive I have seen in England.

Things are just jogging along much the same as usual. I have not been quite so busy lately as I have got rid of a lot of men & there have not been many coming in. You will have seen that Gen Holmes[165] was killed recently. He is a great loss as he was considered as probably our best divisional commander. Gen MacLagan has been appointed in his place & I am hoping that he may be able to do something for me. I know he will if he can. Gen Antill is now stationed just close to me & I see him fairly often.

I am afraid that this is a fairly dull letter but there is really nothing to tell you. We have had some rain lately & it has done my garden a lot of good. I have about an acre of the finest potatoes you ever saw. In fact I almost think that they have too much top but I am told that that does not matter in this country. The rest of the plants are doing well & I expect to have quite a show in the autumn. I am now trying to get a spraying machine to spray them all just to make certain that there is no disease about. With love to all

Your loving son
Tom

---

165 Maj Gen, William Holmes, CMG, DSO, 5th Inf Bde HQ, DOW 2-7-17, [*ADB 9.349*].

Camp 4
Fovant
Wilts
18-7-17

My dear Girl,

I am trying to keep my promise & write to you a little oftener although there is not very much to tell you. I am enclosing a snapshot of myself which the padre took one day just as we were starting out on a route march. You cannot see much of me but it is rather a good one of the horse & the men. It was taken just outside our mess. Last week we had a burglary. It was the night after pay day & a man came thro' all the officers cubicles in one building to see what he could get. It was a hot night & most of us had our doors open. Fortunately I had not drawn any pay and he only got £1 of mine but he also got my pocket book with a lot of addresses in it which is rather a nuisance. He got 15 /- from another officer £7 from another £1 from another & finally he took a pair of trousers & left them outside the door. Then he apparently went to another camp & did the same thing. He left no trace & I am afraid that we have not much hope of catching him. Today it is raining cats & dogs & is most unpleasant. But we have had a splendid lot of fine weather this summer so can't grumble & it will do a lot of good to the crops as it has come just at the right time for most of them. It will do my garden a lot of good too. We have had some very nice radishes from it so far & I think that next week we will be having lettuces from it & after that there should be a regular supply till well into the winter. The only trouble is that the rats are eating a lot of the cabbages before they are fit & I don't quite know how to deal with them.

I have not had a letter from home since one written on the 28th April so do not know what you have been doing for quite a long time.

When you last wrote winter was just beginning & now it is nearly over. From what I can hear the season has been fairly good. Last Monday we had some great boxing contests here. I have started a stadium going and so far it has been quite a success. We are now trying to arrange to have a night every week. On Friday I am having one of Lena Ashwell's[166] concert parties so we are quite gay, in fact with the other battalions round I could go to a concert every night in the week if I liked. Must end this now much love from

<u>Tom</u>

---

166   Lena Margaret Ashwell, actress, OBE, theatre impresario and suffragette, who pioneered large-scale entertainment for the troops despite initial War Office opposition [see Oxford DNB]

Camp 4
Fovant
Wilts
29-7-17

My dear Mother,

At long last there is an Australian mail in & I got two letters from you dated May 21st & 27th; also two Australasians, Bulletins, a Pastoralist Review & a pair of sox from Fuzzie with my initials on. I am afraid that the other letters you wrote in May must have been sunk & it is rather difficult to keep in touch with what is going on when some letters are missing.

The elections seem to have turned out better than anyone expected & I rather think from cable messages that come through that the question of conscription will be reopened shortly. Things at present look very black in Russia but Kerensky[167] appears to have now taken charge & I rather think that the worst is over.

I am very glad to hear that cousin Reg [Futter] was up having a look round & that he found things satisfactory. By the time you get this he should be soon coming again to class the sheep & if he is not too busy I should like to have a line from him just to know how they are coming on & how he thinks the new rams are going to turn out.

I expect the Girl will have enjoyed having Connie White[168] to stay with her, but am wondering if she will pay a return visit. I remember the last time she was at Havilah she did not enjoy it as much as she might.

---

167   Alexander Kerensky, Leader of the Provisional Russian Government in 1917 until overthrown by the Bolsheviks in October.

168   Constance White, d. of Henry Hunter White of Havilah, was at Kambala School with Elma

I gather from your last letter that Mr Champion[169] has gone away & I am very sorry. He was an ideal man to have in Bungendore, he got on so well with everyone & a younger man is nearly sure to upset someone or other before he has been there very long.

If you see or write to Cousin Jean Kater[170] you might remember me to her. We always got on very well together. She has a sense of humour & always sees the funny side of things.

We are living pretty well now & the food shortage is not nearly so acute. All the gardening operations I started when I first came here are beginning to bear fruit. We have been using our own lettuces for some time now, likewise radishes including a white variety (Icicle) which I think is the best I ever tasted. Today we had the first peas from our garden and beet & french beans will be ready in a week or so & cabbage in a fortnight. Potatoes are now only £5 a ton. It has been a very good year for them. I have about an acre in which I have just finished spraying. We have not dug any yet but they are the finest looking crop I ever remember seeing. In fact everything I have put in is looking exceptionally well & the only failures I have had are beet the seed of which came up very badly & a few turnips. I have about 7 acres in altogether & expect to be able to feed the whole camp for over a month without buying any vegetables at all. This is not bad considering I was about a month late in starting operations.

I did not go away yesterday as I was busy & had to interview one of the Staff in the afternoon. Today I set out with two other officers

---

169   Rev Arthur Hammerton Champion, Rector of Bungendore 1913-24. [see Appendix]

170   Jean Gaerloch, née Mackenzie, wife of Sir Norman Kater, [*ADB 9.534*].

for a motor cycle ride. We got about 20 miles from Camp when it came onto rain & we took shelter under some trees. When the rain was over mine was the only bike that would start & after wrestling with the others for a couple of hours without success I came back to camp & sent a man back who is an expert on my bicycle to see what he could do. This was about 6-30 & so far (10-45) none of them have turned up. During the operations I started to tow one of my mates to see if we could get a start that way. We got on pretty well for a while but as soon as I increased speed I felt the tow line slacken & looked back to see him dive gracefully over his handle bars & plow up the road with his nose. Fortunately he was not much hurt.

I have just time now to get into bed before the lights go out & will finish in the morning. The motor cyclists arrived back about midday today none the worse for their experiences. It is still raining & looks as if we are going to get a spell of bad weather. We have just had word that the *Mooltan* has been sunk with mails from Australia dated June 14th so I am afraid that we shall not have any more mail in for about a month. The submarines are still meeting with a fair amount of success but the general opinion is that they can never manage to stop supplies though they may make things a bit uncomfortable. A new push is starting in France today but there is no news yet as to how it has got on.

With love to all

Your loving son
Tom

Camp 4
Fovant
Wilts
13-8-1917

My dear Mother,

I was very pleased indeed to get your letter of July 3rd a few days ago but the last one I had before that was dated May 28th so that there is a considerable gap & I have to piece together events as well as I can.

I should like to get Mr Snell's address very much & next time you are writing you might send it along so that I can see him at the first opportunity. I am very sorry indeed to hear that Mr Cunningham's health is so bad still. He has not been really well for a long time now. I think that you could not do better than to get Cousin Reg [Futter] to have an occasional look round.

He knows the whole business so thoroughly. If wages go up the only thing is to get men who can do a full day's work have fewer of them & see that they do it. Of course as you say we must not be hard on old servants but I think in some cases it would be better to pension them off than to keep them on at exorbitant wages. I can't see, myself, that much can go wrong. Cousin Reg is doing the classing & the place will pretty well run itself. The only thing that needs watching is the rabbits. They have always been a trouble & will remain so until all neighbours get them cleared out. When I left home they were what I was most afraid of & in spite of careful watching they often got ahead of me.

The balance sheet results are certainly splendid & even after we pay excess profits tax there should be something left for

Pat & myself. Then this year we should do fairly well in spite of the losses in lambs as I think that prices in spite of all efforts to bring them down will remain considerably above pre war level. I am very glad that you have decided to give £100 from the estate to various war funds but think you might easily have doubled the amount. The two best funds I know of to support are the War Chest & Y.M.C.A. The latter I am most in touch with just at present & they are certainly doing splendid work in the way of entertainment for the men out of parade hours. I have one of their representatives attached to me here & can speak from experience. As far as possible I would give thro' the local committee as it helps to bring along other subscriptions. I must end now as it is time for bed. With love

Your loving son

Tom

Camp 4
Fovant
Wilts
26-8-1917

My dear Mother,

I did not write to you on Sunday as I have been having rather a strenuous time lately. All last week I was very busy with the battalion. For a month previous to that owing to Courts of Inquiry & Courts Martial I had hardly seen it & things were getting pretty slack. So last week I spent most of my time reorganising & strafing with the result that I have got things in shape again pretty well. Of course you can't recover in a day but I am in a fair way to do so now. You always used to say that I was too easy going & I am still a bit that way but when I really get on the war path, & I can do it now more often, I can hold my own with the best of them. One day last week I spent looking up various detachments all over the Plain & shaking them up a bit.

On Saturday I sent a small draft away & as soon as that was done I went shooting with the Combes whom I have mentioned before. We did not have very much luck but I enjoyed the afternoon & in the evening I dined with them & afterwards played bridge when I won the large amount of 4/6 at 1/- a hundred.

Then on Sunday I went with Col McConaghy[171] who commands here, to Bath. It is a very pretty trip especially the last few miles into Bath but in the town itself there is nothing to do or see on Sundays as the Pump Room is closed. Still I enjoyed myself very much. Today General Sir Henry Sclater was inspecting &

---

171   Lt Col David McFie McConaghy, 54th Battn, DOW 9-8-18.

in addition to fixing up my own battalion there was a special exhibition of an attack in which I was interested. My men had made a section of trenches with shell holes &c as like as possible to the real thing at the front. A platoon carried out an attack on this course using live ammunition & everything was made as realistic as possible. We had rigged disappearing targets over the course and my particular job was to work the targets & make them appear at the right moment. Fortunately everything went off without a hitch & I think the General was pleased. He then came and inspected the battalion & on going away said he had been most interested and did not find anything to criticize. With all this on hand & a concert for the men last night you can guess that I have not had a great lot of spare time on my hands.

I am sorry to say that we are to move again shortly this time to Sutton Very. This will be the fifth move I have had in a little over a year & I really thought that at last we were settled here but it was not to be. Sutton Very is about 20 miles from Bath near Warminster. I have not seen the camp myself but I am told it is not nearly so nice a place as this. I don't know quite when the move is to take place but I expect it to be in about a weeks time. We will march there as by the most direct route it is only 12 miles. The whole thing is a great nuisance. Just as one got used to working under whoever is in command & got to know some of the people living round, it is a case of move on & the whole thing has to be done over again. This time however I don't mind so much as I think that I will be leaving the Battn shortly myself. I think that I am going to be relieved at last and expect to get away some time next month. Where I am going or what I am going to do I have not the slightest idea but I feel that it is high time I got away from here & I have been trying hard to do so for months past.

Gen Antill went back to Australia last week & he has promised to see Cousin Tom Knox & give him the latest news about me & I am sure that Cousin Tom will pass it on to you.

A Major Arnall[172] who has been with me for some time also left here for Australia last week & by him I sent some negatives which I have taken in the course of my travels. I am afraid they are rather a poor lot but they contain views of the temple of Karnac in Egypt, Malta & a few Gallipoli scenes. I only had one print of each & I wanted to keep them but you will be able to get the negatives printed easily. I hope they reach you safely. It is getting near bed time now so I must stop for the present. I will try & finish tomorrow.

Sunday 30th

I have not had a chance to finish this since. On Thursday I went to have a look at our new camp & I cannot say that I am very favourably impressed. The situation is sheltered but I am afraid it will be very muddy in wet weather & the general layout is not nearly as good as this. However we must just put up with it I suppose. On Friday I had a day off & went partridge shooting over part of Lord Pembroke's shoot. It is supposed to be some of the best in England & I must say I enjoyed myself most thoroughly. I was shooting fairly well for me & managed to account for about 10 brace which is considered pretty good when you are walking the birds up as we were. On Saturday afternoon I went out again with Mr Combes, just a small affair. We got 4 brace altogether

---

172   Maj Henry Frood Arnall, Pioneer Training Battn; [RTA 1-11-17].

of which I got $2^1/_2$ brace so did not do too badly & I had a very pleasant time. I expect the coming week will be pretty strenuous as we expect to move about the end or the beginning of the following week. No more news so must stop. With love to all

Your loving son

Tom

Camp 4
Fovant
Wilts
Sat 31-8-17

My dear Mother,

I arrived back from London today. The Court of Inquiry I was on proved longer than I expected but I was not altogether sorry as I was able to see some theatres &c. There was hardly anyone in London that I know & I think the only person I met were the Williams, Mrs Dave Dickson, Mr Forsyth & young Morell[173]. You will remember the latter, a great friend of Keith's who used to come to Gidleigh occasionally from Duntroon. He is in the same artillery as Pat is & told me that Pat is getting on well & was flourishing when he left. It has been miserable weather all the time I have been away. In fact the whole of this month has been bad & in many places one of the wettest Augusts on record. The trouble is that there have been a lot of high winds & coupled with the rain have done a lot of damage to the crops which, in some places, are still lying in the fields cut but they have never been dry enough to cart in. I am afraid that when it will all come to be reckoned up a good deal of wheat has been spoilt. I myself have seen it sprouting in the stook in some places. Fortunately the prospects for the American harvest are distinctly good & I don't think there is any fear of starvation. But it will be a hard winter & I believe that milk will be pretty scarce.

Matches are the latest thing to become hard to obtain. This week in London half the shops were without any & I don't believe

---

173   Maj Throsby Morell, MC, 3rd Div Arty; cadet RMC, Duntroon; committed suicide 27-2-19 in France.

you could have bought a dozen boxes any where. As it was you could get a single box for about 2^d as a great favour. When I arrived back today about lunch time I found three letters from you waiting for me. They were dated July 19th 24th & 29th & all written from Leura. About three weeks ago I got one dated July 5th & you were then just starting for Moree. I do hope that that the baths will do you good. The Girl seems to be getting on very well at home while you are away and it will be very good for her. Of course I will be delighted to give you a spinning wheel or two if you like just get what you want & send the bill in to Mr Yarwood. I knew that the Carrawarra Chisholms[174] had taken it up & were very keen about it. I am very glad to hear that Aunt is pleased with Doff's young man[175]. I think that Doff did the only thing possible. We have known here for some time that Gaza was a pretty bad business & I was very interested in reading the General's letter about it. I rather think that there will be big things doing there about the time you get this. I am sorry to hear that things are not going smoothly at the College [RMC Duntroon]. When the heads are at loggerheads the whole place is bound to suffer.

I met Noel Rutledge when I first came to England & did a little bit towards getting him his commission. I hope you got my cable before you got Gen Jobson's[176] letter tho' you would probably realise he had mistaken Noel for Pat. I would not place

---

174   The daughters of Arthur Bowman Chisholm, grazier, of Carrawarra, near Goulburn, and brother-in-law of Alice Chisholm.

175   Dorothy Chisholm, m. Capt Chaplain J W Wayet, a British Army chaplain, [see J M Champion, *Lady of Kantara*].

176   Col Alexander Jobson, 9th Arty Bde HQ; temporary Brig. Gen, [*ADB 9.488*].

too much reliance on the statement that the Panama Canal has changed the climate here by diverting the Gulf Stream. In the first place the level of the Pacific there is several feet higher than the Atlantic & there are several locks on the Canal which prevent a flow either way. Affairs in Russia are still in a pretty bad way & it looks as if it will be a long time before they get things organised again. But the Italian offensive just at present is doing well & if they have luck they may get Trieste which will be a very heavy blow to Austria. I have always had an idea that the conscription question would be reopened & I think that if it is, it will be carried, tho' there is bound to be a good deal of opposition. The chief trouble with many of the hand knitted socks is that they are too tight round the tops. They are all right if a man has spindle shanks but if he has a decent leg they won't go on. I myself have received several pairs like this. I hope the Gidleigh Mixture will come along safely. I cannot get any tobacco here that I really like. I am very sorry to hear about Miss Uppie but as you say she is a most difficult person to help in any way. I had heard that Bertha Brady[177] or Prowse was to marry Ernest Watt[178]. But it is quite a common thing over here for women whose husbands have been killed in the war to marry again. Nearly every day you see an account of some 'war widow' being married in fact one lady I believe was married in mourning for the late departed. It is time I went to bed now so I must stop. With much love

Your loving son

Tom

---

177   Bertha d. of Dr A J Brady and widow of Captain Prowse RN,

178   Ernest Alexander Stuart Watt, shipowner & pastoralist, [*ADB 12.410*]. Bertha was his 3rd wife.

Camp 4
Fovant
Wilts
19-9-17

My dear Mother,

I have your letter of July 11th written from Moree which arrived a day or two ago. One wandering parcel from you arrived the other day containing some chocolate & was much appreciated. I am now in hopes that others will arrive in due course. I am glad to hear that you did not find the hotel at Moree altogether unbearable. I don't know why it is but it seems an absolute impossibility to find a decent hotel in Australia anywhere in the country. I do think you might have been generous & left your brushes out for anyone who needed them. I have had some of your letters with regard to Gidleigh affairs & I think I understand the position. I would not worry about the recent rise in wages under the new award. High wages mean high prices & although we pay out a bit more in wages we get it back & a bit more in the extra value of our produce. Personally I think that prices are going to keep up after the war. I don't mean that they will stay at the present level but I do not think that they will drop as low as they were before. My gardening operations in the camp have been on the whole successful. From a plot not quite as big as the rose bed near the [Gidleigh] office I have got over two tons of good potatoes & last month I made £20 for Regimental Funds out of what I sold. I had a tremendous lot of cabbages in but unfortunately a beastly grub has done a good deal of damage & I have not been able to get enough nicotine to spray which appears to be the only thing that will do any good.

I have been having a pretty strenuous time lately. All last week I was at Tidworth on a General Court Martial & did not finish it till yesterday. On Saturday however I had a day off & went shooting. All the country round here belongs to the Earl of Pembroke & he had a shoot for some of his tenants to which I & two or three other officers were invited. I was not in too good practice at first but managed to get 8 or 9 partridges & four hares. Our total bag for 8 guns was 37 brace of partridges & 48 hares, not bad as we were walking them up.

We seemed to have dropped into winter suddenly. On Sunday we went back to ordinary time which meant putting the clock back an hour & it is wonderful the difference it has made. Last night it was quite dark at 8 o'clock & before that we never had to have any lights before nine. I am afraid this is rather a poor letter but I will try & do better next time. With love

Your loving son
Tom

Camp 4
Fovant
Wilts
6-10-17

My dear Mother,

I think I told you that we are to move camp again this time to Sutton Very about 15 miles away & two miles from Warminster. I have been going thro' my things & destroying everything which is no use to me. When you are stationary for any time rubbish does accumulate so. I have had quite a lot of letters from you lately & on going thro' them find that I have four written in July from Moree & two in August the 8th & 17th, the last one written from home. Also I have had numerous parcels lately two lots of chocolate, two lots of sweets & cigarettes & best of all two tins of Gidleigh mixture. The last were both registered & it seems to have done the trick. I hope you will keep on sending it as I do not like any tobacco I get here. Also the Bulletin & Australasian arrive regularly & are much appreciated.

I am very glad to hear that you got my cable with regard to Pat before you got Col Jobson's letter. The latter is returning to Australia & has sailed just recently. Your last letters have been full of the strike[179] & it must have been pretty bad. It was a funny thing but except for one or two small paragraphs just when it started, the papers over here had absolutely nothing about it until a small paragraph appeared in the Times saying that it was all over & that the men had been beaten. I suppose that all news about it was strictly censored. Things had to come to a head & it is a very

---

179 Railway workers in NSW went on strike for 6 weeks; it became known as the Great Strike. [see Day, David, *Chifley*, pp 127-145].

good thing that it is over. There may be peace for a little while now although beyond the bare fact that it is over we know no details here of any sort. I am glad to hear the trip to Moree did you good but I think you went home to soon. I am glad to hear that the lambing started so well. As far as I can tell there was a fair rainfall in August & September so the spring should be good.

Mr Cunningham seems to have had a long illness & I am very sorry indeed to hear that he is not well yet. I am afraid that the losing of Tuggeranong & Lanyon has broken him up a good deal. The news this week has been good. We have gained ground considerably and apparently with comparatively slight casualties. If only the weather will keep fine for a little while longer we should have a pretty big gain as everything appears favourable. The air raids on London have been pretty bad lately while the moon has been full. I think there were eight raids in ten days or something of the sort but the casualties have been small compared with other raids & it looks as if the defences are becoming fairly effective. I have been very busy all the week & have not had much time to look round. For about a fortnight the weather has been beautiful but on Wednesday it rained all day & since then we have had our first real winter days. Tonight I have a fire in my room for the first time since April. The food question here this winter I think will be pretty right except in a few things such as sugar & milk. Milk will be the most serious & as far as I can see the shortage has been solely brought about by the efforts of the Government to control the price &c. Nearly everything they try to control turns out more or less a failure.

You will have seen by the papers that both Gen Peake[180] & Gen Maxwell[181] have recently been killed. I have written to Mrs Pat Osborne but there is not much one can say. I am afraid this is not much of a letter but things have been very uneventful lately. I think I will try & get a weeks leave as soon as we get settled down in our new camp. With love

Your loving son

Tom

---

180 Brig Gen Malcolm Peake, CMG, RA I Corps [KIA 27-8-17];.m. Mrs Pat's daughter Louisa Margaeret Atkinson Osborne

181 Brig Gen.Frank Aylmer Maxwell, VC, DSO*, CSI [KIA 21-9-17]; m Louisa's sister Charlotte Alice Hamilton Osborne,

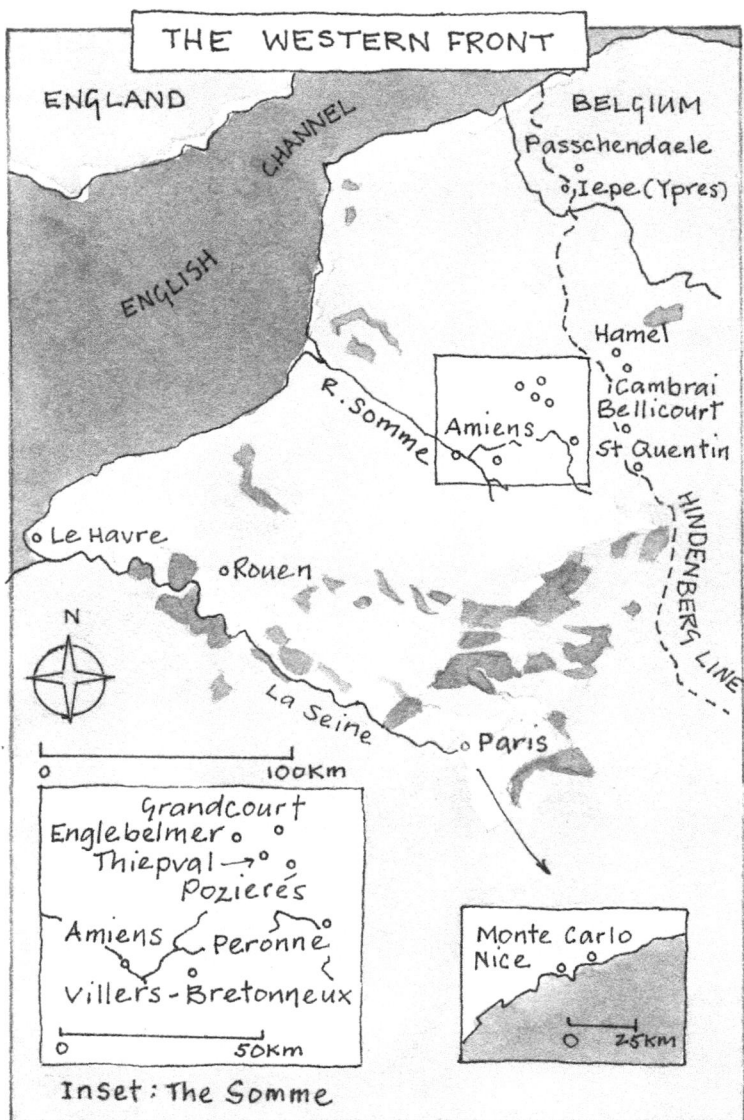

Map by Catherine Gordon.

Chapter Five
The Western Front

Camp 6
Sutton Very
12-10 –17

My dear Mother,

Things have been moving since I last wrote to you on Sunday. The very next day I was warned to hold myself in readiness to proceed overseas & am leaving for France tomorrow. I am joining the 2nd Pioneers & my address will be the 2nd Pioneer Battn, A.I.F., B.E.F., France but I think you had better continue to send mail to the Commercial Bank. I will get it much more certainly & very nearly as quickly. The Pioneers are a very good job & one great thing is that we live back from the front line & get much more comfort which means a lot especially in the winter. I managed to get a couple of days leave in London to buy a few things. I saw Mrs Willie Chisholm & she has promised to write to you & tell you that I was looking well. I did not see anyone else I knew. They all seem to be away in the country still.

Now don't you worry about my going to France. Pioneers are as safe a job as can be found & I simply could not face going back to Australia & saying that I had spent all my time in England without having seen any fighting at all in France. Besides, my work here was getting very monotonous. The weather for the last week here has been very cold & there has been a good deal of rain but I think there is a change on & expect it to be finer for the next few days. This is only a very scrappy letter but I am pretty busy & I will write to you more fully as soon as I get to France. With Love

Your loving son

Tom

21-10-17

My dear Mother

Here I am in France at last but I am still at the Base awaiting permission to join up with my Battalion. In the mean time I am leading a very peaceful existence with nothing to worry me except the next meal. I have been here two days now & expect to be sent on any time. The camp is rather prettily situated. We are on one side of a narrow valley fairly high up & on the other side there are a lot of woods which are just turning colour. Today has been perfect just like our autumn days at home. Not a cloud anywhere & perfectly calm. This morning I was at the church parade & this afternoon I went for a walk of about six miles thro several little villages & woods. There was great excitement this morning when we got our papers & found that there had been another zeppelin raid on England & that four had been brought down as they were returning over France. It will be a very nasty knock to the Germans & they will probably think twice before they try them again but of course there are always the aeroplanes & they are much more difficult to deal with.

I am afraid that I will miss my mail for some time now as I have written to the bank to hold all my letters until I join up with my battalion. Otherwise they will chase me all over the country. This will be your Christmas letter & I am sorry it is such a poor one but of course here again all letters are censored & I cannot talk about the military situation or anything much which bears on the war. After being away from the censor so long it takes time getting used to writing with one again. Wishing you all Happy Xmas & with lots of love

Your loving son
Tom

28-10-17

My dear Mother

I arrived with my battalion yesterday after a very wearisome journey. When I arrived I found a wire from Snowy Parrish telling me about Pat[182]. Mummy dear I know it will be a terrible shock to you but do not grieve more than you can help. You know that the old chap would not wish it & I am sure that he would never have been happy if he had not come away. It seems very hard that he should have been taken but it is God's will & there is the satisfaction of knowing that he has done his duty. I am enclosing a letter which I have just received from an officer in his battery & it will give you all the information which I have at present. I am writing to find out further particulars & will send them on to you as soon as I get them. One thing I am thankful for is that he did not suffer at all. If he had to go it is far better as he could never have felt anything. I am broken hearted & I know it will be an awful shock to you but I also know that you will be the brave Mother you always are & there will be a little consolation after a time in knowing that he died for his country & that he did his duty. I am sure you will find the Girl a great comfort to you & you must rely on her as much as you can. God's will be done but oh it is hard.

At present I am a long way back from the front line & do not expect we shall be going any father [sic] forward for some time. The Colonel is away on leave & Major J. F. Donnelly[183] is in

---

182   Tom's brother, Harry Forster (Pat) was killed at Passchendaele on 13th October

183   Lt. Col. John F (Jack) Donnelly, DSO, 2nd Pioneers An instructor of Commonwealth Forces before the war. He and Tom had both served with the Bungendore troop of the 11th Light Horse. After the war he establish a successful stock and station agency in Bungendore.

command. If you see Mrs Donnelly[184] you might tell her that he & the other two boys[185] are all well & very fit. I cannot tell you very much about this place yet as I have only been here a day & do not know my way about. We have a very comfortable dugout for a mess room & I am sleeping in the cellar of a ruined chateau. It is quite comfortable but rather dark.

Please continue to send me tobacco it is about the only thing I really want as I do not like any of the tobacco I get over here. Socks also I can always do with as if I get too many the men are always glad of them. There has been a good deal of rain here lately & the mud is pretty bad but today & yesterday have been fine & not cold. I was out riding this afternoon & did not need an overcoat so you can see it is not bad. We have a nice fire in the mess dugout & I have a primus stove also which will do splendidly later on when it gets cold to heat my dugout. They have little radiators which fit on & give out a splendid heat. I have also got my fur rug so should keep pretty warm during the winter. I will write again soon. With best love

Your loving son
Tom

---

184 Annie Stuart Donnelly, [widow of Patrick J. B. Donnelly], Douglas, Bungendore

185 Sgt Patrick Joseph Donnelly, MM, 2nd Pioneers, RTA 8-11-18 & Lt Charles Edward Donnelly, 5th Pioneers, RTA 24-4-19.

4-11-17

My dear Mother

My move has upset my mail arrangements considerably & I have had nothing from you for a month or so now but I sent the bank my new address some time ago and I expect them to come along any time now. I have had a very easy week just going round looking at the various jobs & really having more or less a rest cure. I am supernumerary at present & have no definitive job & consequently no responsibility for which I am not sorry after being in command for so long. I do not quite know what is going to happen but rather expect that I will have a definite job shortly. In the mean time I am getting the hang of things generally & having a restful time. I have not been into any of the neighbouring villages yet tho' it is quite possible to get away for an afternoon & have a dinner at one of the cafes where I believe they do you quite well. The mess just at present is not as good as it might be but we have sacked our cook & got another who I think will be an improvement & are generally trying to get things going better. Clara Miller [née Mackay] sent me a box of chocolates which arrived today and I have what are left of them in front of me as I write. The Bosche has been letting us have a fairly quiet time lately & beyond an occasional bomb from an aeroplane has done nothing to disturb our peace.

The weather has been fine & quite mild. In fact I have not had to wear an overcoat since I have been here. Of course anywhere off the roads the ground is very muddy but there is no chance of that drying up until next summer although a long frost would harden for the time. This time last year we had already had snow

& I remember it was bitterly cold in England. The leaves are not yet all off the trees. You cannot imagine the desolation there is round here. The country is mostly flat & the surface has been ploughed up over & over again by shells. I was in two woods (so called) today & all that are left are a few broken stumps that look as if they had been struck by lightning. Every shell hole is filled with water & you will get some idea of what it is like when I tell you that it took me half an hour to go about a quarter of a mile & I must have walked fully a mile to do it. Of course this was across country where there are no tracks of any sort. It is quite a common thing to step into apparently firm ground & go down up to your waist. With love to all

Your loving son
Tom

13-11-17

My dear Mother

We left camp yesterday & have come back for about a weeks rest. Then we go forward again but will only be in reserve for a month at least so I do not expect we will have any forward work to do for some time to come. It was a beautiful day with not a cloud to be seen & I quite enjoyed the march of about 12 miles although in one place we were held up for over an hour owing to a block in the traffic. You can have no idea of what the traffic is like on these roads. There is a continual stream both ways always & if anything gets blocked, as sometimes happens, you soon get miles of vehicles bung up. I lunched at a Belgian farmhouse where we got some excellent soup & coffee. At present we are camped near two farms. Most of the men are in tents & the rest in barns &c. Eleven officers are living in a hut which is quite good but colder than the dugouts we have come from & there is no fireplace which is another disadvantage.

Still it is a long way better than the blue sky hotel as we call it. The chief occupations at present are haircutting & generally cleaning up. The camp is fairly muddy but there are green fields round it & it is a pleasant change from the shell torn ground we have come from. We have sent for our mail today & I hope to get some letters. I got a couple of Australasians yesterday which were very acceptable. The weather so far has been quite mild. In fact yesterday was the first real frost I have seen & yet this time last year we had a heavy fall of snow. I am sending by this mail a sample of the Battalion Xmas card. It will be a bit late but we did not get them until a day or two ago. The drawing on it is the remains of the cloth Hall at Ypres which I have seen. This afternoon I am going to a town about two miles away where I want to get some handkerchiefs, razor blades & one or two odds & ends. With love to all

Your loving son
Tom

15-11-17

My dear Mother

Yesterday I got two letters from you dated Sept 9th & 23rd also one from the Girl. Also two Bulletins & two tins of tobacco so you see that some of the things you are sending me are coming along after all. Altogether I have had about six pairs of sox in the last four months. I am delighted to hear that Marjorie [Ward] has a son & am writing to John tonight to congratulate him. At all events Michael John are two good homely names & better than Algernon or Leonard or any of those fancy names. I can imagine how pleased & proud Marjorie is. Your letter is full of the strike which now has happily been settled and I hope it will teach them a lesson. I was very interested in the two newspaper cuttings. It is just the sort of thing I should have expected from the Dean of Newcastle. He is a man of brains without any of the saving grace of common sense & such men are always dangerous.

Just screwed away in one corner of your letter is the news that Charlie Young[186] has a son. I suppose that he has not been doing too well lately what with lack of ships mice &c. [sic]

I am glad to hear that we have had good rain & just lately the cables have told of floods in the Murrumbidgee & Murray so it looks as if there should be plenty of grass for the summer. It seems that the only thing to do to ensure a crop of peaches is to cover the trees during the dangerous period & I think we will have to evolve some sort of a frame & proper cover.

---

186   Charles E Young. Son of Charles Young & his wife [Mary] Lillian, née Futter & sister of Cousin Reg; Charlie m. Annie Sneddon in 1914.

The Girl tells me that at present they look like attempts at mushrooms & I can quite believe it. Jackson[187] seems to be a good chauffeur in spite of his cranky ways. (The padre is at present playing a gramophone & as every one has a fault to find with whichever record he puts on I have to leave off now & again to join in the argument.) I am rather inclined to agree with his remarks to Jim Gordon[188] with regard to the latter's new car although over here the Fords are turning up trumps every time & are now being largely used for military work. Fred Ward[189] should be back in Australia by this & then there may be a chance of getting the Champions back. The accounts of our new man are not reassuring. I had a letter from John Ward a day or two ago & in it he said that he expected to be going back to Australia shortly. I have absolutely nothing to do just at present while we are resting. Yesterday I got a spare horse & took a nurse from a neighbouring hospital out for a ride. There are more exciting forms of amusement but I think she enjoyed it. Some of the officers go to this hospital every day & have tea with the nurses but it is not a form of amusement that appeals to me very much. Most of them might be described as of uncertain age & small talk with strangers never appealed to me very much.

Today I have written a few letters & loafed the rest of the time we leave here in three days time for a place about ten miles away. We will not be doing any forward work for a while, in fact as far as can be seen at present I do not think that we shall have a very

187 Charles Nelson Jackson, chauffeur, Bungendore.
188 James Henry Forbes Gordon, grazier, Werriwa, Bungendore.
189 Captain Chaplain Frederick Greenfield Ward, MC, Rector of Canberra, [RTA 10-9-17]. Brother of Archdeacon John William Ward.

strenuous time for some months to come. I have found out where Pat is buried & I am sending you the location so that you will be able to keep it. It is about a thousand yards north of Zonnebecke, just north YPRES-ROULERS railway & quite close to a place called TYNE COT. Its exact location is described officially as follows: French Map of BELGIUM SHEET 28 N.E Edition 8.A, D.17.a.0.5-1.0. All our maps are squared & by quoting the figures I have given will bring you to within ten yards of the spot. I have not been able to get there but a cross has been put up & the spot can always be found. All his things he had with him in France are being returned through the military & I am arranging with Dalgety to return a suitcase and tin box he left with Cooks.

I am leaving this letter open & may add to it tomorrow.

Since writing the above we have moved camp again and are now in an old Brigade Headquarters which are very comfortable. Our mess room is a ruberoid building with a fire place & quite cosy and I sleep in another room just the same. We are just near a farm house of the better class & altogether the surroundings are quite pleasant. Yesterday I saw in operation a churn worked by dogs. There is a large wheel outside the building connected to a barrel churn inside. Two dogs are tied inside the wheel & start to walk round it when the wheel revolves & away they go. It takes from one to two hours to make the butter & as far as I can see the dogs enjoy the fun.

Round here we often see dogs harnessed to carts & delivering milk vegetables &c. I want to catch the mail so I am ending this now. With love to all

Your loving son

Tom

26-11-17

My dear Mother

Since last writing I have had a letter from you Aug 27th also two tins of tobacco a pair of socks & some papers so I have been lucky. There is an Australian mail in dated Oct 7th & I expect that my letters will come along tomorrow. Sometimes I get them thro' the Bank before those addressed direct & sometimes the other way about but considering everything the Bank is I think the quickest. Your letter is full of the strike & we can only hope that now they have been so soundly beaten it will teach them a lesson for a while. I am much amused to hear of Aunt Em's [Rutledge] activities at the Railway Station & can imagine how she glories in the work.

Somehow I have missed your letter saying that Charles Shaw[190] had been ill but as you say they are at Brisbane & is better I gather that he must have been away for a change. Do not bother about sending me anything for Xmas. It is very good of you to tell me to get a leather jacket but I do not need one. I have the one you sent me last year & also an issue one so I am quite well off in that respect. In fact there is nothing that I want at the present time at all. I am well set up with plenty of warm clothes &c & I seem to be getting the socks &c better now. I am sorry to say that I have not been able to get either you or Elma anything. The only thing one can get here is lace & I do not know enough about that. I saw a girl making it the other day. Each thread was wound on a separate bobbin & she seemed to do the whole thing by sticking

---

190   Charles Macmahon Shaw, Auburn Street, Goulburn, manager of the Bank of
      Australasia, secretary of Goulburn Golf Club.

pins onto a pad & then working the thread round them. It must be a very tedious business. I may get leave to Paris in a couple of months & I will look out for something then. Yesterday I went to a neighbouring town & had lunch at the Club where I met Jimmy James, Col Abbot.[191] Major James was looking very well indeed & has just won the DSO, so was very pleased with himself. Yesterday the Colonel came back from leave. I had not seen him before. He comes from Brisbane & seems a very nice man. At all events he is very popular with all his officers. Yesterday & today there has been a cold wind blowing but they are the first two days it has been cold enough to wear an overcoat & I am in hopes that we will not have anything like so bad a winter as last year. The days are beginning to get pretty short & it is now nearly dark by four o'clock in the afternoon.

We are still resting well back from the line & have very little to do. I spend most of the day reading the paper & visiting the various working parties & at night play bridge. With love to all

Your loving son

Tom

---

191   Lt Col Percy Phipps Abbott, 12th LH, [RTA 21-4-18], [*ADB* 7.2]

2-12-17

My dear Mother

I have two letters of yours to answer this week dated Sept 30th & Oct 7th. You seem to have been seeing quite a lot of people lately. The Knoxes & Blomfields[192] &c. I am glad to hear that the garden is successful this spring & that the young fruit trees are doing so well. There is no doubt that Hopperton is an excellent man & will be very difficult to replace. The lambing seems to have turned out very well 78$^1/_2$ per cent is as good as we can expect most years & with the grass there is it should give them a good start. I see by the papers that the British Government is taking the wool again & although I don't expect it will reach last year's figures still we ought to do very well & it will probably be heavier. The cheque you sent duly arrived, thank you very much for it. There is nothing I really want at the present time so I am paying it into my account for the present. I have plenty of warm clothes boots &c & watches & over here one's wants do not extend to much more. We get our pay regularly every fortnight & that more than suffices for all current expenses. Another tin of tobacco has arrived since I last wrote & I think I told you in my last letter that a pair of socks had come along so that you will see that I now receive parcels pretty regularly.

I am very sorry indeed to hear that Aunt Gus [Powell] has been so seedy. I get an occasional letter from them & generally answer it.

---

192 Descended from Thomas Valentine Blomfield of Denham Court, Campbelltown, NSW, and his wife Christiana Jane, d. of Captain Richard Brooks, original owner of Turalla, [*ADB 1.156*]

You seem to have had rather bad luck in Mr Ingle.[193] It is a pity he does not come over here for a bit & his views would probably broaden. Here creed has very little weight & a padre is looked up to for his personality rather than creed. One of the best men I have met was an R.C. & another, a Presbyterian. I have seen an R.C. padre read the burial service over a Presbyterian & vice versa when there was no one else available & the whole thing taken as a matter of course. I never did like High Church goings on & have not become any more enamoured of them lately. I won't be able to get you any viola seed just now but will remember it & try & send it along before next spring. The little sugar basin belonging to the tea set is safely at Cook's but I am afraid it is rather risky sending it just at present.

I am very sorry indeed to hear that Judith Osborne[194] is so ill & hope that she has quite recovered by the time you get this. Today has been our first really cold day. There was a black frost this morning & in the shade it has been freezing all day. It looks as if it will be worse tomorrow as it is a bright night & is now freezing hard. There was a shrewd wind blowing from the North West but it is now calm. For a wonder it was a sunshiny day, a thing that we rarely get here. Tomorrow I am going into a neighbouring town to see what we can get in the way of Xmas comforts for the men. Someone in Australia has sent us a cheque for £100 for this purpose so we ought to be able to give them a good time, that is if we are not working. We have got our Xmas turkey for the officers' mess & are pretty well fixed up for other things. Everything is

---

193   Possibly the clergyman who replaced Mr Champion

194   Daughter of Robert T Osborne & Charlotte, née Powell, of Foxlow, Bungendore.

very dear here there, are so many troops. The turkey is to weigh 12lbs & will cost 33fr which is pretty exorbitant. Still the only thing on which to spend money is food so it does not matter very much. With love to all

Your loving son

Tom

8-12-17

My dear Mother

Your weekly letter is due tomorrow (this is Saturday night & I generally try to write on Sunday) I am afraid there is not much news to tell you. I really have very little to do here & am having the best spell I have had since I left Malta. I am attached as supernumerary & as such have no definite job but I do not expect that they will leave me here for very long. They can't afford to pay Major's salary & get no return. Usually in the morning I ride round the various jobs the men are working on & that takes me till lunch time. In the afternoon I read the paper which we get the day after they are published in London. It is dark now by 4 o'clock & in the evening I read or play bridge & get to bed early. We will be back in the forward area shortly & I expect will spend Xmas there. There will be more work then but it does not seem likely that it will be very strenuous. It has been a quiet part of the line for some time & there is no reason to suppose that it will change.

We held some sports this week, but they were not a great success. It was a sunny day but fairly cold. The frost never went off and it was very chilly standing round looking on. My pen has given out & I can't find my ink at present so I have to continue in pencil. There is really not much use in trying to get any outdoor amusements going during the winter in this country. The weather so far has been good. Only one or two cold days & not much rain. I expect we will get it worse later on but it looks as if it is not going to be as bad as last year & at any rate it is starting a good deal later. My lamp is running low & it is after nine so I must stop this now & continue tomorrow.

I got up early this morning & went round the jobs & had just finished a shave & clean up generally when who should turn up but Snowy [Parish]. I gave him some lunch & we had a good talk. I am afraid Snowy is pretty miserable. He does not get on well with his O.C. and wants to transfer to the infantry. I strongly advised him not to but I don't think it had much effect. I feel very sorry for him he seems so prone to melancholy but one cannot wonder. Still I think our talk cheered him up. I think he likes to feel that there is someone about who knows him.

Tomorrow is the Referendum on conscription. As far as I can tell there will be a majority among the troops against it. It is hard to discover their reasons for voting no but as far as I can make out the most common one is a reluctance to compel anyone to go thro' the fighting here. It is rather a mistaken attitude but I am afraid it is fairly common. I am rather afraid of the result as a whole but we must hope for the best. According to the latest reports it looks as tho' Canada will support it & that decision may have some effect in Australia. It is bed time now so I must stop. With love

Your loving son

Tom

17-12-17

My dear Mother

It is Monday & your weekly letter is overdue. I have been pretty busy lately as we have just started work in the forward area again & I have been going round the various works & getting the hang of things generally.

We came here on Friday and are billeted in a town which is still inhabited by civilians. There are no shells & only occasionally a bomb. My billet is in the curé's house but I have not seen him yet & the only sign of his existence is a couple of skull caps hanging on the hat rack. His housekeeper welcomed me with voluble French & has provided me with a good French bed & sheets. With my own blankets I sleep warmly in spite of there being no fire in the room. Some days I have to get up at 4 o'clock in the morning & don't get back till one o'clock & then I generally sleep in the afternoon for an hour or so. Most days I get back about lunch time & after that change wet boots & socks & clean up generally then read the paper do a little work in the way of discussing what is to be done next day which brings me to tea time.

After that I smoke a pipe & then to bed about 8 o'clock. As a result I don't find time hangs heavily on my hands. It came on to snow last night & there was about half an inch on the ground this morning & still snowing slightly. I was out riding & walking thro' trenches all the morning & did not find it cold. In fact if it is no colder than it has been so far I will not complain. Of course we are a good deal better off than most people. We nearly always have comfortable quarters & when we are out we are on the move or working & can get a dry change when we come in. The sector we are in is a quiet one at present & there seems to be every prospect that it will remain so for some time to come at any rate. Snowy Parish came to see me again the day before yesterday. He was just going up to the line with some battery and had all his worldly possessions on his back. It is just tea time now so I will have to stop for the time being.

Later

It is nearly time I went to bed so I will have to finish off now. I am afraid that this is rather a dull letter but there is really not much to tell about. I cannot talk of military matters except in the most general way. With love to all

Your loving son
Tom

24-12-1917

My dear Mother,

It seems only a day or two ago since I wrote to you but here it is Monday again & your letter is due. So far our Xmas mail has not arrived from Australia but it is expected any day now. I got a letter from the Girl yesterday dated Sept 6th which has been chasing me for a couple of months but nothing else. Cousin Clara Gilchrist sent me a tinned turkey which was very acceptable & has already been eaten as we have managed to secure a fresh one for Xmas day. Also we have just got our Xmas parcels from the comforts fund. Mine came from a girl in Victoria & among other good things contained a tin of cream which will come in very handy for our Xmas pudding. I had a slight touch of flu a couple of days ago but took [sic] it in time, dosed myself with quinine & I am quite well again now. I was able to do a ten mile walk this morning so I can't be too bad.

Tomorrow if Fritz wills we are to have a holiday except for a few essential jobs which means most of the men will be off. They are going to have quite a spread tomorrow. There is an issue of Xmas pudding & we have managed to buy enough geese out of Regtl Funds to give every man a good helping while all the officers have put in a bit to give them a glass of beer each. Then they have all got their parcels & have bought one or two extras as well so they are well provided for. It has been freezing for the past week but the frost has broken today & a fine drizzle has set in. I must say I do not mind the frosty weather. The roads are free from mud & as long as you keep moving it is easy to keep warm. You can also get across country anywhere while when it thaws the roads are about the only tracks.

The Colonel[195] is billeted in the Mayor's house who is also the local doctor & we had quite a pleasant evening. Three or four of the officers sing fairly well & the doctor's daughter aged about 15 plays their accompaniments and sings a little so we had quite a musical evening including a few quartettes. I aired my French & found that I could get on pretty well if I went slowly but I find I can understand it a good deal better than I can speak. About 9 o'clock coffee (black) & cognac were provided & altogether we had a very pleasant evening & left with warm invitations to drop in any time we liked for a cup of coffee. It is very nearly dinner time now & as everyone is in the room & talking it is rather hard to write so I must stop. With love to all. Your loving son

Tom

---

195   Lt Col Frederick William Godsby Annand.

30-12-17

My dear Mother

For once I am starting your letter on a Sunday but whether I will finish it or not tonight I cannot yet say. Our Xmas mail has been delayed somehow or other & has not yet been delivered but should be along any day. It is fully a month now since there has been any Australian Mail in, except a stray or two that has got lost. I had a letter from Cousin Jessie today who says she has not had a letter for a month so it looks as if there has been no mailboat in & the troops are not the only ones to be without. Our Xmas passed off very quietly. I have told the Girl about it so will not repeat myself, Fritz did not disturb us at all. In fact I think he put over fewer shells than usual & this locality has never been remarkable for the number of shells since I have been here. I go out to some of the work nearly every morning & since the ground has been frozen that means a ten or twelve mile walk. The ground is too slippery to ride unless the horses have frost nails in their shoes & mine was only fixed up today. I will have to go out for a ride soon or he will be getting too fresh but really it is better to walk if the distance is not too far. It is much warmer & the exercise is most beneficial. I find the leather waistcoat you sent me last year most useful & always wear it. I never wear an overcoat unless it is actually raining or snowing. It makes you too hot walking & gets in the way when going through trenches. There are always pieces of wire sticking out & I should say that a weeks continuous use would reduce any coat to ribbons. Today a thaw has set in but what wind there is still in the north & I don't think it will last very long unless the wind changes. Really so far this winter the weather has been quite good. There have been no bitter winds at all & the weather has been mostly sunny & frosty. Of course we will get some bad later on but it is something to have got this far without it.

I am leading a far from strenuous existence as I have no definite job but I don't know how long that will last. I rather think that they will find something else for me before very long although now that conscription has been turned down it looks as if one division will have to be broken up to reinforce the rest, in which case there will be a lot of spare officers about & no hope of promotion for some time to come. Still I am very well content as I am. I like the Colonel very much & get on very well with him. He is a very well read man & talks very well. Somehow I am rather hopeful that the war will end this year though how it will end is more than I can tell. It all seems to me to hang now on the submarine campaign. The whole question is whether the food supplies in England can suffice & whether America can get her men over quickly enough even with the submarines. With these provisos I don't think there is much doubt that the Germans are beaten & if it can be proved to them that England has sufficient food & that the Americans can get here I am inclined to think that she will try to make peace. Of course her army is far from beaten but I don't think she will ever resist long enough for Germany to be invaded. Of course this is only opinion & I have really no grounds for saying so. At present things are not too bright. The number of ships sunk every week keeps up to a dozen or so & it must have an effect on the imports. The spring will really show us more & it seems likely that the Germans will try a big offensive as

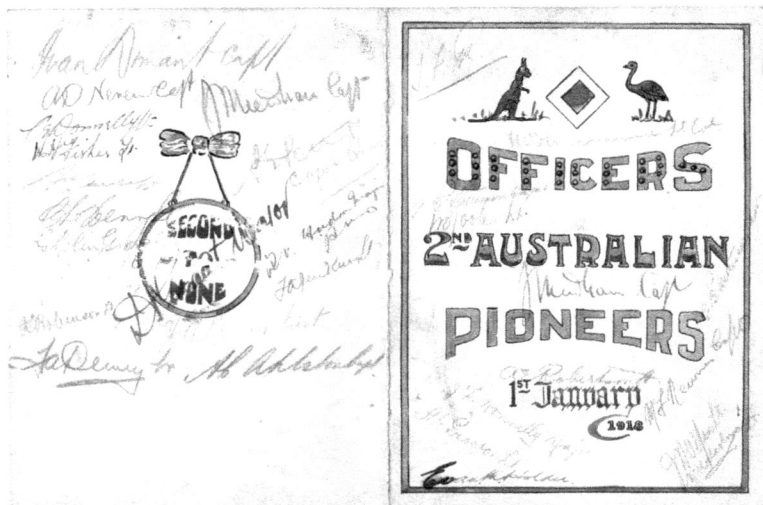

The Menu for the New Year's dinner, 1 January 1918.

NEW YEAR DINNER

1918
MENU

POTAGE
Tomates

POISSON
Merlan Frit
Sauce Mayonnaise

RÔTI
Bœuf à l'anglaise

VOLAILLE
Dindon Rôti
Jambon

LÉGUMES
Pommes de Terre
Petits Pois

ENTREMET
Plum Pudding
Gâteau de Noël

DESSERT
Fruits de la Saison
Noix. Café. Liqueurs.

VINS

GOD SAVE THE KING

soon as the weather permits but where it will be no one can tell as yet. I had quite a long talk with the curé who lodges in my billet. At least he talked very fast & I did my best to understand what he was saying. I gathered that he was a refugee & that he had been shelled out of his town in Belgium early in the war. He still visits some of his parishioners who live in farms around & has a little chapel in one of them. I have seen his church of which four stone columns remain & he told me that the bricks from it had been sold & used for roads by the troops.

The old boy talked pretty fast but I was able to follow most of what he said. He was most polite & told me dozens of times how delighted he was to meet me. On New Year's night we are going to have a dinner for all the officers of the Battn & are trying to get a piano so as to have a few songs afterwards. At present & in fact, always owing to the work being done at all times each company has a separate mess & one for headquarters so that all the officers very rarely meet together. In fact it has taken me till now to get to know them all. Our mess secretary is very busy now borrowing sufficient plates &c to go round. Naturally we have not enough for them all & they are rather difficult things to come by. For some time we only had enamel mugs & plates but just recently we have risen to cups & saucers. I was well supplied with Xmas cheer as Cousin Clara [Miller] sent me two parcels containing a turkey, pudding &c. With love to all

Your loving son

Tom

6-1-18

My dear Mother

Our long delayed mail has arrived at last & I have three letters from you dated Oct 22nd 28th & Nov 6th. The one dated Nov 6th was sent via America & arrived yesterday while the rest came today. It has been rather a sad mail for me. You had just heard about Pat. I find it hard to realise even now that he has gone from us. I am constantly meeting people who knew him & Noel & they all speak so highly of him. I don't think I ever know anyone who was more popular & respected than he was & after we grew up I don't ever remember that we had the slightest disagreement. I hear from all sides how brave you are Mummie dear but I know what your grief must be. As a family we have never been remarkable for wearing our hearts on our sleeves but the feeling is there just the same & perhaps all the deeper even tho' it is not expressed. I had arranged with Dalgety to send me his letters &c even before Cousin Tom wired & I have destroyed all that have been forwarded. I forgot to say that by the last mail I also got a tin of Gidleigh mixture & two days ago your cable came saying that you were well which was a great relief to me. You must really look after yourself & I hope that this winter you will go away to some warm climate during the cold weather.

I am sure that you will find the Girl a great comfort to you & you must let her do as much as she can. I am afraid that you have been worrying a little about the place. I am sorry to hear that you & the Girl do not get on as well as you might with Uncle but above all don't worry. With Cousin Reg to supervise nothing can go very wrong. The place is too sound for anything serious to happen & it will practically run itself. I wrote to Uncle not long ago & I am writing tonight to Cousin Reg from whom I had a letter. As long as the rabbits are kept down & we do not go in for dealing (Cousin Reg will see to that) there is not the slightest cause for any anxiety.

Cousin Reg seems very pleased indeed with the progress the sheep are making & sent me some samples of wool which are certainly very nice. I have also had a letter from Mr Cunningham & am writing to him too. In your letter of Nov 6th you mention having sent one by a different mail the day before this has not yet come along nor have the ones from Aunt Alice[196] or Mr Yarwood. I will write to Aunt Alice in a day or two, just at present I am fairly busy as I have a good many letters to answer. I have thought very seriously of trying to get six months leave to come home but am afraid that there is no possibility of doing so at present. Leave for six months is very rarely given & I am sure that it would not be granted. I am glad that you sent me Mrs Buckley's address. I liked her & will write to her within the next few days. It is still freezing here but so far I have not felt the cold at all. We have been notified that a thaw is to be expected shortly & I expect that then we shall get the mud.

This frosty weather seems to agree with everyone & there is very little sickness among the men. They have good billets & are fed pretty well. I am walking about 10 to 12 miles nearly every day eating like a horse & putting on flesh. We are in a very quiet sector & really there is very little doing. With love to all

Your loving son

Tom

---

196   Alice Louise Rutledge, d. of Thomas & Martha, b Carwoola 1852; d. Sydney 1938.

13-1-18

My dear Mother

The Australian Mail arrived this morning & I got four letters from you dated Nov 4th 11th, 24th & 25th together with enclosures from Aunt Alice & Lizzie Edwards & lots of photographs. I will tell you what little news there is so far & then answer the letters. There is really nothing to tell & every day is very much like another. Last night I had dinner with Dudley Williams. He is camped only about two miles from me & is with an anti aircraft battery. I heard he was near here & looked him up a few days ago & last night I had a great yarn with him. He is not changed at all & was looking well. Mrs Williams is at present in London & has done several small commissions for me & I have written to her to say that I had seen Dudley & he was well. Keith I believe is over in England on leave at present. I have found out where he is stationed. It is some way from here but I hope to be able to look him up later on.

For the last few days we have had a thaw but it froze last night & today has been a beautiful day bright & sunny & I think we shall have some more frost. Really I think I prefer the frosty weather as then there is no mud about. I had a letter from Snowy yesterday. He was gassed & slightly wounded the day he came to see me. The gassing affected his eyes but they have been treated & he says they are now better than they ever were. Still from what he says I don't think he will come back again & really he is not fit for it. I am very sorry indeed to hear about Charlie Shaw. It will be a very bad lookout for them if the bank does not keep his place open. I am sending a line to Aunt Fan within the next few days but I have a good many letters to write just now with this mail in. I have got Mr

Yarwood's letter on business matters & a copy of Pat's will. I have to make a new one & am leaving everything to the Girl. I want to make it as simple as possible & I cannot get a lawyer to make it up at present. It must have been a wonderful spring & from what I can tell from the photographs the Girl sent me the garden must have been a sight. If the wet keeps on much longer the lake should get full again. I will see if I can get into touch with young Arnott & if I do will do what I can for him.

Really so far the winter here has not been bad & I feel the cold far less than I did in England. We have had very little rain since I have been here & only two light falls of snow. I practically never wear an overcoat so you see it can't be too bad. I think we move again about the end of the month but where to I don't know. The socks Dulcie Cavanagh[197] knitted have not come yet but parcels nearly always take longer than letters & they will probably arrive before long. Some time ago Cousin Clara Gilchrist wrote & asked me if I would like any socks for the men & I said that I could do with all she could send along with the result that every fortnight I get about 18 pairs of beautifully knitted socks & I am kept busy acknowledging them. Still they are very welcome as the men can always do with extra pairs.

I don't think I ever knew a cat that had as much character as Brownie. I think 17 years must be nearly a record for a cat. You seem to have been having a very interrupted shearing but rain in November always does a lot of good & keeps to the grass green well into the summer. There will probably be a great danger of bush fires.

---

197   Dulcie Cavanough, b. 1902, d. of Willis Walter Cavanough, stationmaster at
        Bungendore.

I see by the cables in the English papers that there have been very bad ones in Riverina & Victoria. It will be bad for grass seed too with all the grass about & the lambs will want some watching. I am glad to hear that the spinning venture is making an auspicious opening. The next thing will be to start hand weaving as well. I must say that I never could raise much enthusiasm for the Carrawarra girls & I am afraid that you will find it rather a trial having Ruth[198] with you but it is all for a good purpose. If you find you want any more wheels just get them & get Mr Yarwood to pay for them for me. I am quite impatient to get the first pair of socks made from homespun wool. I am glad to hear that everyone is taking such an interest in the matter & are supplying fleeces for the work. I know how glad you will be to have the Champions back again. We were very lucky to get them & must try & keep them as long as we can. I am sorry to hear that Aunt Gus is so sick. She really should see a doctor but I know how they are in such matters. I don't expect that the wool will bring the same price as last year but I am spending nothing beyond my pay in fact not that & there should be more than enough to pay the probate.

I am writing to Aunt Alice [Rutledge] tonight but the unfortunate part of it is that I have forgotten the name of her house & I don't like to send it to you to forward. I think I will just address it Edgecliff Road & trust to it being delivered.

It is funny how after three years you forget the names of people & places that you have been quite familiar with. With best love to all

Your loving son

Tom

---

198   Ruth Maggie Forster, a daughter of A B Chisholm, one of 'the Carrawarra girls'.

29-1-18

My dear Mother

I was not able to write to you on Sunday as usual as there was no mail out & we were busy preparing to move. We moved out on Monday (yesterday) & are now pretty well settled in our new quarters. It is only about seven miles from our last place & although not so comfortable is nothing to growl about. We are all in huts & the men are pretty well off. I have a little hut to myself. It is about 9 x 6 & is made of ruberoid lined with hessian. There is a stove in it and as I have just got the stove going it is very snug. There will be very little for headquarters to do here. There is only one Company with us. The rest are camped at different places & are mostly doing railway work. Beyond getting the men onto the job we have nothing to do with the work & so you can see that we have not much to occupy us. I am taking advantage of the opportunity and am applying for leave to Paris and I have no doubt that I will get it. I am trying to arrange to go with Major Jack Donnelly & think we should have a pleasant four days. Our last week in the old billet was quite gay. On the Wednesday evening we had four nurses to dinner from one of the Casualty Clearing Stations and after dinner we had some songs & a dance or two & spent a very pleasant evening. We got a Frenchman from an Estaminet to play for us but he was not as good as he might be. For piano we had a small five octave portable Kramer that was rather tinny & the pianist although he did not make many mistakes was very mechanical & the music sounded just like a pianola played by a novice without any ear. Still we enjoyed ourselves & that was the main thing. Also one night we called on the Mayor & spent the evening there. I think I told you before that the Colonel is very musical & sings well & there are two or three other officers who have fair voices so we did quite well & were even treated to a quartette. The Mayor's daughter aged about 16 played the accompaniments & also sang once or twice in a very high shrill voice. About nine o'clock supper was brought in consisting of black coffee and cognac & the Mayor was quite excited when the Colonel produced some cane sugar all the way from Australia. He got a lump of it & one of the beet sugar & compared them carefully, then he tasted each & pronounced the cane sugar the best. I was the only one there who could speak any French and as they understood very little English I had to act as interpreter & although I am not fluent I can generally make them understand me.

On Saturday night a pierrot party formed from men in the battalion gave a concert & it was really quite good the most popular items being those given by a couple of men dressed up as girls and their makeup was really very creditable. The Mayor & his family were invited by the Colonel & seemed to enjoy themselves and after it was over they came & had supper with us. The weather has changed again and it looks now as if we are in for a spell of frosty weather again. For the past fortnight it has been exceptionally mild so much so that yesterday I saw catkins on several bushes in the hedgerows. Yesterday I think was the most perfect day I have seen in France or England. There was a slight frost in the morning which soon cleared off & then it was clear all day with a slight haze & absolutely calm. Today is much the same only the frost was harder & there is a very light breeze from the

South. It looks settled for some time to come & then I expect we shall have some more snow. All the young crops are beginning to show thro' the ground & I expect the frost will check them somewhat which should be beneficial at this time of year. Really the winter so far has been far from unbearable & we are getting on now. Already you can see the days lengthening. Last night I missed the bed in my last billet. There, there were two deep feather mattresses but last night I slept on wire netting stretched over a wooden frame which makes quite a good bed when you get used to it. I was too cold to be absolutely comfortable & not cold enough to make it worthwhile to get up & look for more clothes. However I will have more clothes on tonight & will have a fire going so I should be as snug as possible. With love to all

Your loving son
Tom

4-2-18

My dear Mother

Although nearly three weeks have passed since I got your letter dated Nov 24th a couple of days ago I received one dated Nov 18th. All this week I have been inundated with papers & have got various Bulletins & Australasians dated from June to October. Also I got a pair of mauve socks from you with blue & red ring around the top. Today I got another pair of the same sort of socks apparently posted in Bungendore on Dec 13th & also a letter from Aunt Fan [Garraway] dated Melbourne Dec 16th so I expect that there should be some home letters along tomorrow. I am enclosing the little ticket that came with the last pair of socks so you will probably remember when you sent them. I will try them on & let you know how they fit. As a general principle they should be on the big side. They always shrink when washed & if the foot becomes too small they always work down under the heel & the result is a blister after a couple of miles and once the skin rubs off it is very difficult to get it well again besides the danger of infection.

I wrote to Mr Yarwood not long ago & asked him to pay the bill for the two spinning wheels so if you send it along he will fix it up. I don't know how you and the Girl are managing but if you want any more money or anything for a special purpose don't hesitate to see him about it. I have asked him to let you have whatever you want. I am very sorry indeed to hear that Aunt Gus is so unwell. Of course she ought to see a doctor but you know what they are & if anyone urges them to do so I think it makes them more determined not to.

Since we moved from our last Camp I have been having a very uneventful time. I rode round one day to see the various companies & another afternoon the Colonel & I went to a town about five miles away but beyond that I have spent most of my time reading the various papers that have come along. I forgot to mention that I got two Pastoral Reviews which I enjoyed very much. They help one to keep in touch with things. We had two days fog which never lifted for a minute & a couple of frosts but not very hard ones. The weather has now got milder again. Since last writing I have got used to the change of beds & can keep the clothes on top much better. My stove is going well & the only trouble is that if I stoke it at all liberally the hut gets too hot & I have to open up everything and get out until it cools down. As I write there is news of very big strikes in Germany & while I do not think any immediate effect on the course of the war will result I think they are very hopeful signs. To my mind the internal conditions in Germany are a good deal worse than we realise. I think that this strike will not come to anything & that the authorities will suppress it by severe measures but it is a sign of discontent which it seems to me will grow all the faster for being suppressed & is liable to break out in a more violent form later on. There is also a chance that it will spread to the army & the Russian business may be repeated all over again. (I had to stop here to refill my lamp, it is now going again). Of course we must realise that our own Labour [sic] people are also liable to cause trouble but I have enough faith in the British to think that they will see it thro'. It is just a question of which people (apart from the armies) can last the longest & I don't think there is any doubt that we are far better off than the Germans I don't think that we will get nearly all we hoped for at the start but that only time will show. I expect to get leave to Paris in about a weeks time. With love

Your loving son
Tom

12-2-18

My dear Mother

Three letters from you this week dated Dec 2nd, 9th & 14th besides two from the girl & a pile of papers & some tobacco. Now I will just run through your letters and answer them although you will probably have forgotten this time what you wrote. I am very interested in the spinning industry & the progress you are all making. I never cared very much for the Carrawarra girls but I daresay they have improved and I agree with you that Ruth is the best of them.

I saw in an Australasian, I think, that Nancie[199] was engaged. I am now awaiting most anxiously the arrival of the socks made from homespun wool. The two grey pairs you sent me with the black & red stripes arrived safely and are quite O.K. as regards fit. I like them on the large side, they always shrink in the wash and if they get too small they have to be thrown away as they then slip down under the heel & cause blisters. But these are just right, nice & long & roomy. I am not bothering about subscriptions to charities just now it is too difficult to fix up from a distance but the Station can always do it. The shearers seem to have behaved very badly this year but with things as they are at present it is really more or less what one would expect. Still I think that a day is not so very far distant when they will change their tune. There is bound to be a period of depression in the future & I think we will see the time when men will be only too glad to get the chance to work. I think I told you before that I did not expect the same quantity of wool this year or the same price so I won't be disappointed. It is a

199 Nancie Vivian, youngest d. of A B Chisholm, m Ivan S Young in 1918 at Woollahra.

pity about the dipping. I have seen the same thing before & had taken certain steps to minimise it. I think that by other means it could be prevented altogether but that would probably mean an alteration to the dip & is not for the present necessary. I certainly think that the billiard room & garage should be painted although I know that paint now must be very expensive in Australia. In fact the whole house wants doing up but I would be inclined to leave anything that was not especially urgent until things are more settled.

Aunt has certainly done yeoman service in Egypt and by this time you will have seen that she has been given some decoration of the order of St John [of Jerusalem]. I do not think that there is much doubt but she will get the Order of the British Empire later on although to my mind the latter has been made very cheap. I saw in a paper the other day a little bit which shows how people look upon all these orders. A man was telling a friend how all his neighbours had been decorated for driving wounded soldiers organizing charity matinees &c & finished up by saying but what have you got. 'Oh nothing' replied the friend, 'you see I enlisted at the beginning.' Now they are starting to do the same thing with the army. There are 1914 stars, wound stripes, long service stripes, a brass A for those who were at Anzac & which I do not believe in and which have been brought about chiefly by a few newspapers. Really now in England the papers rule the country. They have only to start out after a thing & keep hammering away long enough & they get it. Whether their object is beneficial or not I think the principle is bad. I am very glad to hear that Doff's wedding went off so well. I know that the soldiers would make things lively as they were there. I had a line from Mark Beresford

Pat Rutledge's grave at Passchendaele. He was later re-buried at Dochy Farm Cemetry.

about a month ago. He was still in England but I should say that he would probably be sent over here any time now.

I am glad to hear that you like Mrs Frank Osborne.[200] It makes such a difference if the neighbours are people you can get on with. Foxlow certainly can do with the improvements she has carried out.

The Girl seems to have enjoyed her trip to Michelago & I am sure it would do her good. The men seem to have behaved very badly with regard to the referendum. I cannot understand the motives of the opposition. There was a strong opposition here & for the life of me I could not get to the bottom of the reason. It seemed to me to be blind prejudice. Still I am sure a day of reckoning will come & that before very long. I am very glad to hear that Mr Cunningham is better, he has had a very long time of it. He is quite right not to stock up too heavily. There is always a temptation to do so in a bad [good] season but I am sure that it does not pay in the end. Besides I think that the light stocking will do the place a lot of good for a year or two. What with the dry years & rabbits the grass did not get much of a chance to seed and now it will get a chance to thicken up & the finer grasses will get a show again. The snapshots of the garden arrived safely & I am very pleased to get them.

At present it is impossible to do anything with regard to Pat's grave. It is still in no man's land but as I have mentioned before, I know where it is and as soon as it can be got to I will have a temporary cross erected. Nothing more can be done until after

---

200   Frank Marshall Osborne, 6th s of Robert & Charlotte Osborne of Foxlow, Bungendore , m. Daisy Gollan at Woollahra in 1904.

the war. As you probably know the care of graves has been taken up by a commission but they do not go any farther than erecting a temporary cross & registering the place & the intention is to leave the erection of a permanent headstone to relatives but not until after the war. I am enclosing two photographs of Noel Rutledge's grave which I have managed to get for you to send on to his father as I do not know his address. I found out from some of his brother officers where it was & visited it about a month ago. There was only a small cross then marking it but they were getting the one in the picture made & it was put up a few days later. It is just on the edge of Ploegsteert Wood in a military cemetery. I would write to Cousin Tom[201] if I knew his address but I am sure that he will like to have the photos.

I am glad to hear that you did so well for the Red Cross. £200 is certainly a good amount for Bungendore more especially coming as it did so soon after the War Chest Day. I am rather amused at the hive of bees & should very much like to be present when the honey is being taken. I'll bet that the Girl is much amused.

You will probably have heard that Evelyn Gilchrist[202] is engaged to a Mr Jackson[203] who is in the navy. I saw the announcement in the Times a few days ago & next day got a letter from Cousin Jessie telling me of it & also that Cousin Clara had been ill but was better. Cousin Jessie seemed very pleased with the engagement & with the fact that they had known each other for some years & it was not a 'war engagement'. Today I got a letter from Sister An

---

201   Thomas Forster Rutledge, of Werronggurt, Warrnambool, Victoria.

202   Clara Evelyn, d. of W. O. Gilchrist and Clara, née Knox

203   William Lindsay Jackson; they married in 1918.

[sic] telling me that the MacCormicks[204] had all gone to Australia & that she had heard from them from Honolulu.

I have managed to get <u>eight</u> days leave to go to the South of France by way of Paris & I start on Saturday next the 14th. I am going with Major Donnelly & expect to have a pleasant trip. With love

Your loving son

Tom

204   Sir Alexander MacCormick, surgeon and yachtsman, , and family, lived at Kilmory, Point Piper, [*ADB 10.236*].

Hôtel-Edouard VII
Rue & Place Edouard VII
Paris
18-2-18

My dear Mother

I have only time for just a line to let you know I am well. We arrived here on our trip to Nice late on Saturday night & were unable to go any farther until 8pm tonight (Monday). I spent yesterday trying to see as much as I could of Paris in a general way without going too much into detail & am now writing this just after breakfast this morning before going out again. With the time at our disposal it is hopeless trying to really have a good look at anything. Will write you more fully later. With Love

Your loving son
Tom

Nice
20-2-18

My dear Mother

As all paper in this hotel is sold for the benefit of the French Red Cross I have just had to pay 20c for a packet & drew only a few envelopes & letter cards no paper, so you will have to be content with this. Had a poor trip down. It took from eight one evening till six the next, no sleeper and the train very crowded. Have been loafing on the promenade most of today & enjoying the sun & sights. This is a most luxurious place & is supposed to be the best hotel here. Am enjoying the trip very much. Will write more fully later. With love

Your loving son
Tom

Thurs Feb 28th
1918.

My dear Mother

We arrived back with the battalion last night after having had a most enjoyable trip. I found a lot of letters awaiting me including three from you dated Dec 23rd, 30th & Jan 6th also the copies of letters you sent me about Pat. I will just skim through them & then go on to tell you about our travels. Your first letter is full of the referendum but I have touched on that so often that I do not think I have anything more to say. I am very much amused at your account of the Bishop [Radford] and the lily. I never expected that the Bishop would be popular but he has his good points. He is extremely energetic & there is no denying that he is a very clever man. Possibly he may not be altogether practical but he is very obstinate & a great fighter & I do not think that there will be any stagnation while he is in charge & with such a man there are always ways of getting things done provided you have the right sort of power behind the throne. His wife[205] will probably be a handicap to him I admit. At college we always considered that she was boss.

I am very sorry to hear of all the trouble on the place over the referendum but we must certainly stick up for Hopperton & Jackson. I certainly think it would be a good thing to get rid of Red Mick Flynn[206] some way or other even if the housemaid has to go too & there are always ways if you only go about it properly. It is a pity that Uncle is not a little more energetic. I can see that the men are getting out of hand a little as they will unless you

205   Bishop Radford had married Maud Isabella James in England
206   Michael Flynn, station hand, Gidleigh, Bungendore.

assert yourself occasionally. Jack Wark was always a good man as far as actual work went but he never had any control over the rest. I always realised this so it did not much matter but if he is given too free a hand I can easily realise what will happen. He had it once before & it took me some time to get things straight again. If I were you I should talk things over will Cousin Reg & I am sure he will give you sound advice. I know how glad you will be to have the Champions back again. They are such nice people it is a pleasure to have them living near. It seems to have been a wonderful year for all growth & I am always interested to hear particulars about the garden. The dindyums[207] [sic] does not seem to be so troublesome as usual. You have not mentioned them in your letters & you say that there have been plenty of loganberries. There is no need for you to worry about how the place is going with Cousin Reg supervising things. There is nothing very much that can go wrong & our financial position is very satisfactory. I can imagine Marjorie's joy at John's [Ward] return. He wrote me just before he left but I am afraid that he could not have got my answer. My parcels come along fairly regularly. I get Gidleigh Mixture nearly every mail & this mail got a pair of mittens from Fuzzie. I have had one lot of chocolate from England & I told you that some time ago I got two Pastoral Reviews while at the present moment I have several Bulletins & Australasians unopened waiting to be read. The mittens were made of homespun wool & are the first samples I have had of it. It seems excellent and should wear well. Now I must tell you about my trip to Nice. I sent you a letter card from there announcing my arrival but not giving any details. We stayed at the Hotel des Anglais &

207   Probably Dindymus versicolor, the harlequin bug

Ruhl a most luxurious place right on the sea front & the centre
of the fashionable promenade. It is one of the best hotels in Nice
& you can imagine it was rather expensive but as it was only a
few days we remained there chiefly to see what it was like. It was
rather interesting to live in a place which in happier times was a
great resort of American millionaires &c. We really had a very
quiet time but I thoroughly enjoyed every moment. Generally a
French breakfast in our bedroom. Then after a bath (bathroom
attached) & leisurely dressing appeared on the promenade about
10-30.

Here we basked in the sun, it was perfect weather all the time until
lunch. After lunch we went for a drive up into the hills & saw some
splendid views. All the hillsides are terraced & the chief things
grown seemed to be wattle which was in full bloom & scented
the place everywhere & carnations. After tea while waiting for
dinner we generally talked to American officers of whom there
were a good many about. I rather like what I have seen of them &
think they should give a good account of themselves. The general
idea of the Americans is that they are very boastful but I have
certainly not found them so & I met a good many while I was
there. They quite recognize the fact that they have a good deal to
learn & seem most anxious to pick up any information they can.
I really rather like what I have seen of them. After dinner we used
to have coffee in the winter garden & watch the people who were
always interesting & so to bed. I never realised that such jewelry
existed until I saw it in the Paris shops but at Nice you never saw
a pearl smaller than a good sized pea & they were everywhere
while I don't think it is the least exaggeration to say that I saw at
least 20 emeralds as big as a pigeons egg. It is really an education

to go there for a few days & just keep your eyes open which really formed my chief amusement.

Nearly all the women had dogs and really you could only recognize the fact that some of them were dogs from the fact that they were being led. One day we journeyed to Monte Carlo. We went by tram all the way along the coast which took an hour & a half & is as pretty a trip as can be imagined. We looked over the Casino & had a peep into the gambling rooms but officers were not allowed in so I could not even put on five francs to try my luck & had to be content with a peep through the door. It is very hard to describe what the whole place is like. All the buildings are magnificent & the streets very well kept but I think that the chief charm of all is the climate which is comparable to Sydney in the winter. We had a very tiring trip back. We left Nice at 12 o'clock on Monday Morning & did not arrive at Paris till 11-45 the next morning. The train was very crowded & we were lucky to get seats. Then we had just 12 hours in Paris before catching a train on here which did not arrive till yesterday evening. This meant two full nights & two days almost continuous travelling so you can guess I slept soundly last night. With love to all

Your loving son

Tom

28-2-18

My dear Mother

I wrote your letter in rather a hurry this morning and as
there are one or two things I forgot to tell you I will start this
now while I think of them and continue the letter later on so
as to get back into my usual weekly stride. First of all about ten
days ago I sent you a pewter jug which I managed to get hold
of very cheaply. I rather liked the look of it although it is a bit
battered. As far as I can see it is pewter & old & I sent it along
on the off chance that it may turn out worth while. Anyway at
the worst it will do to hold hot water & is a souvenir. If you
saw the rubbish which is sold in the shops here as souvenirs
it would almost make you ill. Poor quality silk handkerchiefs
with most gaudy decorations in startling reds & yellows with
'souvenir of France' or some such emblem written large across
them. Most of them look as if they are the cheapest of cheap
Manchester productions but the men buy them largely & they
are to be obtained in every little shop. I do not go in much for
collecting souvenirs; they will be too common and are an awful
nuisance to lug about until you get a chance to send them away.
It is forbidden to send any military articles & if you get them
away at all they have to be smuggled. Since I wrote to you this
morning I got six parcels four of them socks one pair each from
Fuzzie & the Girl & two from you one pair from you & the
pair from Fuzzie were from homespun wool & I am going to
try them tomorrow to see how they go. Yours are made of Al
Edmonds'[208] black wool & look very fine indeed.

---

208   Albert Edmonds, grazier, Ingledow, Bungendore.

I am trying to get the Girl to write me more grown up letters. Her present letters are very interesting & as a rule very clever & original but she very rarely expresses an opinion & confines herself to incidents that have happened. Probably my letters cause it to a great extent. She was such a child when I came away and I cannot get the idea out of my head that she is so still. Don't say anything about it to her as I have written to her myself & asked her to let me know her opinion on various matters. She has such original views that her opinion should be worth having.

I got a letter yesterday from Evelyn Gilchrist yesterday in answer to my letter of congratulations, telling me that she is to be married on the 6th of March. I sent off post haste to England today for a present for her but am afraid it will be too late. It generally takes at least four days for a letter to get to England. She seems very happy & was tremendously busy getting her trousseau together. He was getting a fortnights leave & they were going to Devonshire for the honeymoon.

I don't think I told you before that I did not see much of Paris when I was on leave. I only spent two days there & most of the museums were shut up while all the monuments &c are being covered with masonry to try & protect them in case of an air raid. I did not try to see anything thoroughly but spent most of my time going round the city getting a general impression of the boulevards &c. Nice I found most interesting. You can see that the whole place has been laid out simply for pleasure purposes & although it is now shorn of most of it glories in that no gaieties are on still one can realise what it must have been before the war. It is really an education to have been there & seen it at all. I never tired of watching the crowd on the promenade a crowd is always an interesting study & this one was especially so. Nearly every woman dressed in costly furs & jewels and generally leading a toy dog of some sort unless it was hidden away in her muff with only the head showing. I should like to see it again when everything was in full swing but think I would soon get tired of the life. We are still working in the back area but expect to go up into the front area in about a week or fortnight but for how long I do not know.

By this last mail I got a most interesting letter from Hopperton telling me all about the garden & how his fruit trees are doing. He writes a very good letter indeed. I will answer it in the course of a few days.

8th.

No time to add any more to this now will write in a couple of days. With love to all

Your loving son
Tom

17—3—18

My dear Mother

I have only written two letters in the last three weeks for which you must blame me, the Army & Fritz in about equal proportions. We were to have moved here on the fifth but owing to a change did not come till the 9th consequently we were all packed up & in a state of unrest for three or four days. Then when we got here & had just got nicely settled down Fritz sent four shells in which got some of our men in their billets. These villages are simply mantraps when the shells come so we cleared out & bivouacked the men in the fields. Three days later at breakfast time Fritz started again & sent in 14 big ones which have pretty well wrecked the square & church. I was in bed when the first one came as I had been out till 4 o'clock the night before but it did not take me long to get dressed & move to a safe distance. Since then we have been building shelters for ourselves in the fields which are now practically finished & are really quite comfortable. I share one with the doctor & will try & describe it to you. First of all we dug down into the ground a rectangle about 9ft by 12ft & 2ft 6 deep. For roof we have curved corrugated iron very strong which is high enough to enable us to stand upright upright. The ends are built of sandbags & the earth is heaped up round the sides to give additional protection. The finished article is really very snug & looks something like the sketch. I am afraid it is a very bad one but you may be able to imagine the rest. We have a bed along each side & a small table between them & our belongings live at the foot. They are very safe as only a direct hit can affect them and as we are out in a field & Fritz does not know where we are so it will only be an accident if he gets a shot in. The trouble with villages is that he can shoot by the map and when he does get in the bricks will fly in all directions for at least five hundred yards and we all feel much happier now we are not in one. Last Thursday night I had to take two companies out to dig a trench in the front line. It was a most exciting job as Fritz was not very far away and if he had heard us there would probably have been something doing. Fortunately he left us alone & we did not get a single shell or bomb near us the whole time. We finished about one a.m. & I finally got back to bed about four. It is not often that we have to do that sort of job in fact this was the first time since May & it was really my first stunt with this battalion so I am very pleased that we carried through successfully.

Today I got a great mail. Three letters from you, Jan 13th 20th & 27th, one from the Girl one from Turalla & a piece of Evelyn Gilchrist's wedding cake. I sent the latter a present, a pair of silver fruit dishes but unfortunately they did not arrive until after the wedding. Also in the paper which we got today my name appeared as 'mentioned in dispatches'. Of course it is not very much still it is something & it is a satisfaction to feel that your work has been recognized. Although so late in coming it is really for the work in England last year. I don't know how long it will be before you hear of it but I know you will be pleased.

Today I got a letter from the Commercial Bank saying that they had received a cable enquiring as to any news they had of me & I am rather mystified as to the reason. About a fortnight ago I got a cable from Mr Yarwood asking if I was well to which I replied & the reply was sent the day before the bank got there [sic] cable. I can only suppose either that there is some rumour that I have been wounded or else my letters have been going astray. I have written every week since I have been in France & only missed one week so some of the letters should be delivered. I have not been able to make as much progress as I should have liked with this letter as there have been some people in here talking most of the evening so I will leave your letters & answer them in my next which will be begun on the first suitable occasion. Really I have been busier the last ten days than any time since I came to France. One of the Majors is away on leave & I have been doing his work & what with building the new camp there has been a fair amount to do. If at any time you don't get news of me for some time there is no need to worry as no news is good news always. We are having beautiful spring weather now. All the hedges are starting to come into leaf & the grass & crops are growing fast. Just a touch of frost in the morning & then bright sunny days. With love

Your loving son

Tom

19-3-18

My dear Mother

I will now proceed to answer the letters which I received a few days ago. Please excuse the writing being in pencil but I am sitting up in bed writing this (I am not ill) & ink is difficult. It has been raining steadily all day & though our dugout is fairly dry a little rain dribbled in under the door and as we have an earth floor it is rather messy. My feet were wet & so I decided bed was the best place so here I am about 8pm sitting up writing this. We have two Primus stoves going, one belongs to me & one to the Doctor who shares my dugout. We have an acetylene lamp burning also & are really very snug & about 9 o'clock will have some Bovril for supper. Yesterday I was out classifying some roads & had a very enjoyable day. I rode about 20 miles & as it was a perfect spring day with a gentle breeze & all the hedges just coming into leaf it was hard to realise that there was a war on except for an occasional shell in the distance. Today I was out again in the rain but as I had a good coat I did not get wet. Now for your letters. I am glad you got the films that Major Arnall took out safely. But I don't want the prints as I have copies of all of them here. However if they come along I can give them away. I am afraid you will not care for Major Arnall if he accepts your invitation. His occupation before the war was secretary to a Coal Miners Union. He is uneducated & very narrow minded so I don't think you will have much in common & if you get onto politics there will be trouble. I know how glad you must have been to see John Ward & Marjorie must be delighted. John did very good work while he was over here & everywhere I go I hear nice things about him. In a way I am rather glad that Uncle is leaving you although I am very sorry for Aunt Meg. But I have seen from your letters for some time that you did not think he was managing the place as it ought to be run. Tom Knox[209] seems to be reliable & there is no reason why he should not be able to carry on with Cousin Reg to supervise but he may need some help in dealing with the men just at first. However that is a point which I am sure Cousin Reg will see to. With Mr Yarwood too, in control of the finances I know that there will be no speculation & I don't think things could be in safer hands. The Girl told me about the Micalago trip in her letter & also how pleased she was with the alteration of the rooms. I think it is an excellent idea. Ever since the new room has been built no one has ever used the drawing room & it seems a waste to have a room that is never used. Really in the country a drawing room is a white elephant & most houses would be much better without them provided a decent bright living room is put in instead. The little spare room should make a very cosy sitting room. But I can appreciate Hopperton & Jackson's feelings while helping to rehang the pictures. I am glad to hear that the apple crop is such a success but you do not tell me which are the varieties that have done best & which are the best flavoured. I am rather curious to hear how the Jonathon trees have turned out. I hope that this year the nectarine crop will be large enough to go round. My parcels are coming regularly now. Yesterday I got two tins of Gidleigh mixture, a pair of socks which I have not opened yet & some chocolate

---

209   Thomas Hope Knox, 2nd son of T F Knox & brother of Nell

ordered by you from England. I am glad Aunt Chaddie[210] & Stephen[211] have been able to stay for a while. I think the last time I saw Aunt Chaddie was in Sydney a good many years ago. She was very deaf then but I think must have got worse since. I always remember her as a very cheery person.

There is no doubt that the people of Cooma have taken to John Ward & I am sure he deserves all his popularity. John Chisholm seems as suitable a name as they could have chosen for the baby. I have always wished to see a window in the church to Dad's memory & will certainly help you to do it but things are so uncertain now with the submarines that it would seem better to leave it till after the war. With regard to the supposed German offensive in the spring, I don't think it will be successful even if it does come, which personally I am inclined to doubt. I mean in this way. I expect that Fritz will attack somewhere on the west front but I rather believe that it will only be to try & keep troops here, while he makes his main attack in Italy & what success he will meet with there is more than I am prepared to say. Of course this is only guess work & I have really no reason for thinking as I do. But I am exceeding doubtful if it would pay the Germans to try and break through on this front & I think the Germans themselves realise it. The chances of success are very slender & if it was a failure it would mean too much to them. At present each side is more or less sitting down waiting for the other to make the first move.

---

210 Charlotte Hogg, Aunt 'Chaddie' m. Francis Henry Rutledge.
211 Their youngest son, Stephen Crane Rutledge.

Continued on 20th

I don't think the little car served us so badly. It cost £300 when new & to get £144 after nearly four years of constant use I consider pretty good. What make to get to replace it, I don't know. So many firms have given up making since the war but I certainly agree with you that a small car is needed and is really an economy. Some American cars are all right but they need very careful choosing unless you get someone on whose advice you can absolutely rely & who has no interest in any motor agency. I would not go for one. That is unless you get a Ford. They are certainly the best value on the market but they are not very pleasant to drive in. Still before you get this you will probably have made up your mind. Don't forget to apply to Mr Yarwood if you want any financial help in buying the new one.

This season seems to have been even wetter than the last we are constantly reading of floods & cyclones. The last one at Innisfail only a few days ago seems to have been pretty bad. Truly it always seems to be a feast or a famine. You speak of the grass being too green to burn in the middle of January a thing which I can never remember seeing. I am rather surprised to hear of Howard Hepburn's[212] engagement to Mary Bryden[213]. She always struck me as rather a silly little thing but she was very young & may have improved with age. I met him once in London while I was on leave. He did not look well then.

I am sorry to hear that Charles Shaw is no better. It must be a very anxious time for poor Aunt Fan [Garraway].

---

212 Howard A E Hepburn, b. Cooma 1884, grazier of Coolamatong, Berridale.

213 The only Mary Bryden born in NSW was born in 1886 in Sydney. There is no record of their marriage in NSW.

Today I have been in Camp all day it was very misty & cheerless this morning with mud everywhere but it cleared up this afternoon & looks as if it will be fine tomorrow. The camp is pretty muddy at present & a fine day will do a lot to help dry it.

Monday.

Must finish this now to catch a mail. We are moving again tomorrow which means that mail arrangements are upset for two or three days. With love

Your loving son

Tom

28-3-18

My dear Mother

We expect to be moved from our present spot shortly & if so I may not have a chance to write for a few days so I am sending this now even if I don't get a chance to write a proper letter I will try to send a note just to say I am well. As far as we can tell the German offensive seems to be pretty well held up for the time being but we get very little news & I have not seen a paper for over a week so it is hard to tell what is really going on. We moved here from our last camp two days ago & are very comfortable just at present. I think this is really the best camp I have been in yet. Things are pretty quiet just at present here & I do not expect that they will liven up at all while the push is on elsewhere. I really have no news to tell you. I answered your letters in my last. There has been no further mail in & I do not expect it for some time; generally we get about three weeks mail at once. After a long spell of beautiful weather the last three days have been cold & windy. Today it looks like rain but the wind is south so it should become warmer. With love

Your loving son

Tom

6-4-18

My dear Mother,

Since I last wrote to you I have spent most of my time travelling. We have been in a different camp every night & are now not very far from the line but I am rather doubtful if we are going to stay here for very long. We only arrived here about four o'clock this afternoon & have just got settled down in tents. It has been raining off & on for the last week & as we have been always moving it has not been as comfortable as usual. Fortunately today was fine but it came on to rain later in the evening & is coming down steadily now. It is quite likely that here we may have a fight instead of our usual work & if so I feel sure that the men will give a very good account of themselves. Needless to say I could not tell you anything about operations even if I knew very much which I don't. By the way, since I last wrote I have been appointed 2nd in Command of the Battalion. The previous man in the job has been appointed to command another battalion & I have moved into his place. I like the Colonel [Annand] very much & think that we will get on very well together. Last night I had the worst billet I have had since I have been in France; a tiny little box of a room right under the tiles & the only light I could get came from a small piece of glass in the roof. However I was very tired after spending the whole of the night before in the train & most of the day as well & I slept like a top in spite of being awakened two or three times by people who were looking for someone else. The country round here is looking very well now. All the trees & hedges are just coming into leaf & in a little wood just near the camp the ground is simply covered with wild anemones. White are the most common but there are also purple ones. You would love to see this part. Every inch is cultivated & there is absolutely no waste. Even the trees are cut every two or three years & the prunings carefully collected in bundles & I think a lot of them are used for baskets &c. There is no doubt that the French are a thrifty race but the trees are rather spoilt as after the pruning operations are finished only bare trunks are left. Still I think we can learn a good many lessons from them & there are a few things we can teach them. I am travelling fairly light just at present having left most of my things in a box but I am still carrying round a Primus stove which I find most useful both for warmth & for making tea or soup when travelling. There is nothing like a hot drink of Bovril or cocoa when you are cold & tired. I intend to have something tonight before I go to bed. By the way I raised a sore heel the other day through having on too thick socks. If socks are very thick part of the socks rubs off & collects in a lump & then if you keep on walking a blister is the result. I like medium weight socks best, Fuzzie sent me a pair made from merino wool that are just about right also I have two pairs you made, a sort of mauve colour with a line of black & red round the top. The ones made from black wool are just a little thick especially for summer wear. When I left some of my things I found I have 24 pairs of socks so I cut myself down to eight & gave the rest away to the men who were very glad of them. Bed time now. I am very fit & well. Love to all.

Your loving son

Tom

11-4-18

My dear Mother,

After being without mail of any sort for nearly a fortnight it came in yesterday & I got a fine bunch. Three from you, 3 from the girl two pairs of white socks (homespun) & two tins of Gidleigh Mixture as well as English Mail. Since my last letter we have moved again in fact we moved the day after I wrote in the rain & when we arrived at our destination there was no cover of any sort. We are in open downs country & the only thing in the way of shelter are a few banks made apparently by centuries of ploughing. You will probably have seen the sort of thing I mean in England. We did not arrive till about four o'clock in the afternoon & then had to set to work & make dugouts in the bank for the night. Fortunately it did not rain that night but it has done so every day since except today which has been fine & sunny part of the time but it is very sultry & I am afraid the rain has not done yet.

Since our arrival we have been busy improving our quarters & are now quite comfortable. Fortunately there was a deserted aerodrome not far away from which we were able to salve corrugated iron & timber in plenty & we are now living in buildings which are half dugouts & half huts. I am sharing one with the padre & will try & describe it. At the back there is a bank about 10 feet high. We dug into this until we had a terrace about 10ft long & 7ft wide. As only 7 foot lengths of iron were available & tools limited we had to build according to the material at hand. The two sides consist of one sheet of iron & then the roof begins as we had to use the same iron & the building is only 7 feet wide it runs up very steeply & looks rather funny but it is dry & airy especially as we do not bother about lining & there are plenty of cracks under the eaves. The back consists of a sheet of iron at the bottom then come two boxes built in for shelves & the rest is boarded with a small piece of celluloid at the top for a window this shape• $\triangle$. The doorway is in the centre of the front & the ends boarded up. Then we cut a trench down the centre from the doorway 2 feet wide & 2 feet deep which left a bank on either side just wide & long enough for our beds. Some nails in the rafters to hang things on completed our first days work & we had a most eligible residence but the trouble was there were so many things hanging about that we could hardly move. So the next day we added to the front in the following way. On each side of the doorway we added small structures about 2 feet high where they join on to the building & running down to six inches something like this only steeper. They serve as wardrobes for stowing all our possessions which at present are not very great as we stored a good deal of our belongings before coming here & now we are as comfortable as we could wish. The whole thing looks something like this. While we were building it someone came along & chalked on the front 'THE SINNERGOG' or 'THE PIGEON LOFT' but that is only because they are envious. For a door we have a piece of old tarpaulin which hangs down in front & I am sitting in it now writing this by acetylene light so I am not so badly off. Today being fine I got all my belongings out & aired them well which they needed being more or less damp in fact I have not had dry socks or boots for over a week but beyond the discomfort wet feet don't seem to signify in this country except to make you liable to trench feet & the season for them is pretty well over now. Since we have been here Fritz has been very quiet & his offensive here seems to be finished for the time being but today we have news that he has made an attack in another sector & met with some success but how much we don't yet know. Last night I was out with the men digging some trenches fairly well forward & we did not get a single shell near us the whole time. It was a very dark night & I fell into several shell holes while one of the officers fell into the trench we were digging. Coming home we started across country but it was so dark we felt we were in danger of losing our way so made for the nearest road & then came all the way back by road. It took us three hours instead of the one it had taken going out & was misting pretty heavily. It was just on one o'clock when I got back to camp & you can imagine I was not feeling as good tempered as I usually am but after getting into bed & having a cup of cocoa I felt up to a small philosophic discussion with the padre before going to sleep.

Today I have loafed around all day doing nothing in particular. About five o'clock there was an aeroplane fight overhead which I missed as I was busy trying to brush some of the mud off my breeches. The result was that Fritz was brought down in flames & ours landed immediately afterwards. One of the men had a bullet in his knee & the other a cut lip so we appear to have had the best of it. I have never yet seen an aerial fight & am very sorry I missed this one. I think that is about all the news I have for this letter so I will now proceed to answer your letters taking them in order. Today I got no more letters but got 2 Australasians & a Pastoral Review none of which I have opened yet. Now for your letters written on Feb 3rd, 10th, & 17th. I am glad to hear that the Trustees 'gave' Uncle a gratuity when he left. As you say the running of a station in our district is an altogether different thing to doing it in the hot country & he would be better off if he could get something

(2)

something like this ... running down to six inches.
something like this ... only steeper. They
serve as wardrobes for stowing all our
separate possessions which at present are
not very great as we stored a good deal
of our belongings before coming here
& now we are as comfortable as we
could wish. The whole thing looks
something like this.
While we were building
it someone came along
& chalked on the front
"THE SINNERGOG" or THE PIGEON ☆ LOFT
but that is only because they
are envious. For a door we
have a piece of old tarpaulin
which hangs down in front & I am sitting in
it now writing this by acetylene light so I
am not so badly off. Today being fine I got
all my belongings out & aired them well
which they needed
in fact I have not
over a week but
fact don't seem to
to make you liable ...
them is pretty we
been here fifty ...
offensive' have ...
time being but toda...
has made an
& met with some

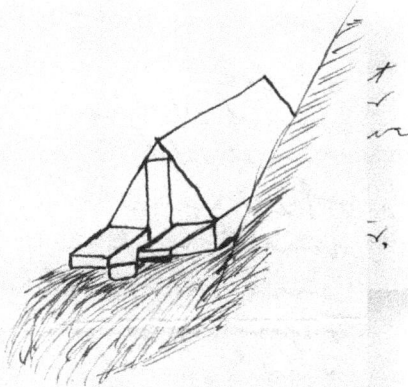

Margin sketches in the letter, dated 11-4-1918.

to do in the district he knows. The present arrangement should work fairly well i.e. Tom Knox looking after the books & store & keeping a lookout generally & Wark looking after the rest. The only thing is that Wark is not as good as he might be at keeping the other men up to their work & Tom will want to keep an eye to that so as to let Cousin Reg know.

I think the best way to have turkeys is to do as we have always done & pay someone on the place so much a head for all they can rear. About the house there are too many disturbing elements. The question of a small car seems to be worrying you a good deal. Of course the choice now must be strictly limited as so few firms are making them but that should really make the decision easier. I agree with you that a small car is needed & after all they have now got beyond the experimental stage & nearly any make you can get is reliable & will do good work. The last socks that arrived made from white wool (one pair has a band of black & red round the top) seem to be just about right although if anything they might be a little lighter. Still these are quite light enough & making them any lighter is only a refinement. I have not worn them yet but intend to put a pair on tomorrow. Soon I will be able to discard all except homespun. One officer to whom I showed them considered it a great pity to wear them in ordinary working boots at all & thought that they should be kept for best. The pair you sent me made from wool spun by Fuzzie is certainly excellent & it is very difficult to detect that the wool is homespun. The amount of Gidleigh mixture that is arriving now is quite sufficient for my needs. Even if an occasional tin misses I can always make a smokeable mixture by mixing it with other tobacco so do not worry about sending it more often. I am very sorry to hear that Aunt Ada [Powell] has been so unwell. She really should see a doctor but that I am afraid is too much to hope for. There is a big gun near our camp & whenever it fires all our lights go out. It has just fired & I have had to light the gas again. It is amusing at first but becomes wearisome after a while especially as sometimes tho' fortunately not often it averages about one shot every five minutes.

I know that the old dairy & cook's room must be about done. I am certainly in favour of pulling them down & putting up a stone building in their place & joining it on to the rest of the house. With regard to getting Hopkins[214] to do it, I think it would be advisable to make sure that he can do a satisfactory job. It is no use putting up a second rate affair for the sake of saving a few pounds especially as it is to be joined on to the rest of the house. The only trouble I can see is the window of the present maids room but it might be possible to overcome that by putting a small boot room there & then building on a dairy & two maids rooms. Someday I would like to see the billiard room replaced by a stone building to join on to this proposed on thus closing in the yard with possibly an archway to take the place of the present gate but it is no use talking of that now. Still if you have not yet started to build when you get this it would not be a bad idea to build with an eye to possible developments in the line I have spoken of. It is far better to have a separate room for each maid even if it is only a small one. Anyway I think it would be a good thing to get it built as soon as possible and there is no need to wait[215]. I expect though that you will have to talk to Mr Yarwood round. I am afraid that the building of it will not

214   William Leonard Hopkins, carpenter, Gidleigh , Bungendore.

215   Tom is referring to major extensions to the Gidleigh homestead which were completed c 1920

save any taxation but that I cannot say definitely from here and it really after all does not come into the question. I get very little news of the members of the Cunningham family in England & had not heard that Mary had a daughter. I am very sorry for poor Tommy losing her baby. I had not heard of that either. The season seems to have been very wet right through & I am afraid that there will be trouble with the lambs in the way of seed & worms. I always made a practice of drenching the lambs at this time of year as a preventative & I think it gave good results. The bush fires seem to have been pretty bad in Riverina. You say that Mr Circuitt[216] lost 20,000 acres at Uabba & that he got off more lightly than anyone in the district. I think it would be a very good idea indeed to get a parish car for Mr Champion & then allow him so much a year from the proceeds of Easter Monday to maintain it. A Ford is what I would recommend. They are very easy to drive, cheap to buy & maintain & I don't think there is the slightest doubt that they are best value on the market where utility is the chief consideration. I should say that a special subscription should cover the first course [sic]. I had to get out of bed just now to get this paper. I have finished my block & I am afraid you will only get scraps for a while until I can get another block which is not particularly easy just at present. It seems a pity the Church wardens made a mess of the new Church Hall. I was always against brick as I knew that to put up a decent brick building would have been too costly & I am sure that a hardwood building would have cost less & if properly painted would have lasted as long. I know you don't like wooden buildings but for certain purposes I don't know of anything that is as suitable as wood.

---

216   George Cameron Perry Circuitt, of Uabba, Lake Cargellico, formerly of Bungendore

I am in a writing mood tonight so am going to keep on going till the inspiration is exhausted. I don't think you need worry very much about keeping Jerusalem. I would lay a shade of odds that we don't whichever way the war goes. I hear sounds of the rain on the roof & am afraid that we will have a wet day tomorrow. Still it does not matter so much now as we are all under good shelter & can keep our belongings dry, that is those we are not wearing. No one troubles very much about keeping dry during the day. In the first place if you have to go out at all it is hopeless and in the second even if a coat would keep you dry it is extra weight to carry & when ploughing through mud every extra pound counts. A dry change is an advantage although even that is not necessary. The other night I dried a pair of trousers by the simple method of going to bed wearing them. They were quite dry in the morning & I have suffered no ill effects I have known men sleep in wet clothes for a fortnight & thrive on it. I think it is the open air life we lead & certainly generally speaking there is less sickness here than there would be in civil life. There has been an interlude here while the padre & I have been discussing educational matters & as he has finished writing & is in a talkative mood I am afraid I must stop now. With love

Your loving son
Tom

19-4-18

My dear Mother

Since writing my last letter I have found that there is one of your letters I did not answer so I have kept it instead of burning it as I generally do. I started to keep all my letters but found that they got all over the place so now I make a practice of burning them as soon as they are answered. Result I have very few unanswered letters & my writing case keeps reasonably empty. The supply of writing paper is very scarce just at present & it is hard to get more. The padre succeeded by sending [sic] ten miles in getting an ordinary pad but he had to pay five francs (3/8) for it. I have written to Cousin Jessie & asked her to send me one and I hope to have it within a week.

Since last writing to you in a way I have had the busiest time since coming to France. The whole battn has been on the same job (trenches in the forward area) at once, a thing which very rarely happens, & the result is that I have been going out with them instead of just going along afterwards to see if everything was satisfactory. I have had three nights this week which means leaving camp about 7 o'clock in the evening & returning at 2, 3 or 4 o'clock next morning. Still that is all I have been doing. After I come home I make myself some cocoa & then turn in, have breakfast & sometimes lunch in bed. It would not be so tiring only we have to make our way back across country with a good deal of ploughed fields while if it is at all dark one is continually falling into shall holes trenches &c. We have had a few casualties but on the whole have been fairly lucky & I think we have got the worst of the work done now. Of course there is always plenty of work for us to do but from now on I think most of it will be

where we can work in daylight. Yesterday the General rang the
C.O. up and expressed his appreciation of the work the battalion
has been doing since we have been in this area. Of course it is only
a small matter but I think everyone likes to feel that their work is
appreciated & I know that the whole Battalion feel pleased about
it. All this month the weather has been vile. Cold northerly winds
with a good deal of rain. Today the wind is very cold & every half
hour or so we get a snowstorm which lasts two or three minutes
& then the sun comes out again. Our dugout was not built for
this sort of weather & tho' we have a stove in it made from an oil
drum it is very cold & chilly because the roof does not fit tightly
& our doorway is a piece of canvas which does not quite reach
the ground. Still we are good deal better off than lots of others
& we can always keep warm by getting into bed a simple matter
which only involves the removal of boots & tunic. I have just had
a look outside. It is bright moonlight & the wind has dropped
so we may have a fine day tomorrow. I hope so. I have not had
a bath for three weeks & if it is fine I can have one in the open.
I don't think I have much more news for you this week. From
the latest news we seem to be holding Fritz pretty well but that
does not signify very much & I think he is probably preparing for
another attack. This week I have got three Australasians to Jan
13th 3 Bulletins to Jan 18th & a Pastoral Review. They have come
just at the right time as I was getting very short of reading matter.
Now for your letter dated Feb 17th. I am rather surprised to
hear that Frank Chisholm[217] has got himself into difficulties
financially. I always looked upon him as beyond danger in such

---

217   Frank Kerr Chisholm, son of Charles Kerr Chisholm & nephew of W A &
      AB Chisholm.

matters. From what you say he seems to have got himself into a position where he has not much chance of doing anything to extricate himself. I think he was wise to leave Kippilaw.

Big places like it take a fearful lot to keep up and he will have to go cannily for some time to come. Still I have no doubt that he will be very contented at Narrabeen & the new cottage with all its electrical contrivances is sure to be a perpetual source of joy to his mechanical & inventive mind and expect he will spend most of his time effecting improvements and repairs. Still there is no doubt that in a properly designed & conveniently fitted & arranged house a tremendous lot of work can be saved. Such things as hot & cold water & built in wardrobes should be in every house. Since being over here I have almost become a convert to central heating for cold climates, not necessarily to the exclusion of fires in living rooms but to warm the house generally.

22-4-18

Since I wrote last rather surprising events have happened. Yesterday morning I received instructions to report to the 4th Pioneers to take command. I came yesterday evening & took over so here I am writing to you as a battalion commander and a Lieut-Col. My promotion is only temporary at present but I get the pay & probably after I have been here three months my rank will be confirmed. Gen MacLagan is the divisional commander and when I saw him this afternoon he told me that he was very pleased to have me. He also asked after you and wanted to be remembered to you. Today I also saw Col Ross who used to be

Capt Ross[218] at Duntroon & Major Dunlop[219] who married Tommy Cunningham.

I am pretty busy just now getting the hang of things here & I expect that I will be so for some time to come until I get things going as I would like. I have no time for more now. I have to write to the Bank & ask them to send you a cable. With love

Your loving son

Tom

---

218   Lt Col Arthur Murray Ross, CMG, DSO, 3rd Infy Brig, HQ; Disch from AIF 30-5-19. Imperial officer. As Capt in West Yorkshire Regt, was instructor at RMC, Duntroon,

219   Major Dunlop married Mary Cunningham, Tommy's sister.

25-4-18

My dear Mother

I am not very busy this afternoon & so am starting your letter but I will not finish it for a few days yet. I forgot to tell you that about a week ago I got your cable saying that you had received mine & that all was well. I am sorry I let so long elapse without sending you one but will try & get them away more regularly in future. Really here one loses all count of time & very often I have to refer to my diary before I know the day of the week or the date. It is not that the time passes slowly because it doesn't but one day is so very much like another that it is only by keeping a diary that you can tell where you are. I am afraid that I have not very much news for you this week. I am getting settled down with my new Battalion now & as far as I can see they are a pretty good lot. Of course no two people think alike and it will take me some time to get things running just as I want them more especially as I do not want to be too much of a new broom. I always think it is better to feel your way a bit & introduce any reforms gradually. Commanding a battalion is a very good experience, it takes a good deal of organization & tact to get things going really smoothly.

27-4-18

We have just got word that we are to move again & I think it will probably be tomorrow. After a while one becomes quite accustomed to moves & takes them as all in the days work. The last two or three days have been very muggy but today is finer & I think that perhaps now April is nearly over we may get some decent weather. Anyway there is dust on the road just outside our billets and that is a thing we have not seen for six months.

1-5-18

Since writing we have moved again & have only just got settled in our new location. At first the men were camped in dugouts under a bank but headquarters had to go into billets in a village nearby. I don't like billets for two reasons when in the shell area. In the first place they are generally dirty & smelly & if Fritz does shell they are risky, not so much from the shells themselves as from the bricks & things they throw about, so I have had dugouts built in the bank with the rest of the Battalion and we are occupying them this evening for the first time. Mine is quite comfortable a corrugated iron erection about 7 x 6 lined with hessian. There is just room for the bed along one side & with a small table & chair it is fairly full but quite comfortable while I have a board floor. These dugouts are the safest habitations one can have as a direct hit is the only thing that can get you & that will get you anywhere. I am afraid this letter is two days late but while we are unsettled moving it is very hard to sit down & write. It is rather fortunate in a way as yesterday I got your letter dated Feb 22nd. I think there are more on the way. Australian mail dated 12th March has been delivered within the last day or two but the Bank have not got my new address yet so my letters take a day or so longer. I had a letter from Snowy not long ago in which he wrote much more cheerfully & I think he is getting on slowly & thinks his sight will be no worse than before. He says I have not changed much & I don't think I have except that a few grey hairs are beginning to show.

I am very much amused at your account of Algar Parish[220] & the telephone. Really Snowy has much the same characteristics & he seems to have a genius for getting at loggerheads with people. By the way I got my present job chiefly because my predecessor had the same trait. He could not agree with anyone of the staff & that is fatal.

The latest news from Russia is that the Tsarevitch has been made Emperor but I don't know how true it is. Really there have been so many changes that nothing would surprise one now. The Girl can easily tell if her lonely soldier[221] is a Lieutenant. If he is he will censor his own letters & his name will be on the envelopes. I hope in a way that John Ward does come back. There is no doubt that he did good work while he was here. A padre with the forces is a most difficult job to fill properly & unless a man has personality he had better stay away. Unless a padre is a good one I am sure he does more harm than good & no one finds out what he is really like better than the soldier. I am very glad indeed to hear that Charles Shaw is better & hope that he will continue to make progress. I see by the latest reports that the recruiting figures in Australia are improving & there is a chance that the present situation may help to keep them up. With love

Your loving son

Tom

---

220   Younger brother of Maurice Samper 'Snowy' Parish.

221   Young women were encourage to write to servicemen fighting on the front line – some eventually led to marriage [*Daily Mail 28th Oct 2013*]

5-5-18

My dear Mother

It is only three days since I wrote to you but it is my regular day for writing & since my last letter my mail has come in including two from you (March 3rd & 10th) some photos of the garden, two pairs of socks from you, one brown & one white, two tins of Gidleigh Mixture and a parcel from Cousin Jessie containing some magazines, chocolates and a writing pad of which I was sadly in need.

I am very sorry indeed to hear about Cousin Tom Knox. Cousin Jessie told me that he had been in hospital for some weeks but I don't think she knew about the operation. I think that some time has to elapse before a wooden leg can be fitted. The ones they fit now seem to be most satisfactory. When I was in England I had an officer who had lost his leg above the knee & had an artificial one. You could scarcely notice it when he walked & he was able to ride with it quite well. I am afraid Cousin Tom will not be a very good patient however & it will be a trying time for his family for a while.

I am just getting a door fitted to my dugout and every few minutes I have to get up and assist my batman when he needs any help. However it is nearly finished now and I don't think I will be interrupted any more. I am rather amused at your account of old Mrs Dowling's visit & can imagine the way you disagreed with her.

I am very glad that you have decided to give £50 to the Fund for Soldiers relatives. I sometimes feel that we don't give enough but I can't attend to it while I am over here. I will be writing to Mr Yarwood shortly & will arrange with him about allotting a certain sum for these various funds. The Y.M.C.A. & Comforts Fund

are both worthy of support in the work they are doing over here.
Yesterday I got 30 cases of comforts for the battalion consisting
of tobacco, cigarettes, cocoa & milk together with some odds &
ends. The tobacco & cocoa are especially welcome. Tobacco we can
always do with & now, when a good many of the men are working
at night & do not get back until 2 or 3 o'clock the next morning,
the comfort there is in a hot drink of cocoa when they get back can
hardly be exaggerated. I wrote to you about the old dairy before
& there is no need to go into the matter again. I also wrote about
the parish car. I certainly think it would be a most excellent thing
to get one and am sure that satisfactory arrangements can be made
to pay for the upkeep & I am sure that sufficient could be collected
to pay for the original cost without any trouble. Mr Ingle certainly
seems to have made a mess of things. He must have known that a
faculty was necessary before anything could be put in the church.
Now it seems that we have either got to have a tawdry brass cross &
unsuitable oak table or offend some of the best church supporters
It is an awful handicap to a man when he has not got the saving
grace of common sense. Of course the Girl & I will help to put
in a stained glass window to Dad & Pat's memory and, if you can
get the work done properly in Sydney, I think that it is better to go
there for it[222]. I will write a line to Cousin Florence Darnley[223*] to
let her know my address & will go & see her next leave but I don't

---

222   The window is now the West window of St Philip's, Bungendore

223   Florence, daughter of John Stephen Morphy and Elizabeth, née Styles , was
      born at Beechworth, Victoria, on 25 August 1860. She was one of the young
      women responsible for the presentation of 'the Ashes' in 1883. She married
      [1884] Ivo Bligh, the English cricket captain, who succeeded as Earl of Darnley
      in 1900. [see Berry & Peploe, *Cricket's Burning Passion*]

know when that will be. At present all leave is cut out & tho' I am about due for it now I don't know how long it will be before I get it. A good deal would seem to depend on Fritz. The Girl is certainly most enterprising the rides she takes & she seems to like going off the beaten track. I am very glad indeed to hear that Charles Shaw is slowly getting better. Even if the Bank don't keep Albury open for him they will surely give him another place when he recovers. Gidleigh seems to have done very well at the Braidwood show & I expect the Girl is very interested in it all. You will have to take Alf Taylor back when he is well enough. He is such a decent fellow and a good driver. Jackson should have no difficulty in getting another billet.

This morning we had church parade but I was not able to be there as I had to go see a staff officer about some baths which we have built for the men. This evening I am going to dine with one of the Companies. Each Company has a separate mess & it is a good opportunity to get to know the officers. As they have to go out to work tonight dinner is at 5-30. It is now quarter past five so I must finish this & then go along. With love

Your loving son

Tom

13-5-18

My dear Mother

　　Yesterday was your letter day again but I was kept pretty busy all day & was not able to get off my usual letter. Really I have very little news for you. The same routine goes on daily only varied by whether I go up to the works or don't. Yesterday I went to see the Division in the morning and in the afternoon went round most of the work. We have rather an interesting job on hand just now about which I cannot tell you unfortunately. We have had a good deal of rain lately & it is still threatening. Yesterday morning was wet & in the afternoon it was misty but it cleared up in the evening & I don't ever remember seeing it so clear in this country. Generally it is more or less hazy and you cannot see very far. The trees have all got their leaves on now & are looking very fine. Spring is so different over here to at home. It starts fairly early & then for about two months there is no appreciable change. But as soon as May comes all the trees seem to burst into leaf in one night & you realise it has really come at last. When we came here a fortnight ago there was not a leaf to be seen & now all the trees are covered.

It is daylight now at 4 o'clock in the morning (summer time) & it is still light enough to read by outside at half past nine at night. This evening at mess we are going to have asparagus. One of our Companies is in the forward area where there are no civilians and they got some from a garden there. Since I last wrote I have had 2 Australasians, 2 Bulletins and a Pastoral Review so am well off for reading matter just at present. I had a visit from General Birdwood two or three days ago.

He was very pleasant & as he was going away we had to turn some men out to push his car out of some mud it had got stuck in. It is all chalk country round here & gets fearfully greasy whenever it rains but fortunately it dries very quickly again. Had a most interesting evening last night. A couple of English officers came to dinner and one of them was a keen Unionist who had done a lot of political work in England. First of all we got on to Free Trade v Protection then on to Empire politics generally & did not finish up till after eleven. This is a very poor letter but I will try & do better next time. With love

Your loving son
Tom

19-5-18

My dear Mother

I did not get my usual letter to you on Sunday as we moved out on that day & I was too busy. Yesterday I was pretty well occupied getting things settled down. The men are having two days rest yesterday & today & then we start on rear work for a while, but it won't be as strenuous as what we have been doing. In a way it is lucky I did not write. Yesterday an Australian mail came in and there were three letters from you dated March 17th, 23rd, & 29th. I do not know how long we will remain out but hope for a fortnight. The weather has taken a decided change for the better & we have been having a succession of bright hot days with hardly a cloud. We are near a river now & all day long the men are swimming in it and thoroughly enjoying themselves. I am glad Uncle sent on my letter to him. I wrote it before I knew he was leaving but there are a few things in it I want to know about & am looking forward to hearing them from Tom Knox. I think Uncle has a fair chance of making a success of Stock & Station Agent in Goulburn. I know that there are a lot there at present but there are not too many good ones and I have always thought there was room for a good man there but whether Uncle can be that man remains to be seen. I am glad you have had Edie Cropper[224] staying with you for a while. I always liked her. I know it must have been a fearful trial to Cousin Amy [Knox] when Cousin Tom was laid up. I don't suppose you could find a worse patient. Probably it will be better when he is able to get about again. Also when he gets an artificial leg he will probably be less sensitive. Gidleigh certainly seems to be in the boom as far as shows are concerned. I really think it is rather a good thing they're

---

224   Edith M., d. of James Cropper; b. 1890 at Lambton, NSW.

Monica Spencer (Fuzzie) and Jean in the strawberry patch at Gidleigh.
Tom's young fruit trees can also be seen.

going in for them provided of course that it is not carried to excess. Hopperton seems to be most strenuous in his pursuit of bees. I think he is rather wise getting all those hives for himself. All these little side lines bring in a good deal of money if worked properly & they are not a great deal of trouble when they are properly managed. The young fruit trees seem to have been a great success. I am glad to hear that the Jonathons have been such a success. But you don't say if they are the best flavoured or not. Personally I think the Irish Peach cannot be beaten, that is if we have got the same apple that used to be at the top of the orchard years ago. I think the Girl told me in one of her letters that it had a few apples on it. It seems to me that Duntroon should be rather a good place to build an internment camp for German prisoners but it must be a fearful nuisance to get any work done round there while they are paying such wages.

I know that a lot of improvements will be necessary when I get back. I have long realised that the old engine shed has seen its best days & it is not now suitable for requirements. There is also a lot to be done in the way of subdividing some of the larger paddocks & general improvements. Then too shelter belts should be planted in Jeanfield & Greenhill[225] while in other parts there is a bit more ringbarking yet to be done. Charles Shaw does seem to be having a very long illness and as you say it does not seem likely that he will ever be very strong again. I am much amused at the size of the new parlormaid [sic]. I expect the Girl derives quite a lot of fun from her increase in bulk. I am sorry to hear that you have been run down & hope that Dr Williams[226] will do you good. You must go to Moree

---

225   Jeanfield (also called Janefield) & Greenhill were Gidleigh paddocks
226   Probably Ralph Osmand Williams, Bourke St, Goulburn, medical practitioner.

again this winter for a couple of months. As I told you in my last letter I thought we might do a little more for the various patriotic funds & am very glad that you Mr Yarwood & Mr Cunningham have decided to give £200 to the Red Cross. I am going to try & write to Mr Yarwood shortly but I have not had a great deal of time on my hands for letter writing just lately.

With regard to the war you must not put too much reliance on what you see in the papers. Their accounts of what is happening are very often inaccurate to say the least. We are expecting Fritz to renew his offensive on a large scale very shortly but I do not think that it will meet with the same success as the first for many reasons. For one thing I do not think that his troops are as keen now as they were at the start & they are certainly not as fresh. Then during the last offensive we learnt a good many valuable lessons & I think that this time we will profit by those lessons very considerably. Of course if he really pushes home his attack we are bound to give ground in places but although it is bad it does not really signify so long as the line remains intact which I think it will. If this offensive is to a great extent a failure it can be looked on as his last effort tho' he may have a go at Italy afterwards.

The Americans should be able to make themselves felt in a couple of months & from what I have seen of them I think they will be excellent troops. They are most methodical & very keen. I am afraid however that the end is not yet in sight & it will almost certainly drag on over next winter. With love

Your loving son
Tom

227

Appx. Nº ___1___

4th AUSTRALIAN PIONEER BATTALION
Report on operation on 4 July.

With the exception of some signallers who were attached to the wireless Coy. and Divisional Visual Station the Battalion took no part in the actual attack.

The day previous to the attack 'C' Coy were detailed to provide continuous patrols on the main traffic routes in Divisional area North of river SOMME. There were two of these on the road along the river valley from CORBIE to SAILLY-le-SEC and the tow path along the SOMME. A branch road from VAUX-SUR-SOMME to riverbank was also patrolled. During the day and night before the operation and on the day of the operation itself, these patrols were continuously on the move , but had very little work to do. There was a remarkable absence of hostile artillery fire and during the period under review only four shell holes required filling in.

On the evening following the operation 'B' and 'C' Companies were detailed to dif the communications trenches leading back over the skyline from the front line and joining up with the support line.

'B' Coy were employed near the South East corner of VAIRE WOOD and dug 360ft of C.T. leading back from the front line at P.21.a.8.3 They were delayed some time getting on to the job by hostile artillery fire but were able to complete their work for the night with only one casualty.

'D' Company were detailed to dig a C.T.back from the front line in P.16.a. As they were going out to work they were caught in a hostile barrage while in the valley in P.15.a and suffered severely. Owing to the dust smoke and casualties the rear platoon lost touch with the rest of the Coy, and were not afterwards able to find the work. Owing to the shelling the Coy. was seriously delayed in getting on to the work but they remained on it until 3.A.M. and succeeded in completing 160 yards of trench leading back from the front line at P.16.d.45.90. They suffered the following casualties 3 O/Rs missing, 12 O/Rs wounded, and 6 O/Rs wounded and remaining on duty. On the night 5th/6th July both Companies went out and continued the trenches started on the previous night. Neither Company suffered any casualties and the work was carried out without any special incident.

Reports attached.

Lieut/Colonel.
C.O. 4th AUSTRALIAN PIONEER BATTALION

4ᵀᴴ AUSTRALIAN
PIONEER BATTⁿ
No.
Date

---

227   4th Australian Pioneer Battalion, July 1918, p4. (details in Bibliography)

My dear Mother

I arrived back yesterday & found the Battn just going into the line again. Now I must tell you all about my leave. I think in my first letter I got as far as telling you what I did while in Edinburgh & had just about finished it. Now I must first explain how I came to go on farther north at all. You will probably have heard that there are several organizations in London which arrange for the hospitality of various sorts for overseas officers. As soon as you arrive in London on leave you receive a letter from Lady Harrowby[228] asking you to call & saying that if you want to do anything she can probably arrange it for you. So I went along & said I should like to see something of Scotland. In a few minutes it was all arranged for me to stay a few days with Lady Lyell near Kirriemuir. All I had to do was to send a wire giving the date of my arrival & the train I was coming by. Well when I left Clara [Miller] I proceeded on my way & finally arrived at Kirriemuir which is near Forfar somewhere about six o'clock in the evening. I found a cab to meet me & was driven out to Kinnordy which is quite close to the town. I did not see much of Kirriemuir itself but its chief claim to fame seems to lie in the fact it is the original Thrums in J. M. Barrie's book 'A Window in Thrums'[229]. I think we have the book at home although I have never read it. I received a most warm welcome from Lady Lyell & just had time to have a cup of tea & a talk before it was time to dress for dinner.

---

228 Probably Mabel, Countess of Harrowby, DBE

229 Kirriemuir was Barrie's birthplace and childhood home [see K.Telfer, *Peter Pan's First XI*]

Tom, probably taken on his last leave, August 1918.

There were three other Australian officers staying there & they with Lord Lyell completed the party. The latter is very interested in forestry which he had studied deeply & I had some very interesting talks with him on the subject. The following day we went by motor to a place called Ballantore where Lord Lyell has a moor. The heather was just coming out but it was really too early to see the moors at their best. The next day we went for a motor trip up two of the neighbouring glens which were very fine. The first was Glen Clova and is chiefly noted as being one of the hiding places of Prince Charlie. Then we came back and went up another glen the name of which I forget but at the head of it we had tea with a friend of Lady Lyell (Mrs Ogilvie) at a house called Bal-na-Bosh. Part of the house dates from the 13th century and would have interested you very much. The rooms were very low & had a regular old fashioned look about them. The whole house reminded me of a mixture of Carwoola Turalla & Foxlow. It is built on three sides of a square quite unpretentious & is covered in stucco coloured a light pink. Everything seemed to be in keeping with its age. The garden was beautiful but suffering from want of attention owing to the scarcity of labour. On the following day I was to have seen Glamis Castle[230]. You are sure to have heard of the famous secret in connection with it which is told to every heir after which he is supposed to never smile again. Unfortunately it poured with rain and I could not go & I had to come back to London in the evening so I may not get a chance again. Now I must stop as I have a good deal to do. With love

Your loving son

Tom

---

230   Childhood home of Queen Elizabeth, the Queen Mother.

Kinnordy House, Kirriemuir, Scotland where Tom spend part of his final leave in July 1918.

13-8-18

My dear Mother

Yesterday I got a letter from the Girl telling me all about your illness. Naturally I feel very anxious but fortunately before I got her first letter I received a cable saying that you were convalescent so I am not worrying so much as I would otherwise have done. But I won't feel really happy until I know that you have gone to Sydney & are within reach of a doctor until you are quite well again. You must get away as soon as you are fit to travel & stay there until you are quite yourself again.

Since I came back from leave I have been having a very busy time & have not had a minute for writing. You will know long before this reaches you that we attacked the Germans & have driven them back a considerable distance. Incidentally we have moved camp six times in a period of ten days & have not really had a home during that time. We move again tomorrow but I have no idea how long we shall stay at our next resting place. Fortunately the weather has been exceptionally fine and there has been no hardship attached to our moves. Naturally we have got rid of all surplus gear & are carrying with us simply a change of underclothes & a couple of blankets. Our attack was most successful & I am glad to say that the casualties were very light. The first day I was well back & the whole landscape seemed to be covered with German prisoners, some being marched back in parties & others carrying back their own wounded or ours. On the following days we pushed on still farther & although there is a lull for the moment it is quite on the cards that we may make another move before long. Of course this is mere guess work as we never know when an attack is coming off until just before the time arranged.

I sent you a cable yesterday saying that I was well & hope it reaches you in a reasonable time. Nowadays it often takes three weeks to arrive at its destination but I fancy that they go quicker if they are sent through a Bank.

Today is one of the hottest days we have had this summer & there is not a breath of wind but the evenings over here now are perfect. We have to go to bed about 9 o'clock or else undress in the dark. Fritz is rather too attentive with his aeroplanes just at present to make it safe to show a light after dark & in our present camp which consists of a hole scooped out of a bank with a piece of canvas over it to make it weather proof you cannot screen a light satisfactorily. I am afraid that there is not much news for you. I really saw nothing of the recent operations and anyway the war correspondents get far more information than we do & can really write a better account. With love

Your loving son

Tom

18-8-18

My dear Mother

Here it is Sunday again and time for your weekly letter. There is not much to write about however. Since the offensive started on the 8th we have been having a pretty strenuous time not so much in the way of work, as a matter of fact we have done less work than usual, but we have been more or less constantly on the move and with no settled camps to go into there has not been a superabundance of comfort. Really we have no cause to complain, the weather has been fine & warm & really it would have been no hardship to sleep in the open. All the time I have had a dugout of sorts with a tarpaulin covering but what you miss is a place where you can sit down at a table & write &c in moderate comfort. For the last few days there has been a lull & we are getting back to more or less normal conditions although even now we are not so busy as usual. When things are in a state of flux as they are at present there is really not much work to do in a Pioneer Battn as there is when we are just holding the line, that is in summer time. In winter of course it is different & the keeping of roads in repair is a job in itself which keeps us pretty busy. Fortunately Fritz left all the roads in excellent repair & we have only a small amount of maintenance work to keep them in good order. Just at present we are living in a couple of dugouts which were originally built by the French. They are not very commodious but have the advantage of being fairly safe from bombs & I think we have had more attention from aeroplanes in this respect than I have heretofore experienced. The country we are on now is rather bad from a camping point of view. It is something like the country round Canberra only flatter & there are very few convenient banks to dig into. We always avoid villages if we can, although they afford a certain amount of cover from the weather they generally come in for an inconvenient amount of attention from Fritz shells and are good places to avoid. It is wonderful how quickly the men make themselves a camp. We came here three days ago & had no shelter of any sort. Now the men have built dugouts for themselves and are really quite comfortable.

Fritz skinned this part of the country pretty thoroughly & gathered all the crops but I don't think that they did him a great deal of good. All the grain crops are making a good deal of second growth which seems to show that they were very green when cut & although they might have made hay I am sure they were too green for grain & that is what he chiefly needs.

I have still got the wallaby rug you sent me & when I went on leave I took it over with me. I am having it lined with waterproof canvas & when that is done it will be invaluable in winter for my bed. I had it all last winter & felt the benefit of it but I think that the lining will improve it. I am afraid that some of our mail must have been sunk. I have had only one letter from the Girl in the last five weeks. I know that you were ill and could not write but there must have been more from her. Papers & tobacco come along pretty regularly & I think that I really get most if not all that are sent. By the time you get this it will be the beginning of October & you will be just about beginning lamb marking. Here we are just beginning to remember that winter is coming again and we will probably be starting fires in our dugouts in another month or so. I hope that you are well again now & that you are taking proper care of yourself. With love

Your loving son

Tom

29-8-18

My dear Mother

I got quite a batch of letters from the Girl this week and was very glad indeed to hear that you were getting on so well. Mind you must take great care of yourself & be sure not to take any risks until you are quite strong again.

At present we are well back from the line having a short rest & doing some training at which I am kept fairly busy. Still I don't think that we shall be out for very long. Things are going very well just at present and I rather fancy that we shall make every endeavour to keep on striking while the iron is hot. Today we got news that we are nearly back to Peronne. It rather looks as if the German will try and make a stand about where he is at present but if he fails anything may happen & it is quite possible that the next two months will see France practically cleared.

I saw Ted Rutledge today, the first time since March, he is looking very fit & well. I am afraid that this is not much of a letter but I will write again in a day or two. It is now possible to write in some comfort as we are in billets & are really seeing something approaching civilisation again. With love

Your loving son

Tom

3-9-18

My dear Mother

Just lately I have had a whole host of letters from the Girl about you & in the last week I got a cable from you saying that you had received mine and that all was well which has made my mind much easier. Mind you will have to take great care of yourself until you are quite well again. I was interrupted here this morning and am continuing just before going to bed. After leaving writing this I was kept busy till lunch & after lunch we had a sports meeting which kept me pretty well till dinner. After dinner I had to play in a bridge tournament which we have going & that has only just finished. I and my partner are doing very well & with luck we should win.

Our Battalion sports meeting has been going in the afternoon for the last two days and has been a great success. I came second last in the officers hack race yesterday & fifth in the mule race today. We have bookmakers at these meetings, I know you won't approve but the men enjoy them. I won 55 francs today from one. I only had two bets & won both of them. Also I have on hand the initiation of an educational scheme for the men & so am kept pretty busy. I don't know how it is but everyone I know seems to have chosen this particular time to write to me & the heap of unanswered letters is growing daily. I shall grow desperate soon & lock myself in my room for a day till I can get rid of them. Tomorrow I have to go & meet some Australian Pressmen who are visiting the front & that will take up the whole morning.

We are still in alleged rest far behind the line but that really means training in the mornings & sports of some sort in the afternoon. I do not think however that we shall be out much longer.

The news is very good & while we have the Bosche on the move I think we will try & keep him going as long as we can. (Another interruption here while I answered an invitation to a Boxing Competition tomorrow). This probably means that we shall be in it again before long. This evening we received word that he is retreating over a considerable distance in front of Cambrai. This is one of his strongest positions forming part of the Hindenburg line which we got into yesterday. There is no telling now how far he may go back & you may be sure that we will assist him all we can. Our men have been doing great deeds lately near Peronne & it makes one feel proud to be among them. The German history of this present offensive will prove most interesting reading & I rather think that the part played by Australians will bulk much larger than most people, who are not in the know, imagine. With love

Your loving son
Tom

9-9-18

My dear Mother,

We are on the move again and are living in pretty sketchy quarters. Tonight we are in a small copse. I have a hut with deal walls & a tin roof which lets in nothing but the wind so am fairly well off. There is another Australian Mail in but mine has not come along yet & now we are moving I may have to wait for a day or two. Fritz has been going back the last day or two on our front & while he keeps moving we have to follow & we won't get comfortable conditions until the line settles down somewhere. Today I set out to find a new camp immediately after breakfast and have been riding over evacuated country nearby ever since but now we are settled & I am feeling rather inclined for my high tea but it won't be ready for another hour and a half yet. Fortunately the weather keeps good & really it would be no hardship to sleep in the open air. A lot depends now on whether we can get Fritz over the Hindenburg line. If we can I think it is probable that he will be out of France before the end of the year. With love

Your loving son

Tom

16-9-18

My dear Mother

A fine Australian mail came in today. There were two letters from you dated July 7th & 14th two from the Girl & one from Fuzzie.

I am very glad indeed to hear that you are getting on surely but slowly. I expect that by this time you will have been to Sydney & possibly will be back home again.

I am very glad to hear that Aunt has at last got permission to start a club at Jerusalem. I know how much she has wanted to do it & I also know what a great benefit it will be to the men there.

I am very amused at the incident of Grace. It is a good thing there is someone to keep the Girl up to the mark when you are not there.

I don't think that you need worry too much about the IWW. The men here are pretty sick with them and when they get back the IWW will have to take a backseat or they will most likely strike trouble. I hope the girl will take to her new car. If she will only apply herself there is no reason why she should not be able to drive it herself & then she could go up & visit the twins whenever she liked. I am sorry to hear that the car you got for Mr Champion has disappeared but it will surely turn up before long. If John Ward is not medically fit I don't think he should try to come back here. The winter is just setting in & unless a man is really strong he cannot stand it & is really more a trouble than anything else. It is good news that the carved oak altar the Lundies[231] gave is not the monstrosity I was led to believe. I am developing quite a taste in furniture and am

---

231   The altar was in memory of Pte Leslie Lundie, 2nd s. of Mr & Mrs Charles Lundie, KIA 9-5-1915 at Gallipoli. Charles Lundie owned a butcher's shop in Bungendore. [see G. Ellis *Our Soldiers*]

very hard to please. You would have loved to have seen Kinnordy where I was staying when on leave. It was a big house but Lady Lyell had not made the mistake of putting too much in it. But practically everything there was a gem. My bed room was very big & there were only two small pictures in it. One was an artist's proof of a good picture & the other was a very old print. In a wide hall longer than the long hall at Gidleigh here were just four cabinets & I would have given a good deal to possess even one of them. One especially was very handsome indeed. I [sic] was old Spanish made of some dark wood & ornamented with dark red lacquer work. It was not a bit gaudy but the more you looked the more you liked it & there were dozens of other things much the same. I am sending by this mail a postcard of the house & some groups taken by Lady Lyell which she has just sent me. My room was the one over the front door & contained the little round tower (the window looks straight out at you). It formed a sort of recess in which stood the writing table. I think it quite a good idea to plant an avenue of trees in Bungendore to commemorate those who have volunteered. But let them be Australian trees[232]. But what is really wanted in Australia is forestry which is a different thing altogether to tree planting. While I have been away I have been learning a little bit about it & have some ideas which I may put into practice. The trouble is that so little has been done in Australia that one can get no information as to its special application there. I don't know where you got your information with regard to the Y.M.C.A. from but it is totally wrong as far as the Australian Y.M.C.A. is concerned. The English Y.M.C.A. which is really a branch of the American although it does do good

---

232 Jean Rutledge organised an avenue of chestnut trees to commemorate all the volunteers from Gidleigh. [see Biographical notes]

work, is really a vast business concern & is out to make money. But some time ago the Australian Y.M.C.A. which at first was working with them, broke away. Since then they have been doing excellent work and from my experience here the last five months, I can say that they have done as much if not more, for my men, as any other organization. Whenever we come out of the line for a few days the Y.M.C.A. representative invariably comes to see me to find out what he can do for us. He probably erects a tent where the men get reading material & conveniences for writing, runs a canteen which is better than anything we can do. For the last three months the Y.M.C.A. has been the only place where we can get matches & they have cigarettes when everyone else fails. They also give us issues of cigarettes, provide sporting material for the men, run coffee stalls where men can get free drinks, arrange concerts & entertainments &c &c (free). I have written at some length because I know there is an impression abroad at home that they are not as they should be & I think it should be combatted in every possible way. As I write we have had news of the big American success near Verdun. Things are fairly quiet on our front for the present but I do not know how long it will last. I am fairly busy just now & it is bed time. With love

Your loving son

Tom

23-9-18

My dear Mother,

The question of writing paper is rapidly assuming an acute stage hence this is on what is not usually considered suitable paper for one's private correspondence. We were pretty busy all last week making preparations for an attack which was completely successful & which resulted in the capture of two villages & the penetration of part of the outposts of the Hindenburg line. We were on our usual work on roads & communications generally & had a pretty strenuous two days. Since then we have moved camp again but not very far. I did not write yesterday as it was raining & my home was being built so that really I had nowhere to write. Fortunately just about where we are now was a previous camping ground before last March & there is any amount of corrugated iron about although fairly well ventilated. Still with a little care it makes quite good building material & I now have a very nice corrugated iron hut about 7'x7' perched on the side of a gully in a small copse. I have a wire netting bed which makes quite a good substitute for a spring mattress, a table & a box to sit on. The only requirement now is a floor of some sort when I will be well set up, while if the weather becomes much colder I will have room to put in a small stove. All this month we have had pretty bad weather. Regular equinoctial gales accompanied by driving showers & rain & it has been fairly cold. Still it is too early for winter yet & I am hopeful that we will get good weather next month. I answered all your letters last week & I have had nothing further in since, although there are rumours that there is another Australian mail about. Everything seems to be going very well here. In addition to our own effort the French have been moving forward while in addition considerable advances have been made at Salonica while today we have had news that 18000 Turks have been taken prisoner in Palestine & that they have not yet been all counted. I am now beginning to be very hopeful that the Germans will be practically out of the whole of France by the New Year. The next three weeks will decide. But I think that if we can make a decent advance now anywhere on our front he will have to withdraw a good way. I was talking to a shrewd staff officer this morning who said he considered the situation had never been more hopeful. Fritz is still fighting well in spots but a large number of his men have surrendered recently without firing a shot & the morale generally has not been the best. Of course this does not mean that he is breaking up because numbers of his men still fight as well as they ever did but the proportion who do not is growing & I don't think that the coming winter will help to encourage them to any degree. With love

Your loving son
Tom

30-9-18

My dear Mother,

The news this week has been very good indeed.

The Turks in Palestine practically wiped out, the Bulgarians in full retreat & apparently disorganised & advances made practically on the whole of the western front. Yesterday an attack was made on this front which although not being quite as successful as we hoped in some respects was more so in others. It is being continued today & now we are standing by waiting to go forward to do any necessary work.

Unfortunately the weather has turned dog on us. Yesterday was brilliantly fine in the morning but it was raining in the afternoon & at night & today is showery & overcast with a cold wind blowing. Somehow I don't think that we shall have much more good weather. The summer all through has been so remarkably fine that there is bound to be a reaction sooner or later.

We have had a very pleasant rest in our present camp for about a week and have had nothing to do except make ourselves comfortable. Rather an interesting thing happened the day before yesterday. About 5 o'clock we looked out & saw an aeroplane land quite close to the camp. The pilot & observer came over to ring up for a car to take them home. It appears that they had caught fire while in the air but by cutting off the petrol had managed to get it out. Then they had to come down & in doing so nearly ran into some horses. To avoid hitting them the pilot had to risk the fire breaking out again & start his engine which he did & managed to make a good landing, when he found that his petrol pipe had broken & caused all the trouble. They both seemed to take the whole thing as a matter of course including also a fight with a Fritz aeroplane which they had with indecisive results. I may say that their plane was not a fighter but only an observation machine which usually avoids a fight. We gave them some food & were just about to make up some sort of beds for them when a very annoyed officer arrived in a car who had been looking for them for three hours & had come away without any dinner. They went off but next day when they came to take away the plane we heard that they had collided with another car on the way home & the pilot had some ribs injured. The moral of which is that it is safer in an aeroplane than in a motor car at night on the roads here. With love

Your loving son

Tom

Editor's Note:

The letters end here abruptly because it was at this point that Tom was granted home leave as a result of the Australian Prime Minister, Mr Hughes insisting that this should be given to all the troops who had been away since 1914.

The Armistice was signed on 11th November while Tom was at sea on HMT *Port Lyttleton*.

Pioneers

Pioneer battalions performed construction work in the forward areas such as digging trenches and dugouts, maintaining and repairing roads and bridges. They were also trained as infantry and could serve in the front line if required.

ACCt

ADDRESS LETTERS TO
  BOX 530 G.P.O.
        SYDNEY.
№ 50 A

The Commercial Banking Company of Sydney Limited.

Sydney 17th October 191 8

Mrs. Rutledge,

   "Gidleigh"

      Bungendore.

Dear Madam,

          As advised you by telegram this
morning, we are in receipt of the following cablegram from our London Office dated
15th instant :-

   "COMMUNICATE THIS TO MRS. RUTLEDGE,"
   "BUNGENDORE.   RETURNING ON FURLOUGH"
   "QUITE WELL. RUTLEDGE ."

        Yours faithfully,

               Manager.

A very happy day
for me 5/13

Postscript

HMT Port Lyttleton
22-12-18

My dear Mother,

I am just sending a line to say that I am well & to wish you all a Merry Xmas. We arrived in port this morning & went straight into quarantine. There is no influenza on board however & unless it breaks out we will be released in three days which means we will land on Wednesday afternoon or Thursday morning. I will probably be detained a day or so but with luck I should be with you by next Sunday. Needless to say I am very disappointed & it seems useless to write anything when I shall see you so soon.

Your loving son
Tom

To: DISTRICT COMMANDANT PERTH

Serious trouble with West Australians on board men will guarantee not to break quarantine if allowed to land Albany instruct by wireless urgent

O.C. Troops Port Lyttletonn

T.F.Rutledge Lt-Col

To: District Commandant PERTH

Men threaten to take boats cannot sail until answer received to previous message position serious

O.C. Troops Port Lyttletonn

T.F.Rutledge Lt-Col

To: Military Commandant PERTH

West Australian draft have taken ships boats and are going ashore cannot prevent them other men in sympathy with them They have been warned of seriousness of situation

O.C. Troops Port Lyttletonn

T.F.Rutledge Lt-Col

To: District Commandant PERTH

Four boat loads have taken boats in spite of orders and left ship police informed pay books also taken

O.C. Troops Port Lyttletonn

T.F.Rutledge Lt-Col

Gidliegh from the air circa 1960.

Appendix 1
Biographical Notes
and Family Trees

Tom, in his beloved workshop with a working model of a windmill he made as a birthday present for his son.

Rutledge, Thomas Lloyd Forster 'Tom'

Tom Rutledge was born in 1889. Tom was educated at King's College, Goulburn and the University of Sydney where he was a resident of St Paul's College. He studied Arts and Engineering but did not complete a degree as he had to return to Gidleigh due to his father's deteriorating health. His father died in 1912 leaving Tom at the age of 23 responsible for the management of the family property.

When war broke out in 1914, Tom was very quick to enlist. He had been a member of the Citizens Military Force and obviously felt it was his duty. However it could not have been an easy decision. It was apparent from the copy of a letter that he had written, that the family accountant, F N Yarwood, had told him that he was being very irresponsible.

In 1920, he stood for election to the New South Wales Legislative Assembly for the newly formed Progressive Party, which in due course became the Country Party and then the National Party. He was elected as a Member for Goulburn. In 1921, he was one of a group of Progressive members that refused to support Sir John Fuller in forming a Government. This group became known as the 'True Blues'[233] Tom told his family that he had been offered a ministry as an inducement to support Fuller, but declined. He did not stand for re-election in 1925.

In 1935, Tom married Helen Stephen, the daughter of Sir Colin Stephen and his wife Dorothy. Sir Colin was senior partner of the Sydney legal firm, Stephen Jaques and Stephen

---

233   Graham, B D, *The formation of the Australian Country Parties*, Canberra, ANU Press, 1966. P 170

and Chairman of the Australian Jockey Club. Dorothy was the daughter of E W Knox who was general manager of the Colonial Sugar Refining Company and lived at Rona, Bellevue Hill. Tom and Helen were cousins through the Knox connection [see the Family Tree]. They had three children: Martha who married Charles Campbell, Caroline, married David Parker, and William married Julia Ryrie.

Tom took a keen interest in his Merino stud, and tried relocating it to Coonamble by purchasing Calga West: this move was not a success as it was overtaken by the depression. He was active in the New South Wales Sheepbreeders' Association serving two terms as president. Tom also established an Aberdeen Angus herd in 1920 and his son and daughter in law have their descendants. He recognised the need to improve the carrying capacity of the land and was an early pioneer of pasture improvement, using super phosphate with subterranean to boost soil fertility and sowing exotic grasses, particularly Phalaris tuberosa which flourished at Bungendore.

He also had city business interests, holding a number of directorships, including a long term on the board of Anthony Hordern & Sons. He was a keen follower of horse racing, serving for some years on the Committee of the Australian Jockey Club.

He was a keen fisherman enjoying deep sea fishing off the South Coast of New South Wales and dry fly fishing in the Snowy Mountains where he and three friends had a hut on the Thredbo River. He spent many happy hours in his workshop and leather room, where he made many things and including toys for his children.

In the Second World War, he commanded the 7th Light Horse reserves from 1940 to 1942. They were at one stage based inland from Kiama. His orders were to defend that area if the Japanese invaded. He told us that he did not know how they would get on if an invasion happened as they had little more than broomsticks for weapons.[234]

Rutledge, Harry Forster '*Pat*'

Pat was two years younger than Tom. Like His brother, he started his education at King's College, Goulburn, but then went on to The Kings' School, Parramatta where he distinguished himself at rugby and cricket, and was a member of the team that helped with the construction of the swimming pool.

After school, he spent time jackerooing in Queensland before returning to Gidleigh to take on the management after Tom enlisted. Pat enlisted in December 1915 and embarked on 11th May 1916 with the 28th Battery of the 7th Field Artillery Brigade. He was commissioned as 2nd Lieutenant, August 1916 and Promoted Lieutenant, March 1917. He served in France from the beginning of 1917. He was killed in action at Passchendaele on 9th October 1917[235].

My father once said to me, 'Pat is the one who should have survived; he was a better bloke than me'.

Rutledge, Jane Ruth '*Jean*'

Jean Rutledge was born in 1853. After her marriage to William Forster Rutledge, she settled at Gidleigh, managing

234   See Nairn, Bede, 'Rutledge, Thomas Lloyd Forster', in ADB 11.488
235   NAA: B2455, RUTLEDGE HARRY FORSTER

the household and establishing a large garden which included a vegetable garden and orchard. Some of the roses she planted are still growing in front of the old office building, which was the original homestead, and around the old tennis court.

She became well known as the author of *The Goulburn Cookery Book* which was first published in 1899. The royalties were given to the Anglican Diocese of Goulburn. Over two hundred and five thousand copies in thirty six editions were printed giving the Church a profit of more than six thousand pounds.[236]

Eleven men from the Gidleigh community enlisted in the First World War. To commemorate their service, Jean organised the planting of a flowering chestnut tree for each man; pink for those who came back, double white for the three who did not return. The trees were planted each side of the Turallo Creek bridge at Gidleigh.[237] Sadly the chestnuts did not survive, succumbing to frost. They were replaced by Lombardy poplars which are still flourishing.

Jean had the double sadness of losing two sons. As well as Pat, her third son Lloyd was killed when he was dragged by a horse when he was only seven. After Pat was killed she always looked sad.[238]

Rutledge, (Alice) Elma 'The Girl'

Elma was the youngest of the family, born in 1895. She was educated at Kambala School, Rose Bay. She also received artistic instruction from Datillo Rubbo.

---

236   Rutledge, Helen, 'Introduction' to *The Goulburn Cookery Book*, compiled by Mrs Forster Rutledge, 40th edition, Sydney, The National Trust of Australia, 1973

237   *The Queanbeyan Age*, 4 July 1919, p.2.

238   Rutledge, Helen, *My Grandfather's House*, Sydney, Doubleday, 1986.

She spent the war years at Gidleigh. She had a lot of energy and spirit and would ride her horse to Michelago to visit her great friends, Da and Dee Ryrie, the twin daughters of Granville Ryrie.

After the war, she married Captain John Raymond Broadbent, an early graduate of RMC Duntroon. After ten years in the Mittagong district, they settled at Merigan, Mount Fairy. Ray Broadbent returned to active service in the Second World War and reached the rank of Brigadier; however Mrs Overend, the operator of the Mount Fairy telephone exchange continued to refer to him as 'The Captain'.

Elma was much involved with Community organisations, particularly the Red Cross and Country Women's Association. She founded the CWA Children's Library which provided a most valuable service to Bungendore. She inherited her mother's interest in cooking. I particularly remember her rock cakes.

Others Mentioned Often In The Letters

Birdwood, Field Marshal Lord, GCB, GCSI, GCMG, DSO.

Birdwood had served in India and South Africa. In 1914, Kitchener appointed him to command the Australian and New Zealand forces. After Bridges was killed on Gallipoli in May 1915, Birdwood took command of the Australian Imperial Force, a position he retained until handing over to Monash in May 1918.[239]

Champion, Rev Arthur Hammerton.

Rector of Bungendore 1913-24. He had previously been Headmaster of Launceston Grammar School 1185-1895 and The Kings School, Parramatta 1895-1906, Rector of St John's, Canberra. 1909-13. His three sons enlisted and two were killed on the Western Front. The remains of Christopher were discovered by a French farmer in 2003 and buried in the Outtersteene Communal Cemetery.[240]

Chisholm, Dame Alice Isabel, DBE 'Aunt'.

Jean Rutledge's younger sister who married as his 2nd wife William Alexander Chisholm. At the age of 59, she went to Egypt to be near her son who had been wounded. Seeing a need, she opened a canteen for the soldiers which grew into a large establishment at Kantara where 4,000 soldiers were fed and 60,000 eggs cooked in a day.[241] She was created a Dame in recognition of her services.

---

239   See Hill, A J, 'Birdwood, William Riddell', in *ADB* 7.293

240   See Ellis, Glenda, *Our Soldiers* & Waddy, Lloyd, *The King's School 1831—1981*

241   See Hill, A J, 'Chisholm, Dame Alice, Isabel', in *ADB* 7.642 & Champion, Janet M, *Lady of Kantara: A Biography of Dame Alice Chisholm 1856 -1954*, Sydney, Janet Maxwell Champion, 1977

Chisholm, (Harry) Bertram 'Ber.'

3rd son of Dame Alice Chisholm

Chisholm, Dorothea '*Doff.*'

Younger daughter of Dame Alice Chisholm. She travelled with her mother to Egypt and assisted with the canteens. She married Captain Jim Wayett, a Chaplain with the British Army

Chisholm, (Margaret) Sheila Mackellar.

Only daughter of Harry & Margaret Chisholm of Wollogorang, nr Goulburn. On 27-12-1915 she married Lord Loughborough, 'Luffy', later 6th Earl of Rosslyn. The marriage broke down due to his drinking and gambling. Her close friendship with Prince Albert ended in 1920 when the King intervened.[242] [*ADB 13:423* & see Robert Wainwright, *Sheila*].

Cunningham, James.

Grazier who owned Tuggeranong and Lanyon stations, before Canberra was established. He married Mary Emily Twynam of Riversdale, Goulburn. He was a close friend of the Rutledge family.[243]

Lt Col John (Jack) Francis Donnelly, DSO, 2nd Pioneers.

After the war he conducted a stock & station agency in Bungendore and establish very successful monthly sales at the

---

242   See Simpson, Caroline, 'Chisholm, Margaret Sheila Mackellar', in *ADB* 13.423 & Wainright, Robert, *Sheila: The Australian Beauty who bewitched British Society*, Sydney, Allen & Unwin, 2014.

243   See Horsfield, Jennifer, *Mary Cunningham – An Australian Life*, Canberra, Ginninderra Press, 2004

local yards. An instructor of Commonwealth Forces before the war. Donnelly and Tom had both served in the Bungendore Troop of 11th Light Horse before the war.

Futter, Robert Reginald. *'Cousin Reg'*

Son of John Sedley Futter and his wife Jane, née Styles, Jean Rutledge's aunt. He was a pastoral valuer and sheep classer. He was an adviser to Jean on the management of Gidleigh after her sons enlisted. His son, Reginald Lumley, 'Rex', managed Gidleigh after World War I.

Hopperton, John Chapman.

The gardener at Gidleigh. He later leased a block on Gidleigh on which he established an orchard.

James, Lt. Col. Tristram Bernard Wordsworth James, DSO. *'Jimmy'*

He was the first Adjutant of the Royal Military College, Duntroon. He was the last of the original Duntroon staff to be released for active duty. In 1918, he commanded 7th Bde, AFA until badly gassed.[244]

Knox, Thomas Forster. *'Cousin Tom'*

3rd son of Sir Edward Knox, managing director of Sydney branch of Dalgety & Co, had been a close confidant of W F Rutledge & advised Jean while her sons were away.[245]

---

244 Perry, Major Warren, 'Lieutenant Colonel T.B.W.James, DSO (1883-1939)',; in *The Duntroon Society Newsletter 1/1993*. P. 12.

245 See Rutledge, Helen, *My Grandfather's House*, Sydney, Doubleday, 1986.

McCay, Maj Gen Sir James Whiteside, KCMG, KBE.

Before the war, He had been a Member of the House of Representatives and had briefly served as Minister for Defence. He commanded the 2nd Infantry Brigade at Gallipoli and in May 1917 was appointed to command the base depots in England.[246] [Tom was not consistent in his spelling of this name]

Mackay, Jessie.

2nd daughter of Sir Edward Knox, m. Eric Henry Mackay, Parents of Clara who married Grenville Miller. They lived at Shawford where Tom visited them several times while he was based in England.[247]

Morphy, Harry. '*Uncle*'

Jean Rutledge's brother. He managed Gidleigh for a while after Pat enlisted.

Morphy, Mary, (née Andrews). '*Gran*'

Jean's father, Richard John Styles had remarried in 1878.

Osborne, Elizabeth Jane, (née Atkinson). '*Mrs Pat*'

Married to Pat Hill Osborne of Currandooley, Bungendore.[248] 4 of her 5 daughters married high ranking British Army officers. Two were killed in the war.

Parish, Pte. Maurice Samper. '*Snowy*'

---

246   See Serle, Geoffrey, 'McCay, James Whiteside', in *ADB* 10.224

247   See Rutledge, Helen, *op cit.*

248   See Beale, Edgar, 'Osborne, Pat Hill', in *ADB* 6.377

Grazier of Bungendore. Served with 2nd Mob. Vet. Section, 2nd AVC. Told Tom of the location of Pat's grave.

Powell, Ada Charlotte, Cherry Amy & Augusta Maria. 'The Aunts'

Lived at Turalla, Bungendore, close friends and neighbours.

Radford, Rt Rev Lewis Bostock.

Bishop of Goulburn 1915-1933, Warden of St Paul's College, University of Sydney 1909-15. Tom was still a resident of the College when Radford was appointed.[249] [*adb 11.322*].

Ryrie, Maj Gen Sir Granville de Laune, KCMG, CB.

Commanded 2nd Light Horse Brigade at Gallipoli, MP 1911-27, Australian High Commissioner to Great Britain 1927-32. He lived at Micalago Station, Michelago and was a close friend of the Rutledge family.[250]

Sinclair- Maclagan, Maj Gen Ewen George, CB, CMG, DSO.

A British Army officer, he was posted to Australia in 1901. When RMC, Duntroon was established, he was appointed Director of Drill. He commanded the 3rd Infantry Brigade at Gallipoli and France. From January to July 1917, he commanded the AIF depots in Britain.[251]

---

249   See Cable, K J, 'Radford, Lewis Bostock', in *ADB* 11.322

250   See Hill, A J, 'Ryrie, Sir Granville de Laune', in *ADB* 11.502 & Vincent, Phoebe, *My Darling Mick: The Life of Granville Ryrie 1865 – 1937*, Canberra, National Library of Australia, 1997.

251   Hill, A J, 'Sinclair-Maclagan, Ewen George', in *ADB* 11.616

Spencer, Monica M. '*Fuzzie*'

Spent much time at Gidleigh as a companion for Elma.

Ward, Marjorie.

Elder daughter of Dame Alice Chisholm, she married John Ward [qv]

Ward, Ven. John William.

Archdeacon of the Monaro, 1913-21, married Marjorie Chisholm [qv]. He also served as a Chaplain on the Western Front.

Wark, John.

Overseer at Gidleigh. Four generations of the Wark family worked for the Rutledges at Carwoola and Gidleigh.

Yarwood, Frank Nelson, FCPA.

Yarwood founded the accountancy firm Yarwood Vane & Co which is now part of the Deloittes group and worked hard to get a Royal Charter for accountants in Australia.[252] He was the Rutledge family's accountant for many years.

---

252   Graham, A W, *Without Fear or Favour: A History of The Institute of Chartered Accountants in Australia 1928-1978*, Sydney, Butterworths, 1978

Tom Rutledge with his son William on the verandah of Gidleigh in February 1952. William was about to leave home for his first day at boarding school.

Rutledge

1. James Rutledge of Ballymagirl, co Cavan, Ireland m Martha Forster
   2. William (1806–1876) m Eliza Kirk
      3. Thomas Forster (1846–1918) m Edith A.L. Ritchie
         4. Noel Beresford Forster (1886–1917)
   2. Thomas (1818-1904) m Martha Forster (1821–1909)
      3. William Forster (1850-1912) m Jane Ruth Morphy
         4. Thomas Lloyd Forster (1889–1958) m Helen Roslyn Stephen.
            5. Martha Dorothy (1936–2014) m Charles Campbell
            5. Caroline Phillipa (1939–) m David Parker
            5. William Stephen (1943–) m Julia Ryrie
         4. Harry Forster (Pat) (1891–1917)
         4. Alice Elma (The Girl) (1895–1977) m John Raymond Broadbent
      3. Alice Louise (1852–1938)
      3. Edward Knox (1854–1940) m (1) Francis Hamilton Hume
         4. Edward Hamilton (1882–1974)
      3. Eliza Martha (Aunt Em) (1857–1949)
      3. Fanny Amy (1860–1952) m Arundel Hill Garraway
      3. Jane Eva (1862–1949) m Charles Southcote King
      3. Francis Henry (1865–1925) m Charlotte Hogg
         4. Stephen Crane (1899-1992)
   2. Martha (1821–1897) m (Sir) Edward Knox
   2. Lloyd (1827–1958) m Isabella Bennett
      3. Edward Lloyd (1853–1915) m Hester Annie Denn
      3. Percy Lloyd
         4. Cyril Percy

Morphy

1. John Morphy of Kerry, Ireland
    2. John Stephen m Elizabeth Ann Styles
        3. Rose Florence m Hon Ivo Bligh (later the Earl of Darnley)
    2. Richard John m Mary Emma Styles
        3. Jane Ruth (Jean) (1853 - 1932) m William Forster Rutledge
            4. *[see Rutledge tree]*
        3. Alice Isabel (Dame Alice) (1856 - 1954) m William Alexander Chisholm
            4. William Maxwell (1881 - 1962)
            4. Marjorie m Rev John Ward
                5. Barbara Ward
            4. Bertram (Ber)
            4. Dorothy (Doff) m Rev James Wayett
        3. Harry (1862 -)

Knox

1. Edward Knox (Sir) 1819 - 1901 m Martha Rutledge
   2. George (1845 - 1888) m Jane de Winton
      3. Ruth
   2. Edward William (1847 - 1933) m Edith Willis.
      3. Dorothy (1879 - 1935) m Colin Campbell Stephen (Sir)
         4. Helen Roslyn (1903 - 1991) m Thomas L F Rutledge
            5. *[see Rutledge tree]*.
   2. Adrian (Sir) (1863 - 1932)
   2. Thomas Forster (1849 - 1919) m Amy Hope Ritchie
      3. Helen Edith (1888 - 1956)
      3. Thomas Hope (1892 - 1945)
   2. Clara Elizabeth (1851 - 1930) m William Oswald Gilchrist
   2. Jessie (1853 - 1957) m Eric Henry MacKay
      3. Clara Ainslie MacKay (1885 -1975) m Grenville Acton Miller
   2. Fanny (1856 - 1944)

Chisholm

1. James Chisholm of Edinburgh (1772 - 1837) m (1) Mary Brown.
    2. James (1806 - 1888) m (1) Elizabeth Margaret Kinghorne
        3. William Alexander (1832 - 1902) m 2) Alice Isabel Morphy (Dame)
            4. *[see Morphy Tree]*.
        3. Charles Kerr (1839 - 1914) m Caroline Elizabeth Smith.
            4. Frank Kerr (1878 - 1947)
        3. Arthur Bowman (1842 - 1908) m (2) Margaret Johnston.
            4. Carrawarra girls
1. He (James) m (2) Mary Bowman
    2. John William (1819 - 1899) m Rebecca Stuckey
        3. William (1853 - 1941) m Emma Isabel Mitchell
            4. William Malcolm (1892 - 1914) KIA.
            4. Helen Isabel Airlie (1896-) m
                (1) John Leonard Keep
                (2) Charles Frank Bouvet.
        3. Harry (1858 - 1927) m Margaret Mackellar
            4. Margaret Sheila Mackellar (1895-) m
                (1) Francis, Lord Loughborough.
                (2) Sir John Milbanke
                (3) Prince Dimitri Romanoff

Appendix 2
Summary of Tom Rutledge's War Service[253]

The War of 1914-1918.

Lt:Col.T.L.F. Rutledge, 4 Pioneer Bn., A.I.F.

was mentioned in a Despatch from

Field Marshal Sir Douglas Haig, K.T. G.C.B. G.C.V.O. K.C.I.E.

dated the 8th November 1918

for gallant and distinguished services in the Field.

I have it in command from the King to record His Majesty's

high appreciation of the services rendered.

War Office
Whitehall.S.W.
1st March 1919.

Secretary of State for War.

---

253   NAA: B2455, RUTLEDGE THOMAS LLOYD FORSTER

Prior to the War, he had served with 11th LH in the CMF [Citizens Military Force]

14-11-1914	Appointed to AIF as Lieutenant and allotted to 7th LH
16-12-1914	Promoted Major and appointed to command of 'B' Squadron
20-12-1914	Embarked on HMAT *Ayrshire* In Ma'adi Camp
15-5-1915	Proceeded to join MEF per HMT *Lutzow*
18-10-1915	Evacuated sick and transferred to hospital in Malta. Placed on supernumerary list
20-1-1916	Transferred to Florence for convalescence
19-3-1916	Disembarked Alexandria. Various administrative and training postings in Egypt
13-5-1916	Transferred to 2nd Training Battalion
31-5-1916	Embarked Alexandria
12-6-1916	Disembarked Plymouth. Posted to various training camps on Salisbury plains
1-1-1917	Appointed Commanding Officer Pioneer Training Battalion
18-10-1917	Proceeded overseas to France
27-10-1917	Transferred to 2nd Pioneer Battalion
22-4-1918	Transferred to 4th Pioneer Battalion as Commanding Officer and promoted temporary Lieutenant Colonel
9-7-1918	Promoted Lieutenant Colonel
23-10-1918	Embarked for Australia on furlough. OC troops on HMT *Port Lyttleton*
25-12-1918	Disembarked Albany
31-12-1918	Mentioned in Despatches
25-2-1919	Appointment terminated

Appendix 3
Abbreviations

[A]AMC	Australian Army Medical Corps
[A]ANS	[Australian] Army Nursing Service
ACT	Australian Capital Territory
ADB	Australian Dictionary of Biography
AIF	Australian Imperial Force
Arty	Artillery
AVC	Australian Veterinary Corps
Battn	Battalion
Bde	Brigade
Brig [Gen]	Brigadier [General]
Capt	Captain
Col	Colonel
Cpl	Corporal
Disch	Discharged
Div[l]	Division[al]
DOD	Died of Disease
DOW	Died of Wounds
Dr	Doctor
DSO	Distiguished Service Order
DSO*	DSO and bar
FAB	Field Artillery Brigade
Gen	General
GOC	General Officer Commanding
HAG	Heavy Artillery Group
HMAT	His Majesty's Australian Transport
HMT	His Majesty's Transport
HQ	Headquarters
Inf	Infantry
KIA	Killed in Action

L/Cpl	Lance Corporal
LH	Light Horse
Lt	Lieutenant
Lt Col	Lieutenant Colonel
Lt Gen	Lieutenant General
Maj	Major
Maj Gen	Major General
MB, ChM	Bachelor of Medicine, Master of Surgery
MC	Military Cross
MC*	MC and bar
MG	Machine Gun
MM	Military Medal
mob	mobile
Pte	Private
RC, RX	Red Cross
Reg.	Regiment
Rev.	Reverend
RMC	Royal Military College.
RTA	Returned to Australia
Sgt	Sergeant
Vet	Veterinary

Index of Letters

CHAPTER 1, To Egypt

CHAPTER 2, Gallipoli

CHAPTER 2, Gallipoli (cont)

Date	From	To
11-7-1915	Gallipoli	Pat
14-7-1915	Gallipoli	Mother
22-7-1915	Gallipoli	Mother
29-7-1915	Gallipoli	Aunt
29-7-1915	Gallipoli	Mother
12-8-1915	Gallipoli	Mother
20-8-1915	Gallipoli	Mother
30-8-1915	Gallipoli	Mother
30-9-1915	Gallipoli	Mother
12-10-1915	Gallipoli	Mother

CHAPTER 3, Malta and Florence

Date	From	To
27-10-1915	Malta	Mother
20-11-1915	Malta	Mother
1-12-1915	Malta	Mother
15-12-1915	Malta	Mother
31-12-1915	Malta	Mother
9-1-1916	Malta	Mother
25-1-1916	Florence	Mother
12-2-1916	Florence	Mother

CHAPTER 4, Training Camps in England

Date	From	To
18-6-1916	Perham Downs	Mother
26-6-1916	Perham Downs	Mother
12-7-1916	Perham Downs	Mother
24-7-1916	London	Mother
3-8-1916	Parkhouse	Mother
16-8-1916	Parkhouse	Mother

CHAPTER 4, Training Camps in England (cont.)

Date	From	To
12-9-1916	Perham Downs	Mother
12-9-1916	Perham Downs	Mother
29-9-1916	Perham Downs	Mother
17-10-1916	Perham Downs	Mother
22-10-1916	Perham Downs	Mother
25-10-1916	Perham Downs	Mother
14-11-1916	Perham Downs	Mother
29-11-1916	Perham Downs	Mother
12-12-1916	Lark Hill	Mother
17-12-1916	Lark Hill	Mother
6-1-1917	Lark Hill	Girl
6-1-1917	Lark Hill	Mother
14-1-1917	Lark Hill	Mother
22-1-1917	Lark Hill	Mother
28-1-1917	Lark Hill	Mother
11-2-1917	Lark Hill	Mother
18-2-1917	Lark Hill	Mother
26-2-1917	Lark Hill	Mother
10-3-1917	Lark Hill	Mother
25-3-1917	Fovant	Mother
14-4-1917	Fovant	Mother
21-4-1917	Fovant	Girl
23-4-1917	Fovant	Mother
6-5-1917	Fovant	Mother
13-5-1917	London	Mother
13-5-1917	London	Mother
10-6-1917	Fovant	Mother
24-6-1917	Fovant	Girl
24-6-1917	Fovant	Mother

CHAPTER 4 Training Camps in England (cont.)

Date	From	To
6-7-1917	Fovant	Mother
15-7-1917	Fovant	Mother
18-7-1917	Fovant	Girl
29-7-1917	Fovant	Mother
13-8-1917	Fovant	Mother
26-8-1917	Fovant	Mother
31-8-1917	Fovant	Mother
19-9-1917	Fovant	Mother
6-10-1917	Fovant	Mother
12-10-1917	Sutton Very	Mother

Chapter 5 The Western Front

Date	From	To
21-10-1917	France	Mother
28-10-1917	France	Mother
4-11-1917	France	Mother
13-11-1917	France	Mother
15-11-1917	France	Mother
26-11-1917	France	Mother
2-12-1917	France	Mother
8-12-1917	France	Mother
17-12-1917	France	Mother
24-12-1917	France	Mother
30-12-1917	France	Mother
6-1-1918	France	Mother
13-1-1918	France	Mother
29-1-1918	France	Mother
4-2-1918	France	Mother
12-2-1918	France	Mother
18-2-1918	Paris	Mother

Chapter 5, The Western Front (cont.)

Postscript

Index of Footnotes

Bibliography

Published Sources

Books

Australian Dictionary of Biography, 1788—1850, Vols 1-2; *1851— 1890,* Vols 3-6; *1891 -1939,* Vols 7 -12; *1940—1980,* Vol 13; Supplement 1580—1980; Melbourne, Melbourne University Press, 1974—2005. [ADB]

Abbott, Brian Douglas, *Phillip Parker King 1791-1856—A Most Admirable Australian,* Armidale, Glenburgh Pty Ltd, 2012.

Berry, Scyld & Peploe, Rupert *Cricket's Burning Passion—Ivo Bligh and the Story of the Ashes,* London, Methuen, 2006.

Campbell, Katie, *Paradise of Exiles: The Anglo-American Gardens of Florence,* London, Frances Lincoln, 2009.

Carlyon, Les, *The Great War,* Sydney, Macmillan, 2006.

Champion, Janet Maxwell, *Lady of Kantara: A Biography of Dame Alice Chisholm 1856—1954,* Sydney, Janet Maxwell Champion, 1977.

Day, David, *Chifley,* Sydney, Harper Collins, 2001.

Ellis, Glenda, *Our Soldiers: Bungendore & the Great War,* Canberra, Ginniderra Press, 2007.

Graham, A W, *Without Fear or Favour: A History of The Institute of Chartered Accountants in Australia 1928-1978,* Sydney, Butterworths, 1978.

Graham, B D, *The Formation of the Australian Country Parties,* Canberra, Australian National University Press, 1966.

Griffiths, G.Nesta, *Some Southern Homes of New South Wales,* Sydney, The Shepherd Press, 1952.

Griffiths, G.Nesta, *Some Northern Homes of New South Wales,* Sydney, The Shepherd Press, 1954.

Horsfield, Jennifer, *Mary Cunningham—An Australian Life*, Canberra, Ginninderra Press, 2004.

Maloney, Louise (ed), *Rutledges in Retrospect: From Green County Cavan to The Brown Plains of Australia*, Brisbane, Louise Maloney, 2008.

Moorehead, Caroline, *Iris Origo. Marchesa of Val d'Orcia*, London, John Murray, 2000.

Mowle, L M (ed), *A Genealogical History of Pioneer Families of Australia*, 5th edn, Adelaide, Rigby, 1978.

Oxford Dictionary of National Biography, Oxford, Oxford University Press, 2004; online edn, Jan 2008; Oct 2013; online edn, Jan 2014. [Oxford DNB]

Richardson, Lieutenant Colonel J D, *The 7th Light Horse Regiment A.I.F.*, Sydney, Radcliffe Press, 1923.

Rutledge, Mrs Forster, *The Goulburn Cookery Book,* 40th edition, Sydney, The National Trust of Australia, 1973.

Rutledge, Helen, *My Grandfather's House*, Sydney, Doubleday, 1986.

Telfer, Kevin, *Peter Pan's First XI: The Extraordinary Story of J.M.Barrie's Cricket Team*, London, Sceptre, 2010.

Vincent, Phoebe, *My Darling Mick: The Life of Granville Ryrie 1865—1937*, Canberra, National Library of Australia, 1997.

Waddy, Lloyd, *The King's School 1831 -1981—An Account*, Parramatta, The Council of The King's School, 1981.

Wainright, Robert, *Sheila: The Australian Beauty who bewitched British Society*, Sydney, Allen & Unwin, 2014.

Who Was Who 1929 1940, Vol III, London, A & C Black, 2nd ed, 1967.

Whyte, W. Farmer, *William Morris Hughes, His Life and Times*, Sydney, Angus & Robertson, 1957.

Articles

Beale, Edgar, 'Osborne, Pat Hill', in *ADB* 6.377.

Cable, K J, 'Radford, Lewis Bostcok', in *ADB* 11.322.

Gale, Maggie B, 'Ashwell, Lena [*real name* Lena Margaret Pocock; *married name* Lena Margaret Simson, Lady Simson] (1872-1957)' *Oxford Dictionary of National Biography*, Oxford University Press, 2004; online edn, Jan 2008. [http:/www.oxforddnb.com/view/article/304768, accessed 30 Aug 2014].

Hill, A J, 'Birdwood, William Riddell', in *ADB* 7.293.

Hill, A J, 'Chisholm, Dame Alice Isabel', in *ADB* 7.642.

Hill, A J, 'Ryrie, Sir Granville de Laune', in *ADB* 11.502.

Hill, A J, 'Sinclair-Maclagan, Ewen George', in *ADB* 11.616.

Marsh, Peter T, 'Chamberlain, Beatrice Mary (1862-1918)' *Oxford Dictionary of National Biography*, Oxford University Press, Oct 2013; online edn, Jan 2014. [http:/www.oxforddnb.com/view/article/101358, accessed 28 Aug 2014].

Nairn, Bede, 'Rutledge, Thomas Lloyd Forster', in *ADB* 11.488.

Perry, Major Warren, 'Lieutenant Colonel T.B.W.James, DSO (1883-1939)—A Gunner of the Australian Staff Corps', in *The Duntroon Society Newsletter 1/1993*.

Rutledge, Helen, 'Introduction' to *The Goulburn Cookery Book*, compiled by Mrs Forster Rutledge, 40th edition, Sydney, The National Trust of Australia, 1973.

Serle, Geoffrey, 'McCay, James Whiteside', in *ADB* 10.224.

Simpson, Caroline, 'Chisholm, Margaret Sheila Mackellar', in *ADB* 13.423.

Newspapers and Journals

The Daily Mail.

The Duntroon Society Newsletter.

The Queanbeyan Age.

Unpublished Sources

Australian Imperial Force unit war diaries, 1914-18 War; awm4 Class 14—Engineers; AWM4 Subclass 14/16—4ᵗʰ Australian Pioneer Battalion.

National Archives of Australia.

NAA: Australian Imperial Force Base Records Office; B2455, First Australian Imperial Forces personnel Dossiers, 1914—1920; Items

    H F Rutledge,

    T L F Rutledge [NAA].

Photographs

Fovant Badges Society, Fovant, Wiltshire, Australian Army Rising Sun Badge.

All the other photographs are from the Assistant Editor's private collection.